EVERY
WALL
SHALL FALL

EVERY WALL SHALL FALL

by

HELLEN BATTLE

HEWITT HOUSE
Old Tappan, New Jersey

*To my mother and father,
and to those I left behind the Wall.*

Contents

PROLOGUE

As soon as I reached Europe, I began to question that little girl from Tennessee. Oh, I don't really know why. She was only a naïve girl, from a small town nestled in the heart of the mountaineer country. Her favorite dish wasn't black beans and cornbread, but hamburgers and chocolate malts. She belonged to another generation. She effervesced with enthusiasm when things were going great, and sometimes she displayed a little too much optimism for the disgruntled and more experienced wanderers along life's road. Inside, she was soft, sensitive, even shy, but she radiated the air of a carefree, self-assured extrovert. That, however, was not her real identity. In fact, if you put her on the spot, she couldn't even tell you who she really was. She was in the midst of a search. Why did I reject her? Oh, I guess because Europe made me aware that she was new-grass green when compared with the sophistication of the big city—she was a babe in the woods. Nevertheless, she held opinions about everything. But she was clever and coy enough not to expose her own ignorance before those who assumed a knowing air. And yet, in her restless heart burned a yearning for distant shores—even an idealistic dream that sought its fulfillment at some vague point and place in time. Yes, she ached to outgrow the limitations that space and time in the provinces had imposed on her and embark on the exploration of new frontiers. That's why she resorted to begging, pleading, and crying in order to talk her dear Daddy into allowing her to cross the Atlantic for the first time. Her destination was Spain, where she was to spend her junior year of college.

Her appetite for adventure and her unconditional trust in people caused her to listen to all those voices from without that told her what to become, and proclaimed what was wrong with the world. Hence, she became critical. That was the first step to becoming a rebel, which was her prerequisite to emancipation. The seams of her provincial garments were splitting. She had outworn her past. Thus, she returned from her stay abroad a little wiser, but not much. She was still a restless rebel, in search of herself.

Before I continue, it is only fair to make a confession. I was that American girl. Leaving the borders of the United States for the first time gave me a glimpse of new horizons. Europe, the old man of history, was extremely critical of America for being the inexperienced child. I was a true daughter of America, and faintly Europe's reproaches began to make an impact on my ears. But first I had a long way to travel. I remember so well the summer before I departed for Germany. . . .

The Tennessee sun scorched our shoulders as we loaded the last suitcases into the trunk. August 1962 was retreating in a sweltering withdrawal, and I was not looking forward to the hot, wearisome trip to New York by car. My father and I were driving up to meet the Dutch ship that would carry me across the Atlantic. I had fought a long and hard battle to convince my parents that I should go to Germany. Even though I had returned safe and sound from Spain, they were still reluctant to turn me loose in Germany, especially since I was headed eventually for Berlin. Berlin meant danger. Berlin was the last stronghold of the free world in the midst of a gigantic Communist concentration camp. Nevertheless, they had agreed on one condition—I must first secure employment.

A Berlin language school had offered me a contract as an English teacher, but I would first have to reside in Hanover before obtaining a position in Berlin itself. I had gobbled up the opportunity at once, but with impatient anticipation toward transferring to West Berlin. Indeed, there must have been a mission in the madness that my parents attributed to my decision. It was all beyond them. Why did I want to rush off to Germany and slave away for $100 a month, when America offered everything anyone could want?

"I want you to take good care of yourself, now." Mama stood with tears in her eyes. Her health prevented her from making the trip with us. Besides, someone had to babysit with our two dogs. "And I want you to stay on this side of the Wall when you go to Berlin," she said, hugging me good-bye.

"Of course I will, Mama," I answered, although I was unconvinced as to the intention behind my answer.

Before departing from New York I had the opportunity to visit some acquaintances. I especially remember a conversation with the father of a friend who had requested me to pay a call on his family. Let's call the father Mr. Wood. We got involved in hashing over Communism and the American way of life. When Mr. Wood saw that I was not dogmatic about America's claim on freedom, and certainly not as fearful as he of the potential threat of Communism, he felt compelled to give me last-minute fatherly advice before my journey to the divided land. He felt that I simply did not know what the issues were.

"Our brand of democracy is what everyone needs," Mr. Wood explained. "No country in the world has it so good as the United States. In this country, more than ever, America has been called out to defend the freedom of the world. That's why we must get tougher with the Communists. We must fight fire with fire! In this game of political power, it is 'an eye for an eye, and a tooth for a tooth!' " I was unsure whether it was a glint of fanaticism that flickered in his eyes or impassioned conviction, but I did notice a hint of fear.

As the *Groote Beer* moved out of the harbor, I peeled my eyes for a last look at the Statue of Liberty. I almost missed her, though, because I had stationed myself on the wrong side of the ship. Then I heard people on the deck shouting "Look!" and, running to the other side, I joined them. There she was, standing proudly, with her flaming torch held high. I thought about Mr. Wood's words, "fire with fire," as I looked up at her torch. Was that the kind of fire he meant? A fire of freedom? But freedom, then, was only a trite word in my vocabulary. . . .

EVERY
WALL
SHALL FALL

BOOK I

1

THE LONGEST NIGHT

A PIERCING RING penetrated the apartment, drowning my last words.

Mrs. Braun's face dropped, frozen with fear. "That's the police! Do you want to wait in the next room until I get rid of them?" she questioned apologetically.

My eyes roamed from the two coffee cups on the table to my coat, hanging on the wall hook and to the West German articles lying on the coffee table. The signs of my presence could not lie. "No," I answered, "I'll stay here."

Four burly men barged into the living room, brushing snow from their overcoats. All were dressed in plain clothes. In a grouchy tone Mrs. Braun informed them she was busy entertaining a guest and wanted to be left alone. They ignored her, curiously examining me all the while.

With his back turned to Mrs. Braun, a dark man addressed me. "We're from the Ministry of State Security. We'd like to see your identification papers."

I slipped my passport out of my purse and held it out to him. He snatched it away, examined it closely, and said in a low tone of feigned surprise, "Hmmm . . . an American. When did you enter East Berlin?" The men exchanged amazed expressions.

"This evening."

Still holding my passport, the man questioned me, "Did you know we were looking for Mrs. Braun's son?"

"Yes," I affirmed boldly. "Mrs. Braun just informed me this evening." I drew in a deep breath. After all, my answer was a half truth.

17

A heavy pause fell over the room and the same man commanded, "Get your coats and come along. We have some questions for both of you."

"That's no way to treat my guest," Mrs. Braun protested.

"If you have any questions, you can ask them here," I added.

"No, that's impossible. Get your coats and come on!" His pitch heightened its urgency.

"Well, I'm staying here," I challenged. "You have no right to make me go."

"If you don't come with us, then we'll take you by force," the heavy spokesman of the four boomed.

Mrs. Braun and I exchanged bewildered looks. A silence followed. My thoughts raced to evaluate the situation. These men meant business. They would take me by force, and if I caused a rowdy scene, Mrs. Braun would suffer the consequences.

As if Mrs. Braun had tacitly received my thoughts, she removed her coat from its hanger and began putting it on.

They had said they only wanted to ask a few questions. Perhaps if I cooperated, we could end it all in a hurry, and I would be in West Berlin by midnight. If I resisted with screaming and kicking, which I was more inclined to do, it would only stir the neighbors. No, I would go along silently and get it over with.

"All right." I slipped my arms into my coat. "I'll go along. But I must go to the rest room first."

They nodded a reply.

There was scarcely room to turn around in the tiny bathroom, and I knew the men were standing just outside the door. I flipped the faucet on, but the gushing water was not loud enough to absorb the cracking of tearing paper. Therefore, I calmly removed the letter from my coat pocket, doubled it, and dropped it into the toilet bowl. It was from Mrs. Braun's son to his fiancée. I flushed the water. The thick envelope was too large for the pipe and remained floating on the water's surface. Another flush would arouse suspicion, so I slid my hand into the water and crammed it into the pipe, out of sight. I washed and dried my hands, turned off the running water, and marched out to the group of men who were awaiting me.

Two men remained in the apartment and the other two escorted Mrs.

Braun and me outside. A blizzard roared viciously. We trudged a good distance through the snow, crossed several blocks, and approached three or four parked cars. Suddenly, Mrs. Braun disappeared into a car, and I was left alone with the heavy officer who ordered me into the back of another car. He climbed in and flopped down next to me. The driver, who had been waiting in the front seat, started the engine. I immediately spied the strangeness of the door next to me—the handle had been removed.

We raced across deserted, icy streets, slipping and sliding at every turn. Cold, heavy sheets of snow fell ceaselessly in a flood that showed no sign of waning.

The moments sped away in the chill of the night. As I leaned against the handleless door, I breathed in an air of finality. I was totally unprepared for the encounter and too taken aback by the suddenness of it all to be afraid. Anger surged in me more than fear. Even as the car wheels skated along an icy pavement to an unknown destination and an uncertain future, I accepted the moment as it was. No, I was not busy preparing an intricate alibi; I would depend on my spontaneity to pull me through. It usually did. Therefore, I took no time to reflect on the situation, on how I would react, or even to anticipate questions. I would answer them as they came.

Was I stunned into unawareness? Or was I just consoled by that same false sense of security that seemed to dominate Mrs. Braun's son, Sammy?

The driver turned and attempted to make polite conversation, asking when I had arrived in East Berlin. "How dare he?" I questioned indignantly. Then coldly I asked, "Are the questions to begin here in the car?" A scowl clouded his face, and he remained silent.

"Where are you taking me?" I demanded.

"You'll see," came the response from the back seat.

The empty streets whizzed by, the car almost rotating at times. The lonely black night contrasted sharply with the dazzling whiteness of mounds of snow, and for an instant I could imagine myself a stranger in fairyland. But my illusion was abruptly shattered when the car skidded to a halt before a heavy gate.

The driver climbed out, pressed a button in a huge wall, and waited until two uniformed sentries appeared with slung machine guns. He returned to the wheel and the massive doors of a fortress swung open. The wheels spun around without gripping into the ice, but finally biting into the snow, they rolled forward. The gate swung to and locked. I was in the dark narrow court of a prison.

One of the men led the way and the other followed. I stumbled into a gray corridor, ascended a narrow stairway, and stopped before a wide double door. The first door was ajar, and I observed thick maroon padding on the inside surface.

I still felt no fear—only anger, which swelled into a huge bubble about to burst. How could they treat me, an American citizen, like this? They certainly could not get away with keeping me long, because people in West Berlin would begin wondering. Had I told anyone that I was going to East Berlin? Yes, I probably had. I usually did as a precaution. No, there was nothing to worry about. Sammy had reassured me that the East German police were stupid and inefficient. It was easy to fool them. I would simply answer a few questions to convince them of my innocence and then go home. One thing was certain, I would never return to East Berlin.

My heavy escort pushed open the second of the doors, and I found myself in a large room, furnished in a typically German bourgeois manner.

My eyes immediately met the glare of a small, sharp-featured man in his thirties, seated behind a desk. Cold beady eyes and pale, sunken cheeks were the most marked features of his narrow, triangular face. Long black hair was slicked away from his high forehead. At once the image of a weasel struck me.

He ordered me to be seated, motioning to two bouclé easy chairs on either side of a square table. I obeyed. I sat on the edge of the chair; I did not remove my coat because it would suggest staying awhile, an idea which I offered no sign of accepting.

The two rigid eyes spoke with the hard look of fanaticism, and an urgent tone in the voice that addressed me confirmed my observation.

"How long have you known Herr Braun?"

"I've known him a few months now. But let me explain. . . . It's a terrible coincidence that I happened to come to East Berlin at this time. I've only come to bring his mother some gifts from West Berlin. I didn't know Sammy had deserted the army until his mother told me."

"Zufall!" A snarl curved on his lips. "There's no such thing as coincidence, you know. Why don't you tell me where he is?"

"I don't know!" I exploded at once.

A cautious grin of disbelief spread across his face. "The spider has caught the fly," he replied smugly. When I ignored his sarcasm, he continued, "Why don't you begin by retracing all your moves since you entered the capital of the German Democratic Republic?" Ideology demanded that he refer to East Berlin as the "capital city," for anything less would have minimized East German claims on West Berlin.

I gave a condensed account of all my movements with the exception of my meeting Sammy. He appeared to accept my story and sprang to another topic, again with icy sarcasm. "That's an awful lot of money you spent on Mrs. Braun."

"Mrs. Braun's son has an American girl friend who was recently here for a visit. She left money for me to buy the Braun family presents." I knew that they were already informed about his fiancée, Barbara.

"Did you know that Braun has already served one sentence for trying to escape from the DDR?" He was jumping to another subject, obviously trying to throw me off guard.

"Yes."

"Do you know his best friend, Harold?"

"Yes."

"Have you met Braun on any other occasion here?"

"Yes."

"Had you met Mrs. Braun before tonight?"

"Yes."

"Did you ever talk about escape with Braun?"

"No!" I felt the drops of perspiration collecting on my forehead.

His gaze continued to penetrate mine, his eyes unwavering. I forced myself not to look away, in spite of the deliberate lie I had just uttered. I had never looked into anyone's eyes and pronounced an absolute lie, and a knot twisted in my stomach. Surely my eyes, which always spoke sincerely from within, would reveal that I had spoken an untruth.

"Do you expect me to believe that?"

"Yes." The knot in my stomach tightened. The Weasel's eyes never left mine as bony fingers lifted a cigarette to his thin lips. His gestures were nervous and the pallid aura about him produced a consumptive appearance. He proffered a cigarette which I refused and then exhaled a long puff, followed by a pause, indicating that he had plenty of time to await my answers.

"Why don't you tell me about everything you've done since you entered the DDR?"

"I've already told you." His persistence was making me sick with fright.

Another man entered the room. At first he observed me attentively and remained silent. He was a roly-poly blond with a pleasant round face, which glowed with an ironic smile. His pudgy cheeks and pink skin reminded me of a pig. Then he injected an occasional question, and the atmosphere became one of cynicism, punctuated by outbursts of aggression from both sides.

"I want to hear your story," the Pig coaxed. "I haven't heard it yet."

I traced for the third time my movements since entering East Berlin. I stuck to the same story.

"You really don't expect us to believe that now, do you, Miss Battle?" he sneered. "Your own FBI wouldn't swallow a story like that. How could you expect us to?"

"Well," I answered, annoyed by their stubbornness, "it's your business whether you believe it or not. I've told you the truth!"

"Sure you have . . . just not all of it! We want to know the *whole* story from you."

"That's all!" I protested. My back was wet with perspiration. Something had to give. I could not keep up the pace much longer.

The interrogation took on the nature of a cat-and-mouse game. I was the mouse already in the trap, and the cat was delighted to paw me around. All their responses were interspersed with proverbial sayings, such as "A spider spins a web and gets tangled up in it himself," or "You're more pious than the Pope." The statements were accompanied by sardonic smiles and always the question, "You know what we mean, don't you, Miss Battle?"

Finally, I was too upset to play their game from an intellectual distance. My aggression was mounting. Were they provoking me on purpose? They were, but I had reached the point where it no longer mattered. Finally, they believed nothing I told them, not even the tiny unimportant details. My blood was boiling and I was playing right into their hands when I no longer resisted the inclination to explode.

"You're no different from the Nazis!" I shouted. "You're just like the SS men!"

"Be careful. I don't think you know what you are saying," the Pig warned me.

"Yes. You're criminals!" I went on furiously.

"Did you know that we can imprison foreigners?" the Weasel asked with a threatening glare.

"I'm sure your prisons are full of foreigners and West Germans!"

The tension was increasing, and it was clear that they would not accept my story under any condition.

"What would you say if we told you we had Sammy?" the Pig finally queried.

"I wouldn't believe you," I answered obstinately.

Then a cloud of fear swept through me. I had been confident that they had not caught him. What if they had seen us together already? I had assumed that the appearance of the police at Brauns' apartment was for a routine questioning. It was possible, however, that Sammy and I had been followed.

"No, I'm sure you wouldn't," the Pig answered.

"My, aren't you a good actress, though," the Weasel remarked. "You certainly can 'act' well." He used the German expression *Theaterspielen,* usually denoting someone "putting on a show" that was not genuine.

"I am not a cold German!" I exclaimed.

With those words I wanted to express far more than they could ever comprehend. They had been uttered in response to the reference to my "acting," but I was really thinking of the conflict of ideology versus humanity. The history of Germany had manifested again and again a victory of fanatics of ideology—man in his simple humanity had always been smothered and oppressed by some ideology *about* man—where some ideology had inflamed followers to submit themselves obediently, with all their rigid authoritarian training, to the yoke imposed by a strong leader who took over their wills. They were a herd of sheep searching for a shepherd, but not questioning—just accepting the strongest that came along.

"Where is the justice, the humaneness, the freedom you are always screaming about in your propaganda?" I demanded. "Where are human rights?" I was ready to launch into an attack against all the evils of their system, when the chubby interrogator interrupted.

"We would be discussing different concepts if we spoke of justice, humanity, and freedom. Besides, don't you talk to us about human rights— you, an American, when your country doesn't even recognize Negroes as citizens!" He paused and took a deep breath. "And look at your dirty war in Vietnam. No, you have no right to tell us anything."

It was no use arguing. They were fanatically convinced of the evil of the American government, and clearly held the same opinions "the Party" propagated. I wanted to tell them that the Federal Government itself had been responsible for tearing down racial barriers; the solution to that problem was a matter of time. Already in my lifetime I had witnessed growth between the attitudes of two generations. Many young people rejected the bigotry of their parents. Of course, there would always be fanatics to deal with, but that was not the system! No, it was useless to tell them that I, as an American, had a right they did not possess—a right to criticize the government. Their state did not recognize this right. They claimed one was entitled to his own opinion—but, of course, he was not allowed to express it.

There was no sign of letting up on the interrogation. Although the blond interrogator had left, the Weasel kept pounding me with questions. In one of his long exasperated pauses, he offered me a cup of coffee. When I refused, he assured me that nothing had been put into it. How could I believe him?

I had long since removed my heavy coat. I sat erect with my fur hat still on, wondering what would come next. My purse had been taken away from me and its contents lay strewn on the Weasel's desk.

"Let's begin the whole story from the beginning." The beady eyes challenged mine.

"I've told you everything I remember."

"Not *everything*," he contradicted. "Where did you get your schooling in handling interrogations? From the CIA?"

Fright choked me. The questions had wandered off into the area of espionage, and worry began to gnaw away at my last desperate hope of convincing him of my story. These police were notorious for hanging crimes on innocent victims of the regime or distorting the truth to fit their needs. They needed no proof, or if they felt they did, it could be fabricated easily enough. If they had even the slightest suspicion that I might be a spy, they would detain me a long time.

Maybe it would be better to tell the truth. After all, what had I really done? Almost everyone in Berlin—both sides of the Wall—talks about escape at one time or another. Surely my conversations were not that serious, for nothing had been carried out. Their psychological warfare against me began to play havoc with any sense of superiority I may have had in outsmarting them. I was being edged into a blind alley and their implications of espionage were quelling any hope of my getting away.

Then the Weasel shifted his interrogation to the subject of Harold, Sammy's best friend. I remembered that Harold had been called in for questioning on Sammy's previous arrest, and I felt sure that now he had been brought to the pillory too. I readily admitted knowing Harold and related our one meeting.

"You cannot tell me that you never mentioned escape," the Weasel stated firmly.

"Well, that's natural—of course, only in general terms. . . ."

"What methods were cited? What methods do you know about? You can't deny you know anything about this. Everyone in West Berlin reads the newspaper."

"Oh, I have just heard about false passports."

"Is that all?"

"Yes."

"What else?"

"Nothing."

I found myself on shaky ground, and with quivering uncertainty convinced myself that nothing of significance had really been said. It was a fact that I had lived in West Berlin for some time. That automatically meant I was somewhat versed in the Wall situation.

The Pig returned. The Weasel became silent. I saw that by exercising reserve I could sometimes outwit the shrewdness of the Weasel, but the pleasantness and reassuring manner of the rotund little Pig seemed to minimize all danger, and I found words I wanted to withhold slipping over my tongue when he questioned me.

Now it was clear that he knew something. There was no doubt these police also had Sammy within their clutches. That meant Sammy, his mother, possibly Harold, and I were all being cross-examined at once. Sammy's mother worried me most. She was forced to continue her life in the East and her husband had lost his job as a result of Sammy's past imprisonment. They could remind her of these things, threaten her with new repercussions, and squeeze information out of her.

It was after midnight already and the questioning had been running in vicious circles. Perhaps if I told them how harmless it all was, they would release me. But that choking sensation dammed up any explanation I might give, and I was powerless.

"How long is this going to take?" I asked finally.

An icy and disparaging retort hit me: "That depends on you—when you decide to tell the truth!"

"But I've told you the truth," again I protested.

"Sure you have—but still not all of it. . . . We have plenty of time to wait."

"I've already told that I am the victim of a coincidence! I just happened to come after he deserted the army. If I had known, I wouldn't have come."

"Why?" The Weasel smirked.

"Because I could have expected something like this! I had nothing to do with it! Believe me. I didn't know he deserted!"

"Why don't you tell us about your meeting with Braun tonight, then?"

I swallowed a moist lump. Of course they had him! They had probably been waiting for us at Alexander Platz. They had posted their agents for the meeting. I had no thread of security to cling to. They appeared to be familiar with our conversations, too. Hadn't Sammy told me he had mentioned our meeting to Harold? Yes, Harold!

"It was not a coincidence, Miss Battle, that we picked you up this evening." The Weasel's voice rang with smug assurance. "Anyway, there is a *law* of coincidence, of chance. Sometimes it isn't coincidence at all." He paced back and forth.

I vaguely knew what he was referring to in the teachings of Marx. Marx claims that much of what we term coincidence in history had to happen, because conditions were such that it did not occur accidentally. I saw the uselessness of entering into an argument with him about the philosophical limitations of Marxism and the evolution of history since Marx's time— after all, he was fanatically convinced of his doctrine. In other words, he was saying that my coming to meet Sammy on this particular night at a certain time was no coincidence as I claimed, but the result of some law. Perhaps he was right, but for different reasons than he thought. I was more willing to accept the law of Providence, whose hand was not quite visible to me yet.

"Harold is your agent!" I started violently, no longer able to contain myself. "I thought so! He even said that the Security Police had made him an offer which he refused." Now the jaws of their vise had closed on me. I had said enough to convict myself.

"We never reveal where we get our information. You can rest assured we have our channels. You'll never find out, though," he stated pretentiously. "Now are you ready to tell us the truth about this evening?"

A myriad of question marks dotted my consciousness. I was certain that truth is victorious—even though it takes longer to stake its claim. But I could not open up. As far as I was concerned, the whole matter of helping Sammy was innocent and well-meant, but I was aware of the fact that they could make so much out of it all, twisting and distorting to preposterous proportions. It involved disclosing names. Perhaps others could be arrested. I was overwhelmed with the sensation of facing a major operation in which an important organ was being painfully removed, but ever so slowly.

The remainder of the night is nebulous in my memory. Repetition of the same questions. More details. I stuck to my story and, although they refused to buy it, they wrote it down.

At about seven o'clock in the morning, a guard came and led me into a cell and announced I could lie down for a while. With groggy eyes, I scanned the bare room, where only a freshly dressed bed, a hard-backed chair, and a wall cabinet met me with an indifferent welcome. Nevertheless, it offered a refuge from the harassment.

A policewoman appeared in the doorway, where she parked her buxom body and observed me with hard, expressionless eyes.

I immediately threw myself across the bed, releasing the long tension in loud hysterical wailing. Between paroxysms of tears, I coughed and choked for air. Repugnant nausea filled me, but I was unable to vomit. When the stout policewoman scowled and ordered me to shut up, it only increased my anguish.

I was unable to relax and my thoughts raced to West Berlin. Pangs of nostalgic longing gripped me. "Today is Thanksgiving," I thought. I had invited a German family for an American Thanksgiving meal. I had so looked forward to sharing an American Thanksgiving with them. For a year they had taken me under their wing, providing me with one decent meal a week which my starvation budget did not allow. Now it was impossible. Another flood of tears gushed forth.

An officer entered the cell and sternly ordered me to be quiet. "You're upsetting the whole prison!" I ignored him, crying even louder. I was delighted to be able to upset the prison. It was my only way of striking back at them. Nothing could stop the flow of those tears, which were purging, cleansing, relieving. They alleviated the nauseating sickness. As I lay there I was awaiting one thing. When would they return for me?

Oh, dear, dear Sammy, how did we ever get involved in all this?

2

LAST TRAIN TO FREEDOM

I HAD BEEN STANDING at the Friedrichstrasse crossing in East Berlin, awaiting the arrival of a West German friend. We had both decided to attend Brecht's *Coriolan* at the Berliner Ensemble in East Berlin and had left West Berlin at the same time. However, foreigners were processed much more rapidly than West Germans, and at different control points; therefore, I was left to wait in the bustling station for more than an hour. . . .

Suddenly I turned around and gazed into two of the warmest eyes I had ever seen. They danced with unreserved sincerity, and a round boyish face addressed me boldly in German. "You're an American?"

"Yes," I answered without hesitation to the stranger at my side, "but I didn't think I looked like one. How could you tell?"

His lips curled into a smile. "Oh, I can spot them anywhere."

Somehow that response failed to suffice. No one took me for an American. If I wasn't thought to be German, I was usually taken for Swedish or Dutch.

"I know how you know," I stated suddenly after a flash of recognition. "Those fellows I was talking to. I showed them my passport, because they didn't believe I was an American."

"Well, I must admit you're right. You don't really look like an American. . . ."

It was thus that Sammy entered my life one April afternoon in East Berlin.

Amidst thundering trains, filing tourists, and patrolling guards, Sammy and I exchanged animated conversation. I discovered that he was twenty-one years old, had already served a year imprisonment for attempted escape, had received his nickname from American soldiers after the war, and was engaged to an American girl from California. Meanwhile, Sammy learned that I had been teaching English in Germany since 1962 and studying psychology and theology at the Free University in West Berlin, where I lived in a student dormitory in Dahlem.

I did not generally allow such a conversation with a stranger, but after Sammy told me about his engagement to a fellow American, I understood his frank and outspoken manner with me. I knew how I had felt when I had fallen in love with Hans in Spain three years before. After he returned to Germany I had felt a sort of closeness to all Germans I met and wanted to share a certain confidence with them. In fact, it was this same feeling that spread itself into an admiration for all Germans. It had prompted me to make Germany my home after finishing college, so I could be near Hans.

Hans' vital masculinity, his exploring spirit, eager inquisitiveness, sensitive critical mind, and strong streak of romanticism—all activating a sturdy Germanic body—had introduced me to a new type of man. And I had fallen reeling, head over heels in love, transferring all his positive qualities onto the Germanic people. I finally decided I must discover the land that produced those Teutonic giants.

My first encounter in the enchanted land itself had been a rude awakening, when crude, gruff pedestrians pushed me around the streets, and puffy, arrogant egotists demanded their unconditional rights. The strong and courageous seemed to remain in seclusion, overshadowed by their timid, philistine brothers. And it was not until I found my way back into the university halls after a year's teaching experience in Western Germany's private schools that I detected other Germanic Apollos. Hans had married in the meantime, but there were numerous brothers still at large.

I observed the stranger at my side. For me he was no longer a stranger. His handsome boy-like face, his warm generous spirit, and the sincere, sparkling eyes were enough to make any mother want to cuddle him in her arms. His whole person seemed to evoke a feminine softness and concern. Certainly his story was sad enough to incite a sympathetic response even from the less sensitive. He had lost more than a year of his youth at hard labor for a state he did not accept, was doomed to wasting his days at a job he detested, and now, he revealed, his engagement to a fellow countryman of mine posed an impossible situation as long as he remained in East Germany.

The meeting struck me as too coincidental to be a coincidence. It had to be more. Already an idea began to take shape in the background of our friendly chatter.

By the time Heinrich, my West German friend, had arrived at the crossing exit, Sammy and I had sealed a tacit agreement. We had exchanged addresses and I had promised to assist his fiancée, Barbara, in finding lodging in West Berlin on her arrival in August.

I latched onto Heinrich's arm, and after the two men had been introduced, we three ambled toward the direction of the theater.

The street scene afforded a contrast for any new arrival from the West. Long faces with expressionless eyes cast downward passed by in a depressed cadence. The absence of the activity of cars, the fashions of another decade, the ugly ruins left by heavy bombs announced that we were in another Germany—one that had received a cold shoulder from Dame Prosperity.

Although the performance of *Coriolan* was outstanding, I failed to become engrossed in it. Sammy and his plight still occupied my thoughts. One thing was certain. Those soft eyes had silently spoken to me with a sincerity and pleading I could not ignore.

I do not know what it was that impressed me so deeply. The political imprisonment, the engagement to a fellow countryman, the fact that he no longer had the possibility of an academic career in his state, or simply Sammy himself. . . .

It was only some days after my encounter that Jerry, an American serviceman, dropped by the dormitory for a visit. I wasted no time in reciting the events in East Berlin.

He listened with interest, exhaling casual wisps of smoke, his eyes growing darker as I reached my silent commitment to help Sammy.

"And how did you intend to assist him?" he queried when I had finished.

I hesitated, taking a deep breath. "Your car," was the only explanation I could manage.

Jerry pursed his lips tightly and squinted his eyelids together in narrow slits. He remained silent. Then he briefly relaxed his tense features. "Do you know how the army feels about that?" he inquired soberly.

"No, but I could imagine that they are concerned with helping East Germans," I replied.

"Yes, but if any assistance is given, they want to give it themselves. In other words, it's strictly forbidden. It could cause an international incident if a soldier got caught doing that! And it would certainly involve difficulties for the government, since we don't recognize the regime."

"But you wouldn't have to get caught. Nothing would be simpler than driving to the opera, leaving your trunk unlocked, and driving back to West Berlin," I continued, trying to convince him.

"That's what you think! Not long ago a couple of guys were nabbed. They got busted and sent to the zone. No. Nothing doing." He screwed up his features in tense resistance, a sign that there was no budging. "One thing, though, I would advise you to keep out of such activities for your own good."

I strongly resented the fatherlike warning. I dismissed the matter temporarily, unconvinced of its impossibility. Jerry only lacked courage, for I had heard him mention his interest in participating in the like before.

One afternoon in May I was seated at my desk, drifting in a reverie induced by the spring landscape outside my window, when someone pounded away at my door.

I was surprised to see Juergen, an occupant of the same dormitory. His hurried gestures and grimaces spoke of nervous excitement.

"Hellen, I've gotta talk to you."

"Come on in," I invited him, baffled by the sudden visit. He had never visited me before.

Juergen was a stocky, robust fellow and dominated by a gruff manner that corresponded to his raw masculine appearance. I speculated whether his stuttering speech and limp had been caused by his escape to West Berlin, since I knew him to be an East German refugee.

"I need help." Then Juergen told me the story of his friend Peter Schmidt. Somehow he had been notified that this college friend, who was still in East Germany, was in trouble with the state. Juergen had investigated every escape route that seemed feasible, but to no avail.

"But why have you come to me?" I asked.

"Because you're an American," he responded. "Surely the Americans can do something about it! I've seen a couple of GI's come here in their uniforms. Do you think they can help?"

I reflected momentarily. He had arrived at the same conclusion as I about "the Americans." At the moment it struck me that his plea provided just another piece of a pattern that was being woven into my life. . . .

Again I thought of Jerry. We had nurtured a long acquaintance and often we had discussed the Berlin problem intensely. From him I had learned that the allied military forces had free uncontrolled access to East Berlin. That meant a soldier could conceal an East German in the trunk compartment of his car and drive into West Berlin without being inspected. The American forces took no orders from the East German regime, which our government did not recognize, but were subject only to the Russian military personnel. In all my crossings to East Berlin, I had never encountered a Russian. Moreover, Jerry had bought a car not too long ago. . . .

Struggling with myself about the consequences of the next statement, I finally decided to make it.

"Maybe I can help you," I carefully pronounced the words I knew him to be waiting for, "but under one condition. I would like to know your friend's reason for escaping." I continued by narrating my encounter with Sammy in April and my subsequent discussion with Jerry about the possibility of the former's escape.

"You see, Juergen, that's the status of things. I have no idea whether Jerry is really a possibility for your friend."

"If you want to find out the circumstances, I can arrange a meeting for you," Juergen replied. "He studies in Greifswald, but I can telegraph him to come to East Berlin." His response reflected so much hope that I felt a sense of obligation to help his friend. It was then I agreed to arranging a meeting with Peter Schmidt in East Berlin.

Ironically enough, I had been warned about any kind of escape activity by a student leader of the Christian Student Movement. He claimed that there were too many who attempted escape out of purely selfish motives. Too many were eager to risk all in order to wallow in the excesses of the "golden West" and lacked the maturity or ability to handle their abundance of freedom with responsibility. Time and time again a refugee had reached the Western paradise, only to be swallowed up in the greedy mouth of the "economic miracle."

Although I had agreed with his general stand, the cases of Juergen's friend Peter and of Sammy certainly seemed to be exceptions. Anyway, even if they were not, I felt that every man is entitled to his freedom! Man can only grow and mature when he exercises his free decision and judgment. Yes. Every man should have the right of choice, the right to decide freely, even if he does make the decision to live selfishly. Man has only one life to live.

But I insisted on investigating Peter Schmidt's motivation before even agreeing to approach Jerry.

A few days after the excitement of Juergen's unexpected visit subsided, I found myself staring out the window of the rickety old S-Bahn, with East Berlin my destination. My fingers curved around the edges of the photograph in my pocket, which I removed, examined with exactitude, and replaced in its dark niche. Peter Schmidt turned out to be a small man, with a triangular face and sharp features. He was not handsome, and a high forehead revealed a prematurely receding hairline that disappeared into thinning wisps of hair.

As Peter and I strolled along the deserted cobblestone street, he kept jerking his head around to ascertain whether we were being followed. We had chosen a seemingly secluded area around Mueggel Lake for our rendezvous. As he recounted the dilemma his wife had involved him in, I was overwhelmed by the urgency of his words. The pressing importunity of his plea was not Sammy's "I can't stand it here." It was more. If the story he was relating held the truth, he was the victim of political persecution.

Only for an instant did doubt flash through my mind. But there I was accepting this strange man with the same unconditional confidence I had bestowed on Sammy. What if I was mistaken and everything was a clever trap? For it was no secret that Eastern agents worked their way into the student life of West Berlin.

No, I was sure I could rely on what the Germans called *Menschenkenntnis*—an instinctive judgment of human nature—to decide whether Peter was leveling with me. I prided myself upon a natural endowment of this character trait, and I could not recall a single instance when my judgment had erred.

A trial awaited him, Peter had told me, in which he could expect no justice. A wife, who was divorcing him on political grounds, had set out to destroy him. She was a staunch loyalist to the Communist Party and a judge by profession. In the course of their marriage, she had tried every tactic to win Peter over to the party. He had resisted silently until one day the two launched into a heated wrangling.

Peter had spoken openly about the abuses of the East German regime—the forced opinions, the one-sided ideological distortions of the media, the lack of freedom of the press, the fanaticism and hatred, and the Wall itself. The result of the violent clash was his wife's filing for divorce. Such a divorce had further implications—outspoken strong disagreement was so-called "agitation" against the government and punishable by high sentences.

In East Germany all students had scholarships from the state, and conflict with the government automatically meant expulsion from the university. The least Peter could expect as a result of trouble with the state was the termination of his education. One year remained in his physics study, and his entire future went down the drain if he had to give this up.

Peter had pleaded with his wife to dissuade her from getting the divorce. She remained cold and unyielding. Then he tried a compromise, begging her to state adultery as the grounds. However, she persisted in her hard-heartedness. Moreover, it was useless to try to fight it out legally. His wife had the omnipotent state and the law on her side. There remained only one solution for him now—escape.

I departed from East Berlin with the promise to approach Jerry on the matter—only this time more firmly. I assured Peter, though, that I was very pessimistic about enlisting his aid. Peter, in turn, agreed that he would not attempt escape if his wife withdrew the suit, which seemed unlikely. However, I relinquished any immediate decision to the course of events the future would bring.

At the beginning of June, Juergen appeared at my door once more. Was

Jerry willing to help? No, I was unable to give him a positive answer. In spite of my ranting, raving, and pleading, Jerry had turned a deaf ear to the whole affair. Consequently, Peter was at his rope's end. The only method that now seemed possible was the one Juergen had employed—a difficult procedure with which he himself had been unsuccessful on his first attempt. Great resources in physical endurance were required and Peter was a frail man. Moreover, the probability existed that the procedure had already been uncovered by the police. Nevertheless, Juergen would send a friend to East Berlin to disclose the details of his own escape, which had been one year before. The rest would be left to Peter and Providence.

A couple of days after my refusal, I sat in an exquisite French restaurant eating châteaubriand with Jerry. Midnight had already struck, but we lingered over our crepes suzette. Little did I know what event was taking place in East Berlin.

Peter Schmidt's entire future dangled on a thread. Indeed, his whole life. If he made a dash for it now, the patrol dogs were certain to detect him. But if he hesitated too long, the sentries would be returning on their rounds.

He glanced at his watch. It was shortly after 2 A.M. To make it out into the sprawling railroad yards he had to scale two fences without being spotted. Fortunately the suburban train had just stopped running, because his first obstacle was crossing its tracks. Once he ventured into the yards, though, he had to determine which of the numerous trains was destined for Cologne or Hamburg. That would be a crucial step. There was no time for deliberation. Once in the area there was the danger of arrest for unauthorized persons.

Peter was pressed for time, since the police would be searching for him after he failed to appear for his second trial. He had spent the previous week scouting the layout of the Rummelsburg railroad yards, passing his nights in the dense undergrowth that fringed the area. The success of the operation depended on a precise knowledge of the routines. The timing of the intervals with which the watches patrolled, the number of sentries on duty, the frequency of the rounds, all required observation.

There was the problem of the dogs, too. Juergen, however, had told him how to overcome that obstacle. For it was the very item Juergen had overlooked on his first escape attempt in Czechoslovakia. To ward off the hounds, Peter had soaked his apparel and drenched his body in petroleum. The patrol dogs were then unable to detect any human scent.

The two trains did not depart from East Berlin until 6:30 and 7:00 A.M., but the entrance to the yards had to take place under the shield of darkness.

At midnight Peter had changed his garb in an abandoned garden and then stationed himself in the bushes alongside the fence that enclosed the suburban train tracks. Even though June had arrived, the nights were still chilly. Peter shivered more from fright than from the damp sticky clothes that clung to his body.

After he observed two sentries with slung machine guns ambling through their patrol of the Cologne train, he decided that it was now or never. He crawled out of his bushy seclusion and stalked across the open field, an oily silhouette against a black sky. He rushed to scale the two wire fences and landed with a loud thud in the railroad yard.

The moment was decisive. If discovered now, it was all over. The next step was a risky long stretch to reach the Cologne train. He bent down and stole over to the car. Having reached it, he lowered his body backwards, slinking under the carriage, and grabbed the greasy brake rod. With great effort, he heaved himself into position and sighed with relief.

The struggle this far was a long way away from victory. Hours of waiting in a cramped position might prove fatal to the scheme. To him it now appeared impossible to maintain his grip for four hours on the connecting rods between the brakes with no support for his body. Besides, it hung too low and presented the danger of being seen. A solution had to be found at once.

Squinting in the smutty underskirts of the railroad carriage, Peter detected another niche of concealment. He stretched out his arms and hoisted himself upward into the frame of the car, which braced his trunk considerably better. There he was out of sight. In fact, the thought crossed his mind that he could remain in his newly discovered roost when the train set into motion. This idea was quickly dispelled when it occurred to him that he would be crushed to death by the springs when the movement commenced. It would only supply a temporary waiting station until the heavy wheels rolled forward.

Peter had just adjusted his limbs to the frame when he caught sight of the approaching feet of the guards. Immediately before them were the leashed dogs. A sharp pain raced through his heart, rendering him breathless. Had they spotted him creeping under the car and were they coming to seize him?

The hounds drew nearer, sniffing loudly with their muzzles glued to the ground. Then—they passed. A shudder of relief ran through him at the realization he had not been detected. At least, not yet.

Other guards would return. The same paralyzing fear would seize him again. Perhaps the effect of the petroleum would wear off. The racking pain of cramped nerves and muscles already tormented his body in unbearable anguish. But there was no turning back now, not after he had triumphed this far. To back out now would mean inevitable capture or death.

The engine of the train coughed out a blast of steam, lurched forward, and eased into motion. Instantaneously, a giddiness surged through Peter's cramped body and strained emotions as he stretched down and clutched the connecting rod.

The train was scheduled to stop in East Berlin where it would be thoroughly inspected before arriving at West Berlin's Zoo station. Peter was unsure whether there were one or two stops in the East.

The Cologne train rolled into Ostbahnhof. Peter could hear the heavy footsteps of guards climbing aboard to inspect it. Again, he scrambled up into the frame for the waiting period. Finally, after what seemed an exaggerated interval, the wheels rolled forward once more.

When the train reached the next station shortly afterwards, Peter had to make a hasty decision. He was ready to climb out of concealment when it dawned on him that he must be in Friedrichstrasse, still in East Berlin. Again guards stormed aboard the train and performed their last thorough examination before they dispatched the Cologne train to the West. The next destination was Zoo station, West Berlin! It was the following extended minutes that Peter thought he would not survive. The train finally crawled out of the station, and after an endless period, it screeched to an abrupt halt. Freiheit! Who had ever dreamed he would reach it? Yes, there he was. A free man!

A whole new horizon unfolded before him, flooding him with light, as he clambered out from under his freedom train. He charged forward, his aching legs hardly carrying him, and rushed with all the swiftness his weary body allowed through the barrier, down the steps, through the empty hall, and out onto the streets of West Berlin.

Dawn was just unfurling a warm welcome. The air was fresh and

*still. The first signs of the new day already enlivened sleepy streets, and
West Berliners had begun to bustle about.*

I returned home next day with a heavy heart, in spite of the beaming
rays of the rare sunshine. The day was invested with the promise of a
friendly summer, and the flower-laden spring boughs in the Gelfertstrasse
garden had already shed their last aromatic blossoms. It was the time of
Pentecost, the powerful outpouring of the Spirit. I was still burdened with
the fate of Peter, wondering what had happened to him.

Suddenly, Juergen raced out of the dorm onto the stony walkway. I had
never seen him so excited.

"Hellen! Hellen! Come quick!" He dashed through the door, tripping up
the stairway that led to his room. I hurried along behind him, suspecting
the worst.

He stopped before his room and flung the door open.

There, sitting erect on the bed, breathless and grinning from ear to ear,
was Peter Schmidt!

I rushed to him and enveloped him with a hearty hug of congratulations.
"Man! How did you do it?" I cried out in excitement.

Juergen, another friend who had just arrived as part of the welcoming
committee, and I eagerly begged for the details of his escape.

Peter had appeared at the first proceedings of the case against him, and
when summoned to a second trial, where witnesses were to be called in to
testify against him, he became aware of the course the action was taking.
This behavior was highly irregular in divorce proceedings, and he knew he
had to get out as soon as possible. Then he had made his decision.

Peter Schmidt sat across from me, radiant and proud of his courageous victory. He had lighted one cigarette after another during his fevered
narrative. Yesterday, a frightened fugitive in East Berlin; today, a free
citizen of West Berlin.

I had already told both Peter and Juergen about Sammy. It occurred to
me that Sammy could risk Peter's escape method, and we all concluded that
Peter's freedom train could also become Sammy's. First, however, waiting
was essential. Peter had related his story to each of the allied powers in

West Berlin, and we feared that a leak in information might have occurred. Peter gladly consented to sharing the details with Sammy, but with one reservation. The procedure must otherwise remain secret. Perhaps it could prove a last resort to another in grave danger.

As Peter clarified the particulars by scribbling a rough diagram, I marveled at the brotherhood the refugees displayed for each other. I was especially struck by the sense of responsibility they demonstrated for those they had left behind—even though they were strangers.

It was a sultry July day when I was finally able to arrange my second meeting with Sammy in East Berlin.

A tiny wave of fear welled up when I thought about the sticking sensation between my breasts. I had hidden the sketch of the railroad yards in my bra. What if the border guards decided to examine me? They needed no suspicion to force a physical examination on anyone. They routinely performed random searches. I was disgusted with myself that I had even bothered to bring the diagram along anyway. It was superfluous now—I knew all the information by heart.

Sammy and I met at the designated place, an East Berlin café near Friedrichstrasse. I unfolded all of the details of Peter's escape, and cautioned him not to reveal the disclosed information, neither to his friend Harold, nor to his mother, who was his most trusted confidante. In event of arrest, the parents were always the first ones called in for interrogation.

Sammy readily agreed, pledging absolute secrecy. He decided to investigate the method by nightly vigils hidden in the skirts of the railroad yards. Although he was not enthusiastic about the method, he agreed to explore it, waiting until the nights had grown longer, but not until they had become too cold.

We parted with last-minute "Auf Wiedersehens" at the border. He squeezed my hand in gratitude, and again I felt drawn to him, to help him. Midnight had already struck. The sleepy guards eyed me curiously as they handed me my passport. I was the last traveler to the West in the deserted hall.

As the train rolled into West Berlin, I sighed with relief and a weight lifted from my chest. A heavy oppressing air always overcame me on entering East Berlin. Was my fantasy really too active, as Sammy had implied in the evening, or did the grim atmosphere really exist?

The meshy rows of tiers and snares; the heavy-layered concrete blocks; the stern guards with slung machine guns; the exhausting wait to cross the border. All of that constituted a barrier and offered no sign of friendly reception to a foreign visitor. That silent Wall spoke for itself, proclaiming more than propaganda of East or West could ever declare.

Several weeks had elapsed since Sammy's and my second encounter. Early one morning I opened my door after gentle rapping sounded. A lovely young woman stood in the doorway. Immediately I knew it was Barbara, Sammy's fiancée.

Barbara was a slender, well-shaped 5′6″ and had a lovely, delicately featured face. Her hair was ashy-white blonde, but lacked the harshness that often accompanies bleached hair. Her manner, however, was what struck me as her outstanding quality. She emitted a soft, subdued aura of femininity and all her mannerisms and gestures expressed a suave graciousness. I liked her at once because of her genial kindliness.

I managed to arrange for Barbara's lodging in the dormitory, which rented out to summer guests, and promised her my room when I departed for Paris in just two days. I had enrolled in a French course at the *Alliance Française* for the month of September. I spent long hours briefing her in the events that had taken place in East Berlin before her arrival.

It was a sticky day in late summer when I boarded the train at the Zoo station to depart from West Berlin. The French capital was my destination, and I was full of ecstatic expectation over the reunion with Paris after four years, but I was reluctant to leave West Berlin without knowing Sammy's fate. The train chugged through the city's skirts, the last sign of freedom disappearing before angry watchtowers and hostile barricades. With fleeting dismissal, I whispered "Adieu" to Sammy, Barbara, West Berlin, and Germany. However, I knew I would take them along with me. "Sammy, I am pulling for you," I thought to myself. "That Wall can never stop *you*!"

3

THE SECOND MILE

PARIS PROVIDED a warning I was somehow unable to heed, because I became intoxicated with her lofty, free spirit. There I found myself totally enamored with life, experiencing an exuberance that wanted to reach out with open arms and embrace everyone. I accepted all individuals with the same lack of reserve and unconditional openness with which I had responded to Sammy and Peter. Hence, I returned to Germany a month's income poorer. I had fallen victim to an astute swindler.

The experience had affected me profoundly, since it issued a clear warning about an unconditional trust in human relations. The greater shock for me had not been losing a month's income, but the fact I had so completely erred in my judgment of another individual.

If Sammy's and my scattered rendezvous in East Berlin had provided no ground for suspicion in the past, it was evident that the present operation must have aroused police attention. Barbara had been making daily visits to East Berlin and even spending nights in the family's apartment. Once at the crossing a guard had questioned her concerning her destination. She had responded truthfully with Sammy's name and address. Since he had a prison record, this certainly came to the notice of the police.

A difficulty had arisen, however, in Sammy and Barbara's relationship to each other, which was now very stormy with frequent outbursts of quarrels. While I was away, they had become officially engaged with rings and all. Sammy was now even willing to marry her in East Germany if no other way was open to them.

Barbara, acting on my advice, had gone to the American consulate in West Berlin to investigate the legal aspects of marriage for the two, and subsequent emigration from East Germany for Sammy, which was possible in a few rare instances. The only advice she had received was "Leave that man and have nothing to do with him." The visit strengthened the air of hopelessness that already enveloped the relationship. She was torn by conflict between her American morality, the married life she was already leading, and the improbability of a satisfactory future in light of the whole situation. The tension gave rise to violent misunderstandings, slowly gnawing away the bond that had once united them.

Now another big fight had taken place and Barbara had reluctantly decided to return to America without revisiting East Berlin. She hated to leave without thanking Sammy's parents and apologizing for the abrupt departure, but begged me to do it for her. She left a hundred marks with me to dispose of however Mrs. Braun saw fit, of course with the approaching Christmas season in mind.

The evening before she left I received a telegram from Sammy, telling me to meet him the following day in the city; neither time nor place was given. I assumed it meant at his family's house.

As Barbara and I traveled to the airport in the taxi, I could not help feeling sorry for her, leaving on such a sad note. It was a bleak departure. The sky was a chill gray, and the mid-October weather was crisp and biting, the September sunshine having already vanished as quickly as it had come.

"It's the only way now, leaving like this," she confided, fighting to conceal her melancholy. "Perhaps something can be worked out between us later on. But as long as he remains in East Berlin. . . ." She stopped short, the rest of the sentence trailing into a long sigh. I knew the rest.

She glanced out the window with a disheartened last look before we entered the Templehof airport. "I hate having to go through it all every day. Control every twenty-four hours. The long train rides. The frustrating wait at the border. It's all so depressing. Sometimes I just come home in the evening and cry my heart out for no reason. No, I can't take it all any more." I knew she was seeking to justify her sudden departure. She had resigned herself to the fact that it was all over.

As she walked through the customs barrier before disappearing in the long corridor of doorways that led to the planes, I noticed with a surge of pity that her clothes hung loosely on her now and the glow of her eyes had become dimmer.

Since the airport was just two subway stations from the Friedrichstrasse crossing, I immediately headed there. Sammy would certainly be expecting me.

At the border I became preoccupied with the guard's snarling statement about the purpose of my visit, as he handed me my papers. I mumbled in reply something about a museum visit, but I was certain it sounded unconvincing. I meant to watch out whether I was being followed, but my mind raced away to queries about the purpose of the telegram, and I forgot to take notice.

When I reached Sammy's house it was still early, and only a few people were on the street. I rang the bell at his apartment.

After what appeared to be ten minutes, Sammy's beaming face popped up in the doorway. We marched up the stairs together, immediately retreating behind the closed door of his den, where he started asking questions about Barbara. Indeed, Sammy was upset by Barbara's leaving, and although he was convinced that the relationship had no future, the void she left was painful to him.

An hour's probing conference about the pair's misunderstandings and about the proposed escape charged the atmosphere with a sense of urgency. He handed me a postcard from the East German army. They were requesting his presence at the beginning of November, just two weeks away. What was worse, however, was that, breaking his promise to me, he had included Harold in his plan to escape.

He confided apologetically that his friend was responsible for postponing the operation. Now Harold, whose birthday was the last week in October, was begging him to wait until after the celebration.

"How absurd!" I answered irritably. "This Harold character seems to be messing up your plans. It's not urgent for him to escape, and I don't feel he has the backbone to carry it out! But, you! You keep letting him talk you out of it."

Something about Harold did not ring true, and I knew he had no sympathy for me, either, as much as he had tried to convince me otherwise.

Why did he constantly pump information out of Sammy? Detailed questions about our conversations, the plans, the possibilities? Now Sammy expressed his own doubts about his friend, but there was no backing out.

From Sammy's den we moved into the living room, where I had a chance to meet Sammy's mother. She was petite and lively, almost French in her temperament, but also firm in her manner. She had the appearance of having just come from the hairdresser's, and her trim figure and carefully selected clothing revealed where Sammy had inherited his strong trace of vanity, reduced to insignificance though it was behind the charm his mother had also endowed him with.

After relating Barbara's apology and the account of her departure, I gave them the news of the Christmas present she had entrusted me with, and there was lively discussion of numerous other themes that inevitably pass in conversation between Easterners and Westerners. Mrs. Braun had the knack of putting one at ease, and I soon felt comfortable in her presence.

When Sammy commenced to speak about his proposed escape, I was astonished, and a wave of fear swept through me. Hadn't I warned him countless times about talking to his mother? Reluctantly I swallowed my disapproval, and since there was no way to undo the harm which had already been committed, I joined in the discussion.

As we discussed details of the escape, Mrs. Braun's lively eyes became clouded and her brow wrinkled in deep furrows. She reported hearing a West Berlin broadcast from RIAS, which kept the East Germans informed about escape methods, arrests, and testimonies of ex-prisoners and refugees from the East. She had heard that the trains were now being inspected with large mirrors that were rolled up under them.

Sammy, however, confided that he and Harold had scouted the yards on a couple of occasions and had detected no mirrors, but they had spotted a man wandering around the area, dressed in a uniform with patches—or what appeared to be patches—on the knees of his trousers. It seemed to mean he had been planted to prowl the yard on hands and knees to examine the bellies of the trains. But Sammy was now desperate for time.

Therefore he concluded that, within the next few days, he would definitely risk riding under the sooty, oily belly of a train to his freedom— if the method could still be used. That remained the question! We left the house and ambled aimlessly through the streets. There was still a lot to talk about that we were unable to discuss at the apartment.

It was past ten already, and I was required to be back at the crossing by midnight. So, little time remained for a comprehensive disclosure of all details I wanted to relate. Sammy and I wandered the streets some minutes, seeking a secluded spot for our meeting. We finally decided on the steps of the massive ruins of a bombed building.

The black empty belly of the crumbled building yawned at us like a gaping wound. It stood forlorn, an abandoned silhouette against the night, an eerie stage on which our scene was enacted. A chill wind whispered through its walls, and whisked goose pimples onto my skin.

As I unfolded the details, I felt uneasy about some impending danger, but Sammy reassured me that it was only my Western imagination that exaggerated the dangers lurking in the East. We sat silently for a moment regarding the ruins and contemplating the flight to freedom, when we heard heavy footsteps approaching. Two soldiers with slung rifles appeared over a mound, some meters away, making their path toward us.

Sammy quickly slipped his arm around my back, drawing me to him, pulling my head down onto his shoulder. Nothing looked more innocent in the night than a pair of lovers who had lost themselves in the oblivion of the ruins.

The soldiers passed, ignoring our presence, but the embrace lingered. There was a warm security in Sammy's arms, especially in the dread of possible danger. Neither of us wanted to break away. Moreover, the moment was a tense one; it all appeared so different now that Barbara had walked out on him. Yes, Sammy even needed me.

I shivered more from ecstasy than from the chilly wind that penetrated my spring coat. Sammy's grip tightened. My head still rested on his shoulder and my eyes closed. We drifted silently for seconds, and warmth surged through my blood as I felt his lips brush mine. To have opposed him would have been to say No to all the nature within me. As his lips pressed mine, I felt the depth of my involvement. Sammy, there is no turning back now. You must escape!

As I slipped my fingers slowly away from Sammy's tightly clutching hand, uttering a hesitant *"Auf Wiedersehen"* and *"Alles Gute,"* my words had never been filled with so much well-wished meaning. I was unable to say more. I had done all I could and the rest was his. I climbed aboard the S-Bahn and trembled with a cold shudder of fear at the thought of Sammy's approaching escape. I would live in anxiety until I saw his beaming face in West Berlin.

Almost two weeks had elapsed without sign of Sammy, and each day was dismissed with the silent expectation that the morrow would dawn with a surprise. When a thick, soupy fog covered the city in a dense protective veil one October night, I whispered to a friend with a strong sense of presentiment, "Tonight is a perfect night for escape."

That night, struggling desperately to lose myself in sleep, I found myself combating a swarm of pricking worries. Sammy's future was on the verge of ruin and he seemed unaware of it. He grossly exaggerated the incompetence of the secret police. He hated them too much to fear them. This attempt would also include Harold—who had not impressed me as courageous. If Sammy were caught this time, he was sure to get a high sentence. The odds were all against him. Then I thought of Peter. A little man—even timid—but in danger. No choice but to flee.

A cloud of sleep enveloped me.

The following day's newspaper revealed four new escapees. But no sign of Sammy.

The cool, misty autumnal days of October faded into nippy, frosty November, and still I had received no word from him. I refrained from contacting him, because I knew if his escape attempt had failed, his house would be under surveillance for a good while.

Finally, in mid-November I received a letter from Sammy's mother, requesting certain items from West Berlin. She closed the letter with "Sammy has been in the army since the beginning of November."

So that was it . . . he had gone to the army! I wondered what had happened to his escape plans. I felt a surge of relief that Sammy was still alive, but I longed to see him. Moreover, the move had disengaged me from the whole matter, and I could easily go to East Berlin now without worrying. I was no longer involved in trying to help him escape, and the "impending danger" had passed me by.

Saturday, one day before my birthday, Heinrich arrived from Heidelberg, where he was now studying, to celebrate my birthday with me. Since he always made a trip to East Berlin to visit his friends, I thought it would provide an excellent opportunity to kill two birds with one stone. I therefore had him notify Mrs. Braun that I was planning to visit her on the following Wednesday afternoon.

When I arrived home Sunday evening, I automatically assumed that the bright yellow envelope on my door was a birthday telegram from West Germany.

Still bubbling from the whirl of the gay evening, I ripped open the envelope and read: "Meet you on Wednesday 24th at Haus des Lehrers at 6:00 P.M.—Love, Sammy."

I was seized with sudden perplexity. If Sammy was in the army, how could he meet me? Then it dawned on me. Of course, his mother had notified him of my coming, and they had agreed on the hour together.

Wednesday was a freezing day, and the landscape was enveloped in plush white. In the morning the winds had whipped up a wintry flurry, and by noon another snowstorm had set in. I did not feel like going to East Berlin, but I decided I could not let the Brauns down. I had already spent fifty marks on Christmas presents, and I was obliged to deliver them sooner or later. So, I wrapped up in several layers of clothing, pulled on my high boots, stuffed my hair into my black fur hat, and plowed through the snow, headed for East Berlin.

It was the last night I should have picked for such a visit. The snow had reached a couple of feet in depth, and winds were protesting outrageously, howling as they swept through the streets.

When I entered the Friedrichstrasse crossing, I found it almost void of foreign visitors. The weather had frightened everyone into remaining in his warm living room or taking shelter in the corner tavern. It was certainly no night to be out, and the guard at the window informed me of that as he handed me my passport. Another custom guard made a quick inspection of the contents of my package, made a smug comment, and sent me through the barricade.

As I ascended the long stairs to reach the train to Alexander Platz, I noted to myself that the guards seemed friendlier than usual, almost as if they had been enjoying themselves. I glanced over my shoulder a couple of times to see whether I was being followed, more out of habit than suspicion. What could I fear now? Without taking time or precaution to determine whether I was, I concluded that there was surely little danger of it on a night like that. It was quite impossible for them to have any suspicion concerning me, even though I knew they routinely followed people. No, not even the agents or informers worked in that kind of weather.

It was half past five, and as I hurried to the train I did have a strange sensation. Yes, even that I was being followed. What could I do about it though? Shake them in the crowds? Not go to Mrs. Braun's house? Why shouldn't I? What could they get me for now, anyway?

I neared the tall, modern building at Alexander Platz. It was one of the socialist versions of the skyscraper. There was a loud mosaic on the outside center portion in realistic art, depicting scenes of the working man's life and his belief in science, technology, and progress—the hallmarks of East German socialism. Sammy hated the building.

As I pushed open the heavy glass door of Haus des Lehrers, I wondered why Sammy had wired me to meet him in town, since I was going to his house anyway. Perhaps his mother was unable to see me, I thought, as I eased down into the thick cushion of a leather chair. Others had also selected this warm spot away from the cold night for their waiting room.

There was Sammy, right on time, approaching the building all bundled up in heavy khaki canvas. He wasted no time in leading me out of the lobby into the snow after we had shaken hands.

We slipped on the icy walks, and when Sammy reached over to take my umbrella to shield us from the flying snow, I took a firm grip on his arm. Under the heavy jacket, I could feel a muscle tighten.

"Did your mother tell you to meet me here?" I asked as we wandered in the direction of Leninallee.

"No." He paused a moment. "I've escaped from the army."

"You've what?" I demanded, aghast.

"I've run away from the army," he stated flatly, almost reflecting a sense of pride in his voice.

"How could you do that? How could you be so foolish? You have no way of escaping to West Berlin now."

"I couldn't stand it. The propaganda and brainwashing were horrible. I've been hiding out for a few days already. You see, I was supposed to

has been expecting me since this afternoon, and I would have been there if you hadn't sent the telegram."

"I'll take you to the train. If you're afraid of the police, Mother can come into town and meet you here. They have already been to the apartment several times. Mother said they had even asked about Barbara. They may be watching the apartment now, but I doubt it. It's been several days already," he assured me, minimizing all danger.

"I'm not afraid. What have I actually *done?* They have no way of knowing what we've talked about, and they certainly can't punish me for talking. Until you've attempted escape, how could they have anything against me? Besides, we don't even know of a possibility," I continued, reassuring myself of the safety of visiting the apartment.

We entered the first station we came to and Sammy phoned his mother from a booth. While he was telephoning, I scanned the platform to see whether I could detect anyone who might be following us. The same long, gray, expressionless German faces that frequented the streets and stations crossed my view.

"Yes," Sammy announced, as he stepped out of the booth, "she's been waiting since this afternoon. She said she would meet you at the station. She's using the back door in case the house is being watched."

"Where are you going now?" I questioned, worried about leaving him.

"To celebrate! It's my birthday!" he exclaimed with a warm grin.

"Congratulations! But don't you think you're foolish going out with other people?"

He sighed a long deep sigh and gazed at the ground. "No. They're friends." Then he slipped his hand into his jacket pocket. "Before you go, I have a letter I want you to mail in West Berlin. It's for Barbara. The address where I'm hiding out is inside. If anything should happen . . . uh . . . like the police . . . they'll never get anything out of me. Remember that!" He reached out his hand. The train was screeching into the station.

"Bis Sonnabend," I called out as I boarded the train.

Sparks flashed, cracking and popping, as the train crept along on the snow-covered track. I wondered how Sammy could have been so foolish. . . . Yes, he had probably thought, "Hellen will help me." Of course, I had tried. But it was all so messy now.

My thoughts clicked with the rotating wheels, spinning around in a vicious circle. "Escape!" they cried. The risks involved in an open act of resistance; the consequent distrust and mounting tension between hostile governments; all of this must be carefully weighed before one involved himself in escape help. Besides, German materialism was greedy, stingy, grabbing. A land repeatedly devastated by wars had produced a people who were strongly motivated by fear of the future and who had become obsessed with possession. No, I could not support or encourage this.

With Sammy, though, it was different, wasn't it? He was engaged to an American girl. His prison record deprived him of his legitimate future. But he was also immature, irresponsible. . . . Nevertheless, he had a right—a right to determine his future, no matter how small, insignificant, and imperfect he might be.

Yes, I understood him. He loathed all the force and fanaticism, the aggression and hatred of the political system. It was bondage. Something natural and genuine—the desire for freedom, an innate yearning in man—was ardently alive and burning in his young heart. Then he was required to put his signature on an oath of loyalty to a state he despised and rejected. No, I would have refused, too. A man's name and his word were life's greatest endowments, not to be cast away lightly in self-betrayal. How carelessly one puts his signature to words that are meaningless. No, Sammy refused to bow before the cruel coercion of the system. His protest was an honest one.

Mrs. Braun's face was solemn as her French poodle jumped on me in greeting, when I stepped down off the train. We made our way toward the house briskly, stepping high over the deep white carpet. Occasional gusts smacked and stung our cheeks.

"What do you think about Sammy's desertion?" she asked me. The dog tugged her along, disappearing in soft mounds of snow.

"How could he at this time? He has no way of escaping to West Berlin."

"I don't know." She spoke in tired resignation. "I've tried to talk him into going back, but it's useless." Her eyes darted over her shoulder. "Here we are. I am taking you in the back door in case the house is being watched."

As we trudged up the steps, leaving snowy footprints behind, I observed no sign of life in the building. All was quiet, save for the plodding thuds of our boots on the stairs. Mrs. Braun led me into the warmth of her cosy living room, where the coffee cups stood waiting on the table, and in a few short seconds the aroma of freshly ground coffee floated through the room.

The rest is like fog in my memory. The piercing bell. Mrs. Braun's cry, "Police!" "No, we'll never let you down, Sammy."

I vaguely remember Mrs. Braun's last words, "They'll never get any information out of me!" Those had been Sammy's last words, too.

4

NAKED AMONG WOLVES

"GET UP!" the policewoman, stationed in the corner, ordered. "You are to go for an interrogation."

"Where am I?" I strained to withdraw from my stupor.

"Prison!"

"What time is it?"

No answer. I glanced at a watery soup that stood on the night stand. Droplets of fat floated on its surface. It must have been the lunch that had grown cold waiting for me. I fell back on the cot and regarded the sheet of gray mid-afternoon that lit the dim cell. "It must be after two o'clock," I thought to myself. I had been stretched out in a lifeless daze since I had been thrown into the cell at seven o'clock in the morning.

"Get up!"

My body resisted stubbornly, but this time the Weasel's voice prevailed. He stood in the doorway, anxious to take me to another harassing interrogation. The seven-hour letup had sufficed for his rest.

The same room. The same questions. The same story. The determined Weasel wanted it all detailed again.

"What's the *real* story now? Are you ready to tell me? Eh?"

"I've already told you!"

"What other persons are involved?"

"None!"

"What is your connection to the CIA?"

"None!"

"How much did they pay you?"

"Nothing! Please! Please, how long is this going to take?"

"That depends on you . . . when you tell the truth. . . ." His answer was always the same.

I briefly recounted a couple of meetings in East Berlin with Sammy, without mentioning our conversation about escape. I was convinced that the information appeared too harmless to justify keeping me. I was confused by their apparent knowledge of much more than I had given them credit for. If Harold was on their side, they were sure to know everything! Perhaps confession in that case would be better, but the uncertainty fed my doubts. Maybe Sammy's mother had confided in them. Or maybe Sammy had confessed. It was the third time around for him and perhaps he wanted to save his neck.

At the same time these doubts were sweeping through me, the interrogator was prodding away with implications that confession would be better for me, insinuating that I would be released then. He minimized the seriousness of the whole affair, encouraging me to think that he was just interested in obtaining the why and wherefore and not in punishing me. All his words were loaded with double meanings and snide insinuations, but something compelled me to cooperate. I knew I had committed no moral crime, and I trusted in something basic in all men that surely recognized I had acted only in the interest of humanity—not against it. Wasn't it obvious that I was no enemy of the state, nor a spy? Was it not clear that I was just desirous of helping and not hurting? Could they really take their Wall so seriously? Weren't they capable of compassion? Or were these innate urges perverted in them?

Besides, the truth must be boldly written in my eyes, which could not lie even when my tongue did. Each lie that I uttered increased my tension and nausea had welled up inside.

I had always attempted to build my human relations on the ground of absolute sincerity, and now this encounter struck a blow against everything that was a part of me.

A deluge of doubt haunted me. Sincerity and truth? It was naïve to be sincere with the police, especially when they were trying to hang some political crime on you. Or was it? In Hamlet, Old Polonius had illumined a truth when he said, "To thine own self be true, and . . . thou canst not then be false to any man." No, it wasn't truth I was resisting, but the consequences.

Tears poured out in a ceaseless flow and my body trembled with hysterical spasms. I could take no more of the aggressive attacks and yet I could say no more either. I was torn and paralyzed. Nothing in my life had compared to the mental agony I was undergoing. The desire to confess was strong and burning, although I felt guilty of no crime. But the doubts, the fear of consequences, the danger of involving others, all held me back. Perhaps they knew most of the story, but they would not confide it. I was a caught fish, dangling on the end of a piercing hook, lashing about with the last breaths of hope. They could release the line at any time but that was my decision.

Then the tactics changed.

Without a word the Weasel edged over to me and reached down to my breast. I gasped in fear of the next move. He lifted the silver medallion hanging around my throat, admiring the large Aztec calendar I had purchased in Mexico some years before. He addressed me in soft and friendly words. This new approach frightened me. What did he want from me?

I was unable to stop the flow of tears. They expressed the hopelessness of my situation. I sensed that there would be no turning point, no promise of release, until I related my story. But I could not bring myself to that decision. Again nausea engulfed me, and I was bathed in a chilly perspiration. I began to be more aware of my lot, but I clung to a faint strand of hope. Nevertheless, I saw that they would stop at nothing to get their information.

After some minutes of silently standing near me, the Weasel withdrew from the room, leaving the door slightly ajar. I sighed in relief. The inquisitive eyes of a guard posted outside scrutinized me, tarrying some seconds, and then moved on. I had been oblivious to the sounds in the corridor, but now between the squeaking paces of leather boots, I faintly overheard conversation from another room. I tilted my head at an angle in order to listen more acutely. A door opened, a loud voice boomed, and another voice responded humbly. It was Sammy! The door banged shut, and leather boots marched with heavy thuds in my direction. My heart raced. I wanted to leap up and rush to him, grab him, embrace him, tell him we were in this thing together! The ugly guard at the doorway checked this inclination.

Poor Sammy! It was really over for him. Desertion is a serious matter. I wondered how he was holding out. It no longer mattered. Somewhere they had been supplied with sufficient information. If I could only be sure about Harold. His jealousy, opportunism. . . . No, I had no right to condemn him without knowing. Perhaps Mrs. Braun had offered the key. I folded my arm on the back of the chair, resting my head. I was still trembling and sobbing and still unable to make a decision.

After a long pause both interrogators returned refreshed and ready to continue their probing.

"Suppose you begin the whole story from the beginning," the Pig insisted.

"But I've already told you several times."

"This time we want to write it down." The Weasel kept asking me to repeat my statements, as if he were hard of hearing. He repeatedly extended his left hand to the side of the desk. It dawned on me that he was adjusting the volume of a recorder. The room was bugged!

I no longer cared. A recording only supplemented their evidence at this point, but I was determined to embarrass them with their carelessness about concealing the fact. "You're recording my statements!" I exclaimed.

The Weasel's chalky cheeks reddened. After a perplexed pause, he stammered a justification. "It's an international method!"

If it hadn't been for the tears, I would have burst out in laughter. It's international! Murder is also international—as if that were a criterion for the justice of such a measure! It was evident I had no rights as an individual.

There was no sign of letting up on the probing. The Weasel had already filled his ashtray with dingy stubs and continued to puff away. I stuck to the same story. I was totally exhausted. When the Pig popped up with a surprise, I offered only weak resistance. I no longer knew what to say.

"What did you hand over to Braun?"

"I don't know what you're talking about."

"You know exactly what I mean. What did you give him?" He grinned encouragement.

"I don't understand," I persisted. "You have to be more specific in your questions. Do you mean whether I brought him a book or something like that?"

"You know what I mean. You just want to find out how much we know."

"No, I don't. You are always making bold assertions or snide insinuations without backing them up. You are vague and general. You can maintain anything, but you must be concrete."

"You're just trying to pump information out of us." He smiled. "You won't succeed, though. Now, tell us what you gave Braun."

"Unless you are more specific I refuse to answer your questions," I retorted stubbornly.

"All right, then, a *Skizze*." That was the word for "diagram." He knew! How could he know? Only Sammy knew. Or had he confided in Harold? Just a silly, stupid drawing.

"Yes," it slipped right out. It was the Pig's manner that caused my fears to dwindle into unimportance. He constantly reassured me that there was nothing to fear. Tired, confused, broken, sick inside, I sought the next move.

The Pig then beamed victory, nodded to the Weasel, and strolled out of the interrogation room. The Weasel scribbled down several pages of my statements and handed them to me to sign. I refused. I would refrain from signing anything. Then he conveyed that the questioning could continue forever if I failed to sign. I signed.

Sometime in mid-afternoon I was led back to the cell, exhausted and frantic. The faint hope had dimmed, and I had been provoked to frenzy.

"He's a swine!" I shouted in the strongest language I knew in German.

"Who?" the policewoman wanted to know. *"Ihr Vernehmer?"* I was uncertain whether she asked "your interrogator" or "Herr Weber," since she spoke Saxon. All of the prison personnel spoke in a thick dialect, which I usually took to be from Saxony.

"I don't know who he is," I mumbled.

She must have detected an accent when I spoke, for she questioned, "You're not from here, are you?"

"No," I answered sullenly. She seemed to feel—and not quite hide—a quiet pity.

"I'm not a criminal!" I cried. "Why are they treating me like one?"

"They'll determine whether you are innocent or not," she replied with the intention of consolation. It evoked the opposite response in me.

The afternoon had elapsed in questioning. Darkness fell and I began to realize that the ticket had been one way this time. Would I ever see West Berlin again?

Finally, two guards marched me between them to the courtyard, out into the cold night. Again I climbed into a sputtering Wartburg with the Weasel at my side. When I asked where I was being taken, the driver muttered something in half-swallowed dialect about a prison. So, that was it. I was being delivered to another prison.

The chill air stung my cheeks and burned my lungs, which were already aching. I felt numb and I was unaware of the tears streaming down my face. I ignored the passing scenes on the dark streets which still displayed glittering white mounds. I was unmindful of the last vestiges of freedom outside prison walls because I still clung to a delicate thread of hope that it would soon be over.

Certainly there were no laws that could convict me for having related how another person escaped. In Berlin that sort of information was cheap and easy to come by. Even Western radio stations broadcast methods of border patrol, unsuccessful escape attempts, and methods of refugees. Must a crime be attempted before someone is punished? Maybe they did just want the information from me.

No, they were Communists. The history of Eastern Europe had been isolated from the West and had undergone its development untouched by currents of humanistic reform. Their legal system was dominated by a retributive concept. I could not expect the American brand of justice.

A massive fortress loomed out against the night. It was lighted by glaring spotlights which cast sinister shadows of towers and barbed wire. An eerie city within a city. At a thick panel in the outside wall, our driver pressed a buzzer and a slot slid open. Identification was flashed, and the heavy door rolled aside. With slung machine guns, two sentries appeared, and we continued into the grounds of another prison.

I entered a grim hall and was received by a uniformed policewoman. Her eyes ignored mine as she led me into a bare office and told me to get undressed. I cringed and a flood of humiliation swept through me; I did not try to hold back the tears that again trickled down my cheeks.

Sternly, but with a tinge of pity, she reassured, "No one is going to hurt you here. Stop crying."

Heroes don't cry. But I had never considered myself one. No. My tears were my protest, and I hoped somehow to touch these people with the unnecessary suffering that was being inflicted.

I shivered as I stood naked before the strange woman. If she had only insisted on stripping me of my clothing, the abasement would have been bearable. No. She then proceeded to conduct a thorough pelvic examination, and ordered me to do a couple of knee bends, after which I was told to pull my buttocks apart. All of this I performed with tearful disgust. Then, I had to spread my toes apart, one by one, while her probing eyes carefully inspected the hollows between them. It was all degrading, humiliating, disgusting, it even struck me as perverse, this type of examination by a guard—not by a doctor or nurse.

She then fingered the seams of all my clothing, even ripping some open. Every conceivable hiding place on my body and clothing was examined and when the performance was completed I was ordered to get dressed.

In the adjoining room I faced an officer who requested all my jewelry, watch, and hair pins. I reluctantly removed them, and my long hair fell in tangled strands on my shoulders. My purse and its contents already lay strewn on his desk. "We retain these things in safekeeping for you," he articulated in his best German, aware of addressing a foreigner.

Then the officer, the woman guard, and the Weasel all briskly led the way through corridors and up stairs. They stopped before a heavy, bolted door. The guard slid back the cover of the peephole in the center, placed her eye to it, and revolved the keys in the lock of cell 89. "We don't use names here," she informed me. "You are 'number two,' since you occupy the bed on the right."

The door was flung open and a sad-faced young woman stood at the end of the left bed. Then it banged shut, and I looked into the dark eyes of "number one," my cell mate.

I immediately dropped down on my bed, and a choking nausea permeated my body. It was a "sickness to death." For fear of disturbing the other young woman, I suppressed my wailing to sobbing.

The violent indignation with which I had confronted the Weasel had first been drowned in humiliation. Now, I was in a state of shock. But these three, indignation, humiliation, and shock, alternated in vicious waves. It was unjust! inhumane! They were the criminals, not I. Criminals against humanity. But what was I? A tiny worm, stripped of all possessions and rights, crushed under the mighty heel of evil. Had I even experienced an inkling of justice in all those tormenting hours of interrogation? Had I for one instant been given reason to expect it? Nevertheless, I still clung helplessly to a shred of hope.

My cell mate was a squatty, dark young woman of twenty-six. She sat next to me on the bed, her arm around my shoulders, offering weak words of consolation. She was too dejected herself to be convincing, but there was a certain relief in knowing that I was not alone in my plight. Through the initial hours of arrest, I had been.

She introduced herself as Brigette. Her crime was attempting to escape to her fiancé in West Berlin. The police had arrested her in Leipzig, where she was an engineering student, and had transferred her to Berlin the previous week. She did not have to reveal that she was a native Berliner, for her speech readily disclosed it.

I was terrified when a loud eerie clanging of an alarm began, but Brigette soothed my frazzled nerves. The bell sounded the nine o'clock "lights out." I rushed to wash myself in the dishpan that stood on a stool in the corner. Then I slipped into a tent-like night shirt that had been given me. Totally exhausted I fell into bed.

As soon as the room was in darkness, I threw back the covers and tiptoed over to the toilet in the corner. I had painfully waited until I could have the dark concealment from a piercing eye at the spy hole in the door. That little aperture was the very last invasion of my privacy and rights, and filled me with resentment. Suddenly a light flashed on and remained until I had finished my business and returned to my bed.

The light disappeared, only to flash again at frequent intervals when the guards made their nightly rounds. It added to the miserable aura of the cell, casting sinister shadows across the gray walls.

I stretched my aching limbs on the sectioned straw mattress and bunched up the folded blanket, which provided my only pillow. For hours I lay in an oppressive daze. I must have dozed off, because the next thing I experienced was the piercing clang of that hideous bell, screaming for me to get up. My body was heavy and aching and my eyes swollen. Brigette informed me that it was 5:00 A.M.

I could not imagine what was happening outside until the slot in our door crashed open and an ugly nozzle protruded into the cell. The faucet splashed water into Brigette's dishpan, then gushed into mine, and was withdrawn.

Brigette and I sat at our table, which was covered with a brown checked cloth. She ate the dry sandwiches provided for our breakfast, but I was still too sick to eat. I learned that I was now in an investigative prison in Hohenschoenhausen, in the hands of the secret police, who were feared and dreaded by most Germans. Actually they were the old Gestapo, bearing a new title and wearing a new uniform. I had heard about them in the West. It was rumored that, to get information out of prisoners, they exposed them to bright spotlights, or days in total darkness. I had even heard that one prisoner was forced to stand in a cell filled with water all night until he agreed to disclose a name the police were trying to secure.

The door was flung open numerous times that morning. Each time my heart leapt in fright, and each time a guard stood in the doorway and a gruff voice announced my number, *"Zwei."*

A mug shot, fingerprints, medical exam. The works. I was treated just like a criminal, and it all had an air of finality.

Finally, I found myself following the prison "runner" who led prisoners to interrogation. The interrogation rooms were set off in a separate wing of the building. It consisted of three floors of rows of closed doors. I could not help but recall Kafka's *Trial* and the enormous apparatus of German bureaucracy as we passed the silent doors. I was sure that the prison must be bulging with prisoners, judging only from the number of doors.

It all evidenced the necessary equipment of a police state. The futility of it hit me, as I imagined all those millions of dollars that could go into a positive, productive economy, being squandered on the hiring of agents, informers, secret police, the soldiers at the Wall. . . .

We stopped before room 284—the Weasel's den. The room was small and pleasant. The Weasel motioned me to be seated at the table adjoining his desk.

In one corner was a heavy safe with the door ajar. In another corner a large cabinet rested and in the third, a round table with two arm chairs. The safe and the cabinet had wax seals on their doors. The stone floor was covered with a thin gray carpet and white curtains hung at the window, which looked out on the inner courtyard. Outside through the barred windows I could observe piles of snow.

I stared into the Weasel's penetrating eyes, my heart racing and pounding. I knew what to expect, yet I never could be sure of what question would pop out of the thin mouth or what reaction the nervous little man might make.

It was a harassing repetition of all the previous hours of questioning. This mental torture was to be the daily routine. With cold determination he would hack away until he pressed out the whole story.

I longed for my peace of mind. But that only spurred the Weasel on. He would provoke me to my breaking point. He wrote all my statements down in his words and I had to sign. I no longer had the energy to dispute with him over his distortions of my statements.

This procedure was to take place every day but Sunday—mornings and afternoons. I continued to offer stubborn resistance, but confusion and aggression were mounting in me. Every interrogation was a horrid nightmare which I faced full of dread.

Whether on Friday or Saturday I cannot remember, but I was brought before an elderly man who introduced himself as my arresting judge. In a monotone he read me the charges of my formal arrest. Shocked to insensitivity, I still did not grasp that I had been officially arrested. My mind was alert and active, but I had a sensation of unreality, as of a grim nightmare, where I exercised no control over the situation.

I was arrested on suspicion of *Beihilfe zur Republikflucht* which was simply "escape help." The crime was punishable by up to three years of prison. The judge then read aloud another paragraph, which stated that a person who showed remorse for a crime could be released at any time without serving the whole sentence. Was he stating that with a change in attitude I could go home?

In all seriousness he proceeded to give me a lecture. "Even as a foreigner you must respect the laws of other countries. It makes no difference whether you agree with those laws, but when you violate them, you are subject to punishment. Even in your country you have laws limiting the free movement of your citizens. You could not go to Cuba, for example. if you wanted to."

He had a point. The stern judge continued to inform me, "Here in the DDR we have laws which your country does not have. For example, we have laws against waging an aggressive war. Anyone who tries to go out and spread propaganda to start a war is subject to punishment in this country. Never again can an aggressive war be waged from our state. But look at your country in Vietnam! We have laws against such a dirty war."

I gazed at the floor in silence. "In America we have laws against murdering our own people at a Wall," I thought bitterly. I had been a severe critic of my government's policies in Vietnam, but there was something about a ruthless Communist criticizing my country, despite the Communists' history of abuse of human rights, that cut into my sense of national pride, however weakly it had been exercised until then.

As far as I was concerned, any violence was a primitive way to solve problems. War was the very last step in the breakdown of civilized relations. It was a cankerous sore on the face of history and the paralyzer of progress. Even though war was as old as man himself, man now possessed the power of total destruction with his weapons, and it was high time to re-evaluate his attitude toward war as providing a *solution* to any problem. Besides, was it not a mistake to attempt to fight ideology with weapons? When the consciousness of people is shaped and molded so that men unite their wills and efforts toward a cause they believe in, there is more power than in all the bombs one could take to destroy them. No, weapons offered no solution—but truth. . . .

The stern judge paused in his rambling reproaches. His scolding voice hesitated. "But I see you are a student of theology, and if you take Christianity seriously, then you cannot accept the war either."

I did not lift my eyes from the ground. Big drops rolled down my cheeks, and the terrible sickness never left me.

Then I was told to sign the arrest warrant, and when I hesitated, the judge announced, "Your signature does not mean that you accept the charges. Only that you have read them."

It no longer mattered whether it was a clever trick to get my signature. Signing or not signing did not change my lot. Perhaps it really was better to cooperate—if the paragraph he had read aloud meant anything.

Back in my cell again, I kept pondering what the judge had said about Cuba. Of course it was all part of the Party line which systematically picked out all the weaknesses and contradictions in America in order to poison people's minds, but it bothered me.

Our government's not allowing American citizens free access to Cuba could not be compared to the Wall through Germany. It is certainly different when laws are made to divide families and citizens of one country. I had confronted the same argument with the two interrogators and I was certain to meet it again. What was the answer?

Finally, I decided what I would say. Was it not a mere accident of history where a man was born? What bound a man to his homeland? An American had the right to leave his country and take on a new citizenship, if he rejected the laws or policies of his country. An East German was denied this basic right!

As I stretched across my bed, evening dimmed the faint light of the bare room. It was difficult to distinguish day from night, because the doubled glass briquets at the window shut off the outside world. No clear sky, no snow-covered trees, nor even the chirping autumn birds were longer visible from my sinister cage. And the dull light of depressing days could only cast a gloomy shadow into the austerity of the interior. Enclosed within stone. Behind the ugly Wall.

Oh, Berlin! You are a city standing with a Wall through your middle in the twentieth century. A wall that divides citizens of one country, one people, in enmity. For more than four years its fortified existence has incited, induced, and enticed law-abiding individuals to risk life and security in daring to violate its angry laws. All kinds of people. Some are professional criminals. Many are government agents of the cold war. Many are opportunists. A few are politicians. A lot are idealists. But the majority of those who venture all to act against its laws are common people. Citizens who have never broken laws in their lives. Law-abiding people who fear and respect authority. The people on one side call it the "Wall of Shame"— those on the other side call it the "Antifascist Wall of Protection"!

Yes, Berlin, I am now another of your victims!

5

A SCHOOL OF LIFE

FOUR OR FIVE days had elapsed at a dragging pace since my arrest. The interrogations continued daily, but they had reached a stubborn standstill. I refused to supply any more information. I had repeated the same story again and again. Now my lips were sealed, and the Weasel and I sat staring at each other in long periods of bitter silence.

"Aren't you going to answer any more questions?" the Weasel pleaded helplessly.

I ignored him, but he did not give up. "All I have is time," his narrow eyes seemed to say, "and it is your precious time."

Six days after my arrest the Weasel and I were conducting one of our silent interrogations, when I resolved that not one more word would pass my lips. I directed my thoughts to other things as he pounded me with questions, but his aggressive tone began to frighten me. He kept harping on my connections to the CIA, which he had been doing for days. It was now the same whether I was a master spy or a well-meaning nobody, for either way I was a helpless captive.

Suddenly I recalled the story of a fifteenth-century Russian pilgrim. On his wanderings, he had repeated a simple prayer to himself hundreds and thousands of times until it brought deep meaning into his life and he began to overcome obstacles. The repetition of a short prayer soon became connected with many "unexplainable" incidents in his life. I was desperate. At this moment I would have done anything to shut the Weasel up. I began to mumble the pilgrim's powerful words, at first in a hoarse whisper. When the questions became louder, I raised my voice above them. For more than an hour we conducted this trancelike séance. "Jesus Christ, son of the living God, have mercy on me!" I repeated again and again, but it was a rote phrase, devoid of faith.

Abruptly the door swung open, and a strange man entered the room. He was short, stocky, and had reddish-brown hair. He eyed me quickly and took a seat in one of the arm chairs. He spoke softly to my interrogator, ignoring me all the while. I continued to rest my head on the bend of my arm, which was stretched out on the table.

Without warning the stranger turned, "What's the matter, Miss Battle, aren't you feeling well?" His tone was swollen with sarcasm.

I was taken aback. "No," I cried, "he won't believe me!"

"You're not telling the truth!" the Weasel boomed.

The stranger wielded authority, for he addressed me icily. "Until you answer the questions truthfully and completely you will not be allowed to write your parents." With deliberate gestures he rose from the chair, and marched haughtily out of the room.

Crushed, broken, frustrated, I began to scream hysterically at the top of my voice. I fell to the floor and lay trembling.

"Shut up!" the Weasel shouted, "if you have any sense at all! That was your prosecuting attorney!"

It could have been a king for all I cared. I continued screaming, and hasty steps were heard outside the door. A young woman rushed in and stood over me. I was completely broken.

With violent condemnation, I silently accused the Weasel. He knew no feeling. He was only a political machine, carefully selected, brainwashed in the doctrine of the state, and systematically controlled by superiors who fed him his orders. He had lost his membership in the race of humanity and had forfeited his right to independent decision.

I did not budge from my spot on the floor. The Weasel's tone softened, and an expression of helplessness crept over his sharp face. He placed his hand on my shoulder. "Be sensible," he coaxed. "Let's be reasonable with each other. Why don't you get up and sit in the chair?"

I cannot recall how long I lay sprawled on the thin carpet, trembling violently and sobbing, but I only longed for peace. Finally I was unable to resist the plea in his voice. It was as if he were begging me to help him and my pity was tenderly touched. But that was not it; one could always arouse my compliance with gentle decency and kindness. Until then he had been cynical, sarcastic, cold, and aggressive, and had incited me to obstinate rebellion. Now his voice was pleading, urging me to cooperate for his sake and mine. Somehow his petition got through to my heart, for I slowly rose and eased into the arm chair. A decision had been gnawing away at me for days—confession!

What was my moral responsibility? I found myself engaging in my deepest soul searching in attempting to answer the question. It would have been clear-cut and defined had I been working for a governmental institution. But I alone had made my decision to undertake escape activity—out of my own conviction. I forced myself to clear away all preconceived notions about the evil of the East German government; the illegality of the regime; their prostitution of justice; and confront my mere responsibility as a human being to tell the truth. Moreover, to accept the full responsibility for every decision and every act I involved my life in.

Being responsible meant owning up to what I had done, standing behind it with my person, and not retreating before grim consequences. Anything less would be cowardice! Politics or no politics, the verdict was the same. How would laws ever be changed, if people were shrinking before them, hiding behind them, or running away from them? Especially when the laws were bad and the action that involved the violation of them good? A responsible decision sometimes meant bearing severe consequences, but it was only those who were courageous enough to stand up and take them, who were able to move history instead of being moved by it!

"Yes." I surrendered myself. "I'll tell you everything." I was no longer concerned about myself, but the others who were involved. Those who were not already in the hands of the police were in safety anyway. My decision automatically entailed making a decision for them by bringing them into the case if they were unknown. I would do that as gently as possible, but I knew that once I committed myself to the truth, I had to be consistent. I would plead for their understanding, and, although their laws would condemn me, perhaps I could win their hearts. Perhaps I could manifest to them that what I believed in was superior to their conviction.

The Weasel stopped me from speaking. He handed me pencil and paper and urged me to write it all down. He took on a new nature. His tired face beamed in relief. The victory was his. His job was accomplished. Another criminal had been cowed to confession. Maybe he even received a bonus for it. At least, his masculine drive to conquer and his pride in his profession were satisfied.

And what was his victory? A helpless young woman—maybe even a naïve idealist. She was neither an enemy of the state, nor an international agent. She had wanted to help an irresponsible young man escape to his fiancée. She was an American, though, and that meant a higher price on her head. There was tragic irony in his victory.

I took the pencil and paper. I would write the entire story. Perhaps they would even recognize how ridiculous it all was. I was also supposed to state why I had refused confession until then. I told the Weasel that I feared the truth would be distorted out of proportion, and I was still afraid of that.

Back in my cell, I sat down to write. My hand trembled. Which required more courage, confessing or not confessing? I was unsure which. I was convinced that many of the details were unknown to them. A confession meant supplying them with that information. I knew I could weave a yarn skillful enough to cover some of the facts. All of the details about Juergen and Peter were obviously unknown to them, and I could have invented a good story to cover that. Since that part took place in the West, they had no way of checking it out.

No. I decided to be consistent. Only the truth would exert any moral impact on their lives. Besides, I wanted them to know about Peter's case— how they had driven him to such measures. They claimed there were no real political refugees, that most of the escapees were "economic" ones. Peter's case was a firm denial of their contention. I knew that it would bear greater consequences for me if I disclosed my conversation with Peter before his escape, even though I had nothing to do with the escape itself. They would inevitably distort it, but the truth was more important to me. I would use it as a weapon to challenge them about their own system, or a piece of evidence to convict them of their crimes against humanity. I began to record my story.

As my pencil scratched across the dingy paper, some of the sickness left me. There was still a twisting knot in my stomach, because I had no idea what would be done with my statement. When I noticed I had left some information out, I backtracked and added it. I had made a decision, and it would be a turning point. Not from without—but from within. The outer consequences lay completely beyond my control. If my statement were judged with even the faintest drop of compassion, the consequences could not be too severe.

In the silent darkness I lay on my bed, snatching quick deliberations between the intruding flashes of light. I anticipated the following day. The confession would blow away one heavy doubt that had been hanging over my mind like an angry storm cloud. It concerned my involvement with church work in West Berlin.

Most of the students I had worked with in the German Christian Student Movement and many of the leaders of the church were very intent on paving the way for a policy of reconciliation with East Germany. They were concerned with breaking down the high tension that existed between the two Germanys. It was no wonder that student leaders discouraged participation in any type of resistance activity, for it did not contribute to a relaxation of the political tension.

In fact, leaders of the student congregation had taken an open stand against any organized activity directed against East Germany, especially escape help. The move had been initiated when a soldier had been killed as the result of a tunnel action. More than fifty persons had made the underground journey to their freedom, but an East German guard had been shot to death. The East German Government screamed with indignation. The incident had caused many in the West to reconsider the moral issue at stake in escape help, since a life had been taken. The East praised the dead man as a martyr, and the West claimed he had been shot by mistake in attempting to escape himself.

I had agreed with the general stand and had become dedicated to encouraging new attitudes between the two Germanys. Moreover, any such resistance activity could jeopardize the work of the church, which had struggled to maintain its unity despite a divided land. In fact, when one of the staff members for the student congregations got wind of my involvement, he immediately instructed me to stop. He felt that since I was housed in a dormitory owned by the church, and I had been an active leader in the work of the student congregation in West Berlin, it would automatically cast suspicion of involvement on the church. However, I maintained that the case of Sammy was an exception. My involvement with him had no connection with any church activity, and I felt a moral obligation to help him.

I had been warned in no uncertain terms. But I acted against this warning, convinced that it was my way. Now, only a complete confession would remove any doubt as to my church connections. This had been the main question mark on my conscience.

I dropped the stubby pencil and observed the grim shadows cast by the bars. At once I became utterly aware of my total dependence. I, who had always been so proud of my independence, was now a helpless babe. . . . There is something in a man that rejects his helplessness. The life force that prods him on to maturity and healthy independence rebels against the childlike state of total bondage to others. It makes him want to cry out. Rob me of my possessions; I am able to acquire more! Beat my body to collapse; it can heal! Spit on me in scorn; my pride is invulnerable! But never deny me my liberty; it is my God-given endowment!

"My God, my God, why have You forsaken me?"

Suddenly in the midst of life a blow strikes. All plans, dreams, and aspirations must flow in a different course. But first the floodgates of possibility must be opened. My outer world had undergone an abrupt change which negated all my control over it. The outside world had come to a stop. But life moved on. An inner current took over when the outward came to a halt. Naked against reality, I threw off all the prejudice against my surroundings that had barred me from responsibility. I would act.

I wrote my confession. Indeed, it opened up manifold questions. In future interrogations we would be occupying ourselves with them. But the sickness began to leave me. I began to see my situation with different eyes. The silent victory had been mine, for I had won my freedom. Freedom to be myself.

I had a new relationship to the Weasel. On both our parts, it was one of sincerity, which was not always hearty. He continued to play the role of policeman, but some of the caustic aggression left him, and an occasional twinkle spoke from the beady eyes. With my barriers of defense broken down, we could dare to be human beings with each other and sometimes even venture to approach a dialogue.

Although I considered the Wall an evil, what did that have to do with him? Yes, he was an ardent believer in the state's doctrines, but he himself was only a passive product. His consciousness had been molded to respond in certain ways. He was not free. In fact, I began to feel sorry for the little man. He had placed all his life's energy in a goal he believed in. I knew that history had deceived him, as it had deceived the Nazis, and sooner or later a judgment would be pronounced.

Once I was convinced that my imprisonment was final, I requested a Bible. I had not been a devout reader before my imprisonment, but I simply knew of no other source from which to seek spiritual support. To my surprise, the Weasel agreed readily. However, when after a couple of days one had not appeared in my cell, I demanded an explanation.

With an embarrassed expression, the Weasel explained apologetically, "You understand that our ideology here is . . . uh . . . atheistic . . . There just isn't any demand for Bibles . . . so . . . it is rather difficult getting hold of one." The following day the prison warden appeared in my cell with a German New Testament in his hand.

Even then, I derived little consolation from reading it. For me, even though I was a student of theology, God was "out there," somewhere beyond my reach, cut off by a wall. He had abandoned me—now more than ever. My whole life had been one long intense struggle to find Him, ascending mountains of hope and descending into valleys of despair. I had made detours through philosophy, and I had already arrived at the intellectual affirmation that Christianity must be the ultimate answer to human exist-

ence. However, deep within, I could not *trust*—no, I doubted. The few
moments of illumination in my lifetime had been brief, but enough to convince me of the reality of the Christian God, even though I had no real
inner relationship to Him. Indeed, for me God was impersonal as long as I
had not been existentially grasped by Him. Therefore, prayer had become
meaningless for me. I could not bring a prayer to my lips. Thus, I turned to
my favorite verses in the Bible as to words of wisdom.

The first verse I tried to encompass in meditation was in the first chapter of James:

> *My brothers, whenever you have to face trials of many kinds, count*
> *yourselves supremely happy, in the knowledge that such testing of*
> *your faith breeds fortitude, and if you give fortitude full play you will*
> *go on to complete a balanced character that will fall short in noth-*
> *ing. . . .*

Could one really be supremely happy in the midst of pain, when he accepted it with faith and fortitude? Was there really a certainty of the growth
of character and trust in God in the midst of suffering which gave birth to
joy? Suffering begets perfection. . . . The sister verse to this was in I
Peter:

> *This is cause for great joy, even though now you smart for a little*
> *while, if need be, under trials of many kinds. Even gold passes through*
> *the assayer's fire, and more precious than perishable gold is faith which*
> *has stood the test. These trials come so that your faith may prove itself*
> *worthy. . . .*

Could I take the image of gold with me and purify it in the fire of suffering?

I decided it was only then that suffering could not only become bearable,
but even bring with it a deep sense of joy through the knowledge that
there was meaning in it. It all became a "school of life" for me. My faith
was put on trial. To stand the test meant purification, fortitude, strength. It
was then that I discovered that my real enemies were not from the state,
but from the satanic temptation to let myself go, to give up hope, to be eaten
away in bitter rebellion. Aggression, self-pity, my own instability. Yes, I was

in the most challenging school of my life! But, oh, "Two souls dwell, alas! in my breast," Goethe had said. My stronger one was an untamed rebel!

After several weeks of further interrogation, there came a pause. It was a weekday, and the Weasel failed to send for me. The pause enabled me to experience my "free time": thirty minutes in the outdoors.

I inhaled long breaths of fresh, free air for the first time in days. The boundless sky above was freedom, and it looked down on me in heavy gray mourning. It was in the bare outdoor cage that the bitter reality of my lot struck me most severely. Rows of cages, canopied by freedom. Birds perched on the barbed wire fringe and performed merry antics with their friendly chirping. "We are free to fly away wherever we wish," they seemed to boast.

Then the horrid interrogations continued. But sometimes with a cup of steaming coffee, or in a vein of light conversation instead of verbal attacks. Despite my confession, the Weasel had a thousand other questions. He was seldom prone to trust my answers, especially when they seemed not to follow his own conceptions. He persisted in probing my so-called contact with underground organizations and connection to the CIA. His ceaseless prodding began to affect me psychologically, and I was again tortured with pangs of doubt.

A civilian attorney with the American army had interviewed me for a part-time job shortly before I was arrested. Since I had been in dire need of extra cash, I made application, filling out extensive forms. It had never dawned on me that it might have been the CIA, but the Weasel's cocky self-assurance convinced me that this must be known to the East German police. They were determined to pry out all the particulars. In order to get him off my sleeve, I decided to explain the whole matter.

That initiated a completely new routine. Several days were spent detailing the application form I had filled out. The number of pages, the color, the questions, every conceivable item was of interest. The Weasel was especially interested in finding out who had come to interview me, his description, the part of the country he came from, whether he owned a car, which office of the army had sent him. All the significant answers I had conveniently forgotten.

I assured the Weasel that it was all of no importance. President Johnson was trying to cut down on the outflow of American dollars abroad, and one step had been hiring Americans for positions foreign nationals had previously held. The Weasel was not convinced, and insisted I knew which department of the army the man represented. For lack of a better answer, for I really did not know, I told him that it must have been the "employment" department. Since I was unable to remember the term in German I stated it in English.

The reaction was riotous. With an air of mystery the Weasel probed further. He appeared to be baffled and asked me several times to explain what the word meant. Finally he was convinced I had given him a hot lead on some secret branch of the army. He produced a photocopy of the American army's telephone book in West Berlin. I was told to examine it and tell him which department was meant.

"Oh," I exclaimed as I recognized the proper expression, "it is the personnel services. That's what the employment department of the army is called." This seemed to squelch all the ado he had made on the subject. The confusion had arisen from his total ignorance of English.

In spite of my confession, the Weasel harped on one point and refused to believe my answer. He became cold and caustic, and for two or three days he posed the same question. We reverted to our silent interrogations again, because I had told him the truth. He insisted that Peter and Juergen were planning on helping others escape, and I was concealing their names. I knew of no one. They both had been forced to leave themselves. My denial evoked stormy responses from him, and I was beginning to be shaken again.

"You know how it is . . ." he suggested slyly one day, "one leaves the country, and he then tries to get his friends and relatives out. We, of course, have our ways of knowing just how far along such preparations are. We are already aware of the plans. . . . So, why don't you tell us about them?"

"I told you I don't know of anyone else!" I answered angrily.

"I thought you were going to tell the truth."

"I am telling the truth!"

"Well, I'm afraid you cannot write your parents until I have the truth," he bargained.

I was enraged. "I have told the truth!" To keep from exploding, I refused to answer again.

"I am waiting for your answer," he urged dispassionately.

I looked into his empty eyes and said, "I believe you must have bad ears —or else I don't speak very distinctly. It seems that I have already answered that question!"

The Weasel was taken aback by my rude reply and ended the interrogation. "I'll give you another chance," he threatened as I was leaving. "Think it over and be ready to tell me the truth tomorrow. I'll be expecting it. It is for your own good."

On the following day he received the same answer, and he finally gave up on the question. Then, suddenly, as if he were rewarding me graciously, he produced a piece of pink stationery with matching envelope, announcing I might write my parents. I later learned that the letter was never mailed. Nor was the second letter I wrote. It was only after I decided to write my family in German that they received my mail.

Some days later I was called in for an interrogation. When I had taken my usual place in the Weasel's office, he solemnly handed me a small sheet of paper. Across the top was the phrase "power of attorney." A name and address were stamped in the middle.

"What does it mean?" I asked.

"Your parents are offering you the services of a lawyer."

"You mean they even know that I am in prison?" I asked, fighting back the tears.

"Of course they know. The word of your arrest spread around West Berlin very rapidly—too rapidly!"

The piece of paper was a revelation. It was the first sign from the outside world. It was evidence that someone was trying to help me.

Should I accept the lawyer? I was sure that a lawyer in East Berlin had as much power as a Negro at a Ku Klux Klan meeting. If I did not engage one, then the court would assign one. It was a terrible expense and for what reason? I could defend myself. I glanced at the name. Vogel. Wasn't that the attorney who had negotiated the Abel and Powers exchange? I decided that my family would be frantic if I refused the services of a defense attorney, and for their sake I agreed.

I signed the power of attorney. "But when can I see him?"

"According to our laws you cannot see him until the investigation of your case is closed," the Weasel stated sheepishly. "If you need anything, though, I can pass the word on to him."

I deliberated a moment. "Yes, could I have some clothes sent over from my room in West Berlin?"

"I think it could be arranged."

I returned to the cell with the knowledge that a defense attorney would be working on my case. A famous one, too. But what good did it do me, when I was unable to see him?

The Christmas season was approaching and I was filled with blind hopefulness. Christmas in Germany was the one holiday of the year and had more significance than in any other country of the world. Even the hardest heart was not immune to the warm glow of an advent wreath, or the cosy family circle on Christmas Eve. Surely even the hardened Communists would not keep me incarcerated at Christmas.

As I hastened my pace to keep up with his extended steps, I noticed that the runner had passed the Weasel's door. At the end of the corridor we stopped abruptly before room 248. The door opened into a dark room, where only four candles flickered from the center of a green wreath. With the wide eyes of a child that awakens on Christmas morning, I entered the room and sat down in an easy chair across from the Weasel. His hard eyes were smiling faintly. On the table between us were two small pots of coffee, a dish stacked with cake, and sparkling wine glasses.

The Weasel introduced me to another man who sat behind us at his desk in the darkness. He remained silent. With a subtle smile, he went over to a record player in the corner of the room, and the chords of Tchaikovsky's First Piano Concerto rang out. The eyes of both men were fixed on me, and no one dared to speak. Never had the full rich notes had such an impact on me. My eyes moistened and tears began to roll down my cheeks.

"You know," my voice rasped hoarsely, "it's hard to be bitter when you do something like this for me." I did not question any motives, but only accepted the flow of kindness with gratitude as a dog might gobble up the crumbs spilled from the table.

"Yes," the stranger in the corner spoke softly, "that is the reason we are doing it. I hope you are satisfied with my selection of music. Your interrogator informed me you were fond of Tchaikovsky."

When we had finished with coffee and cake, the stranger carefully removed a bottle of white Hungarian wine from its hiding place.

"See. I told you that we would drink a bottle of wine together someday," the Weasel laughed heartily. "You know they always say *in vino veritas,* and I wanted to test it out on you."

"My, aren't you shrewd!" I laughed at his attempt to loosen my tongue. "Of course I believe that truth is found in a heart made merry with wine, but you got yours from me without the wine!"

He laughed, "Ah, ha! You told me that you feel like embracing the whole world after wine. I'm waiting! Why don't you begin with me?"

I blushed, and I could feel my cheeks glowing. I had never seen the Weasel like this. His eyes were warm and responsive and they never left me. The Weasel's colleague had faded into the darkness of the corner where he sat, and we were no longer aware of his presence. Just the Weasel and I. We sat looking into each other's eyes, uncertain of the destination of the instant.

The warm tones of the music filled the tiny room, which was aglow with dancing candlelight. The melody of the First Concerto waned and *Swan Lake* burst forth melodiously. It was so unreal and far away from the grimness of prison.

"It's amazing," the stranger interrupted us from his corner, "how I can sit down and enjoy a glass of wine and friendly conversation with you without any difficulty, even though you have committed a crime against our state." And even though I was an American, he probably thought. "It would be harder to do this, say—with a woman who had murdered her child. Nevertheless, it would be my moral responsibility to do so."

I felt I was beginning to grasp a profound truth I had already sensed—that in spite of our political differences, we could sit down together as simple human beings and exchange mutual understanding. Perhaps we approached each other in understanding on other issues as a result of this experience. I wondered about the motives, for there was no question about the sincerity of the hour. It was strong and glowing. But I did question how such a sensitive, intelligent man as the one seated next to me could morally justify mentally torturing people into confessing political crimes. Before I left the Christmas-filled room, the Weasel eased his arm under the table and pulled out a paper plate chock-full of nuts, fruit, a package of cookies, and a bar of dark chocolate. "Merry Christmas," he said as he offered me the plate.

"You can be sure I'll never forget this Christmas," I told the two men as I said good-bye, and I knew it was indelibly imprinted on my memory.

Although I was grateful for the small tokens of the season, I cherished the thoughtful kindness more. The spirit of Christmas was even able to penetrate stone walls in East Germany and enliven hearts that had turned cold to human suffering, even if the flame flickered only a brief moment. But in that moment there was an eternal truth, and something was born in my heart. I felt a surge of hope as I anticipated something just beyond my reach. It was my own Christmas Story!

When I entered my cell I was met with a snarl. "Well now, what did 'Miss America' have to do in order to earn a plate of Christmas goodies?" Brigette whined.

I was crushed. I could not share the wonderful feeling with Brigette. The bitterness of her own impoverished soul made her envious and resentful of any crumb of mercy I received from the enemy. She had already claimed that it was to one's advantage to be a foreigner. She had begun to use me as a scapegoat. Life was agonizing on the other side of the cell door, but it had become insupportable within the four walls.

A tremendous flashing, booming, and cracking shook me from sleep. It was midnight New Year's Eve. There must have been a magnificent celebration in town, for the prison was out a good distance and still being shaken by the fireworks. I lay there, wondering how it must have felt being in Berlin in a bombing raid. Then I thought about all those who would be using the occasion for an escape attempt at the Wall. Strangely enough, the fireworks would offer a cover of protection, because the guards could not distinguish them from flares.

Yes, outside in the streets, the signs and sounds of life were exploding, but I was locked in an austere tomb. The Christmas candle had glowed only briefly. Then it had flickered and was extinguished. Now I was engulfed in absolute darkness. Oh, mercy, mercy, mercy! Why so long? . . . To err is human, to forgive divine. . . .

A new year was born—1966. The old year was dead, buried, past. With it had also flown a score of plans and hopes. I had been snatched up from the world unexpectedly, before I had settled my accounts with life. The unwritten lines, the unspoken words, and the uncompleted tasks I left behind said more than the life I had lived. It reminded me of death. Prison was a living death.

6

THE SOUNDS OF SILENCE

THE DIRECTOR stopped before cell 182, stuck the key into the lock, and flung the door open. A slender girl with medium-long brown hair greeted me shyly. Her round baby face was covered with deep scars that caught my immediate attention. The heavy door banged shut, and I was left alone with my new cell mate, Ursula.

My heart was still racing and I felt a sick disappointment as I stepped inside. The cell was about one-fourth the size of the old one and intended for one person. There was just enough room to pass between the two beds and squeeze behind the headboards to fit into the easy chairs on either side of a round table. Directly inside the door was the largest area of free space. It provided enough room for both of us to turn around.

Life in the other cell had become unbearable. Brigette had continually used me as her scapegoat, and I was no longer able to put up with it. After a violent argument in which she called me a vulgar name, I had requested another cell mate, and my petition was honored.

The new year was just a week old, and I could begin it with a new cell mate. Ursula was a welcome contrast to Brigette. She had a sweet shyness, was warmly generous, and exceptionally accommodating. From the very beginning she was delighted to learn that she had the honor of being placed with an American.

"But what are you, an American, doing here?" she wondered aloud. "I thought your country could keep them from locking you up?"

I had wondered the same, but apparently my country had been rendered powerless by the tiny Red regime which it did not recognize.

Ursula had spent the past week in a cell by herself after she had been moved away from a middle-aged woman. Once again new stories were exchanged optimistically, and once again the pain of another's suffering was brought near. The circumstances that had brought us to our present cell we recalled in nightmare, and we agreed it would be more than we could take to change cell mates again.

Ursula's story was not too different from Brigette's. She was caught in an attempt to escape, to reach her fiancé in West Berlin. She had known him long before the Wall went up. For more than a couple of years the two had explored many escape routes for her to join him. Swimming the canal, hiding in a diplomatic car, and daring the Wall itself had all crossed her mind.

Ursula and her fiancé, Dieter, had finally decided on her escape through Czechoslovakia. They had both been spending their vacation there the previous year when the idea struck them. . . . Dieter had secured a West German passport and replaced the picture with Ursula's. She had booked a weekend trip to Prague, which was only a few hours away and a common excursion spot for Berliners. Then Dieter had someone forge the entry stamps and visa in West Berlin.

One item had bothered Ursula, though. He had had the same number that was issued in his passport forged in hers. She had argued that the numerals were probably a significant factor in controlling the papers. Dieter, on the other hand, had felt that the guards would be too busy to examine the stamp in detail. Ursula had reluctantly agreed to accept the papers as they were.

Ursula told me that when she boarded the train in Prague, she disposed of the last trace of her real identity—her East German money, which she flushed down the commode. She said she swallowed a couple of tranquilizers and stationed herself in the railway car.

The rest became just another of hundreds of similar fates. Ursula's papers were not in order. She was pulled off the train and subjected to fiery cross-examinations in the guard room. When the guard left the room Ursula made one last desperate attempt to reach West Germany. She said that she leaped from her chair and headed for the border with all the speed her legs could summon. It was the only chance, and the West Germans would offer her political asylum. A deep voice had boomed behind her,

"Halt or I'll shoot!" At that moment Ursula had questioned whether it all really mattered any more. The urgent authority in guard's command stopped her. He would have fired.

Ursula then found herself in a dilapidated prison in Prague and was taken for her first nightly interrogation on arrival. The procedure was not unlike that in Berlin, but more strongly oriented to propaganda. The harsh interrogator had attempted to fill her head with fables about the West. If his own image of West Germany was as distorted as the one he presented to Ursula, he was the sad victim of brainwashing himself. She could only respond tearfully with Schiller's famous statement, "Sometimes we have to reach up to the stars to bring justice down to earth!"

The day following her arrest a woman guard had led her to a shower where she was told to delouse herself with a pungent powder. Ursula said she was utterly humiliated and had protested. She won her way. All her belongings were removed and she got dressed in a baggy training suit, while two male guards looked on from the outside peephole—even more mortifying than the delousing ceremony.

Ursula described the cell as dingy, musty, and filled with the stench from the corner toilet, which was a mere hole in the floor with flushing facilities, not unlike those in France and Italy. The room was a spacious three by four paces. The only furniture was a folding bench and wall table, and the bed consisted of a thin, stained mattress on the stone floor. It was covered by a yellow sheet and a couple of filthy gray blankets. Ursula received no toilet articles, not even a toothbrush.

Ursula said that her body folded up in exhaustion when she entered the cell, and that she had discovered large boils on her face. They stung with burning needlelike sensations.

After three weeks in the dismal hole, Ursula had been transported to Berlin, where she was handed over to the Security Police. This had been done in compliance with the General Attorney's request to prosecute her in the DDR. Although the sentences were known to be lower in Czechoslovakia, the prison conditions were much worse.

Ursula and I became marvelous companions. After our initial exchange we decided to rise above the tragedy of our lot with humor. Of course, in the beginning it was not easy. We called each other with an old German title for an intimate friend *"Gevatterin."* I was *"Gevatterin-*number-two" and she was *"Gevatterin-*number-one." She was not the fearful Brigette and together we were more prone to flout authority than either of us would have been alone. We soon became in the guards' opinion, "the infamous corner cell."

From Brigette I had already been oriented in all the prison routines. In her better moods she had thrown me into stitches of laughter over her original Berliner jargon. After some time I had begun to imitate it. She informed me that, as prisoners, we were both students of *Knastologie* and *Gitterkunde.* Unfortunately the delightful words are not accessible to English translation. *"Knast"* is Berliner slang for "jug" or "pen." Therefore, we were studying "jugology." *"Gitter"* meant the iron bars. Thus *"Gitterkunde"* would probably be the "science of the bars" in English. She also told me about *"Rotenbestrahlung"*—the state's "red-ray treatment" which denoted the Communist or Red indoctrination of their party members. After a while we would both become Knastologists—experienced prisoners.

One of the first routines that a knastologist had to learn was the "knocking code." The code was very simple, with one knock for "A," two for "B," three for "C," and so on. It was the best way to establish the forbidden contact with other prisoners and connect to the prison grapevine which reached into all cells.

Ursula and I began communicating with our neighbors, who—we learned—were men. Since she had the bed adjoining the neighboring cell, she had to knock, while I was posted at the toilet watchout. The wall beside my bed was adjacent to the stairwell that led outdoors. Each prisoner was assigned to his side of the cell and not permitted to be on the other side.

I was unable to rap on Ursula's wall; therefore, I disappeared to the corner toilet.

An answer of two knocks was returned each time, but nothing else. Then, a series of meaningless and jumbled letters sounded. Finally, the letters n-a-m-e were slowly tapped.

I immediately responded with our first names and "Hellen" seemed to stump the tapper. After all, it was a foreign name and an unusual spelling. I gave up on it. Two names were returned in a quick staccato. Finally, we were introduced to Horst and Peter.

Ursula agreed to replace me, because my long disappearance in the corner was beginning to look suspicious. I began pacing back and forth, listening for the guards, while she sat at the table innocently engrossed in a book, in order to continue our conversation. Her arm rested against the wall.

After several days of our new communication system, Ursula's knuckles were raw and she switched over to a pebble she had picked up outside. It was also more difficult to pinpoint the origin of the faint tapping when a stone was used. We also learned that nighttime offered a better cover for our secret grapevine.

Horst and Peter had both been tried and sentenced. Horst had five years and Peter, three. Horst was twenty-nine, married, and the father of a four-year-old son. Peter was single.

Indeed, the attraction between the sexes was not held back by prison walls, thick as they might be. Perhaps it was only due to the proximity and the fact we had established forbidden contact. Maybe it was because we had exhausted all other topics of conversation. Whatever the reason, we both found ourselves wondering about the two men and constantly bringing them into our conversation. We resented any attention from the guards, but not from Horst and Peter. A warm bond of solidarity and mutual sympathy passed through the thick wall to the strangers on the other side.

We began to talk and laugh louder so they would be able to hear us. They did the same. Their strong accents revealed that they were Berliners, too. It was always the Berliners who manifested an independent spirit against the regime. No wonder the prisons were full of them. The West was too strong and alive for them. They could observe it within the narrow confines of their own city.

Horst's messages became more and more affectionate. "Dearest ones" or "You two darlings" was the salutation, and every night without fail "g-n" was tapped through the thick stone. That was the abbreviation for "Good night."

One night Ursula remarked, "It is a strange feeling to know that a man is lying next to me—just on the other side of that wall. . . ." Yes, women without men. Perhaps that made them all the more interesting. . . .

Peter and Horst met with rivals. The occupants of the cell directly across from us were three men. Ursula's and my noisy antics had attracted their attention, causing them to be loud and boisterous. After the lights were switched off at night, a deep bass would boom out with a cry for freedom. One of the men enjoyed yelling out in the corridor, and we admired his daring.

The manly trio sang songs for us, and Ursula and I followed suit. The slot in the door began to fall open numerous times daily to the tune of a guard's warning to be quieter. Actually singing was not permitted, but most of the guards winked at the regulation as long as it was not too loud.

Ursula was eager to learn the American songs I taught her, and we performed them as loudly as possible for our neighbors. "Unchained Melody" and "On Top of Old Smoky" were two of our favorites, until we heard the three men singing "My Bonnie Lies Over the Ocean." Thereafter, we took turns chorusing it back and forth. Ursula insisted that I write down all the texts for her. Since we were not allowed writing paper, we resorted to toilet paper for our song sheets.

Ursula especially loved all the blues I taught her. Before long she was singing "My mamma done tole me," rolling her big blue eyes, and wiggling her body in a sexy imitation of an American discotheque singer. Then she looked like a voluptuous baby doll.

One brisk winter morning Ursula and I were circling in our stone cage outdoors, drinking up the crisp air, in our exercise period. The armed guards were patrolling with heavy footsteps on the wooden bridge above the cells. Because of deep laughter and scuffling movements which were already familiar to us, we knew that the three men were in the outdoor cell adjoining ours.

Suddenly, as I turned the corner, something plopped in front of me. I bent over at once and picked it up, slipping it into my pocket. It was a note! The passing of notes between prisoners was a more severe violation of the rules than knocking. Instantly a voice from the bridge behind me bellowed, "Give me that note." A wave of tingling fright swept through me.

I hesitated, uncertain of the next move. "What note?" I pretended surprise.

"The note that just landed in this cell," the irate voice continued.

I sauntered on around my circle, ignoring the guard on the bridge. He did not budge from the spot. I could not let go of that note. My curiosity was burning. The movement helped ease my throbbing heart and I assumed an indifferent expression to hide my fright.

"She doesn't have a note!" Ursula defended me. "It was only a stone." I knew that Ursula had not had time to see the object I had taken from the ground, and she was convinced that it was a stone.

"Heh! Come over and unlock this cell," the guard yelled to a colleague.

My fright turned to panic, but a breath of daring struck me as I realized there was no turning back. The men were sure to search me, and in an instant I had decided on the next move. Out of the corner of my eye I could observe the guard on the bridge, who had not taken his eyes off me. When my back was directly toward him, I grabbed the note in my pocket, let out a long cough, and popped it into my mouth. I pushed it into my cheek with my tongue and looked toward the bridge. Had he seen it? It happened right before his eyes.

The cell door was flung open and two angry guards stood outside. I immediately pulled out the contents of my two coat pockets and turned the lining wrong side out. "You can check my pockets," I said confidently. "There's no note in them!"

"What was it then?" the elderly guard demanded.

"Only a pebble," Ursula assured them. She was irritated that they had caused her *Gevatterin* so much distress over a pebble.

Back in my indoor cell, I rushed to the corner out of the range of the guard's eye, and removed the soggy note from my mouth. I carefully unfolded it and pressed it between the pages of a book to dry out. It had been weighted down with two uniform buttons. I expected the door to fly open any minute and to be taken to be searched.

Half an hour passed and nothing happened. I withdrew to the corner again, and removed the dry sheet of paper from the book. *"Nur Mut!"*— "only courage"—was written across the top of the page. Then, "Write me sometime," followed by a name and an address. Ursula and I were proud that I had rescued the sender from punishment—for to have been caught would have brought severe consequences.

A few hours later when we were sure no guards were around, I said, "Only courage" in as loud a voice as possible. Seconds elapsed and "Only courage" came back from across the corridor. He knew we had received his note.

Ursula and I became exceptionally high-spirited as a result of our victory with the note. We even became cocky and decided to name all the female guards one afternoon. To distinguish the various ones, we had always referred to them by physical descriptions, the "fat one" or "grandma." We went to work on appropriate names.

We dubbed an older warder, who notified us of her presence with the creaking of her shoes, "Squeak Shoes." "Door Stormer" was a lieutenant who bounced against the door with her plump body every time she peeked in. "Rosy Cheeks" was a robust, rustic young girl, and "The Nice One" was the friendliest of the guards. "Scratch Brush" was a cross and irritable middle-aged guard, and "The Rogue" was one of the more humorous, impish, and playful guards. "Bowlegs" was a very correct, strict guard who must have had rickets as a baby. I later learned she had spent time in a concentration camp as a prisoner under the Nazis.

Ursula and I became preoccupied with getting information to the cell across the corridor. We were both burning with curiosity to learn more about the trio. Once when we were outdoors, I began knocking to them with a stone. They answered. I got the message across that I was an American, and they informed me they were in for espionage.

The subsequent free times outdoors were spent in loud singing back and forth. The guards threatened to send us back into the building if we were not quiet. After a while the guards established that congenial contact between the men and us existed, and they stopped putting us in adjoining cells. Sometimes, however, they slipped up. Since we had no way of knowing for sure, we developed a new mode of communication—coughing.

Ursula loved to call out when she was sure no guard was around, "Oh, Alfred, darling." Her voice carried across to the men. The response was peals of laughter, and "My Bonnie Lies Over the Ocean" would begin.

Gradually our interest in our neighbors ebbed away because of lack of contact. Then we turned to reading. Once a week five books were exchanged for those who had reading permission. Moreover, not all prisoners had the royal privilege of lying down, and we made the most of ours. Most were forced to while away the long hours of waiting on hard chairs. Ursula and I spent our hours stretched out on the bed, book in hand.

It had taken considerable time and effort to find the inner peace to concentrate on reading. I was also leery of the first poisonous books we received—war stories about the Nazis or Soviet propaganda. Brigette had corrected me at once when I said "Russian authors." "Soviet" had been the modern usage, since the 1917 Revolution, and denoted the present ideology of the Soviet Union. I had always used the terms loosely and interchangeably, but after her explanation I was careful to make the distinction.

Later the books were better and the field expanded to embrace numerous foreign authors, including western European and American ones. Of course, the selections from capitalistic countries consisted of critical social realism and naturalism. At the end of every book was a lengthy interpretation of the novel in line with the Marxist view of history.

I was not surprised to find Sinclair Lewis' *Kingsblood Royal,* or Mark Twain's *Huckleberry Finn.* All of Zola's *Rougon-Macquart* series were also available, and many historical novels which dealt with periods before the Bolshevist Revolution. The majority of authors came from the Communist countries and usually concerned the struggle for power in the Eastern countries. Although other prisoners received a newspaper, Ursula and I were denied that questionable privilege.

With all the books that passed through our cell, there was always something moving in picking up one that had gone through the hands of other prisoners and discovering underlined phrases or passages. Although forbidden, it was our secret language of solidarity. There was a sense of brotherhood behind stone walls and iron bars that did not exist outside. It was silent, but very much alive. All statements concerning freedom, angry despots, or cruel police tactics were underscored with fingernail marks.

It was ironical that the officials could not see themselves in the lucid descriptions in these books which were taken from other periods of history, especially the recent past. They had been carefully selected from past eras to show the prisoners that the injustice they were undergoing was not new to the history of humanity. As long as governments had existed, there had been political prisoners. One police state had only replaced another.

It must have been eight o'clock one evening when Ursula and I were startled by a loud, hollow pounding. It was followed by crashing sounds and deep moans. A male voice cried out, "I'm not a criminal, you dirty Nazis! Let me out of here!" Then wild thrashing against the door. The hoarse lamentation of the man penetrated the corridor. It shattered the tranquility we had managed to find, and not only penetrated the thick walls of the cell but aroused the sympathy of our hearts. Our high spirits were dampened. Silent tears filled our eyes. Another victim had been caged.

A man had been torn from his family; a woman had to abandon her children; a young girl would never lay eyes on her fiancé again; a young man would be denied the realization of his ambitions. There were aggressive screams of "Let me out of here, you Nazis!" Or sometimes a woman's helpless sobs filled the corridor. Someone had said that for every one who successfully escaped to the West, six landed in prison! I knew that literally thousands must be housed in prisons throughout the small country of the DDR.

Our tears of sympathy often became outbursts of rage. Where did they get their right to subject men to such treatment? Oh yes, there were laws—but I could not help asking, "Is man made for law or law made for man?" That was the crucial question! When thousands of respectable citizens felt compelled to violate laws, it was only a symptom of a sick system. Ursula indignantly demanded, "If a government is no longer able to rule its people and finds them all fleeing, why doesn't it give up its right to govern?"

One day as I lay stretched across my bed, a whistling from the corridor caught my attention. The melody was familiar. I jumped up from the bed when I recognized the tune of "The Halls of Montezuma."

"Where is that song coming from?" I asked Ursula.

"What song?" she mumbled, looking up from her book.

"That song! Do you know it?"

She listened a moment and then answered No. I sang it for her to make sure that it was not also a German tune. No, she was certain she had never heard it.

"There must be an American here," I said, "because that is the Marine song." We cocked our ears, and the melody was repeated. I began to sing the words as loudly as I felt I could and get away with it, and Ursula hummed along with me.

"Teach me the words," she begged, "and we can sing it together." I quickly taught her the text, and we both sang out.

The whistling continued. I put my ear against the door to determine its location. It appeared to float from the cell diagonally across from us. Ursula and I had already established that a foreigner was in the cell, because the guards addressed him in broken German. It also sounded as if he had a radio in his cell. We had exerted every effort to discover where he was from. Each time the bolt of a slot was heard to click open, I rushed to the door to eavesdrop. His accent seemed to place him from a Scandinavian or English-speaking country.

Now there was no longer doubt. He must be an American. We decided to call him the "Ami," the German's colloquial abbreviation of American. What a feeling to discover that another countryman was locked up! Since I was completely cut off from contact with the outside world, I once more became aware of the fact that my country must have abandoned me, too. Surely, when the news of my arrest had crossed the Atlantic, a country as powerful as the United States could have done something to secure my release—especially since I was a victim of her foreign policy. Both December and January had elapsed with no sign. The painful recognition that the United States Government must have been rendered helpless by a tiny Communist state was swallowed up in the evening sounds of silence. . . .

7

A SHOCKING DISCOVERY

"Saint louiee woman . . ."—a blouse flew through the room; ". . . with your diamond rings . . ."—a brassiere landed on the bed. "Got that man . . ."—a pair of lace panties fell to the floor; ". . . by your apron

getting completely lax. After supper we both slipped into our black leo-
tards and performed gymnastics on the bed, since it provided the largest
surface.

By this time the guards were becoming amused by the strange antics in
cell 182, and as long as they disturbed no one, they were quietly ignored.
Once more we became high-spirited. Ursula had read somewhere that a
good exercise for relaxation was propping the legs up over the head. There
we lay one evening, our fannies parked against the wall with propped legs
extending upward. We closed our eyes and breathed deeply.

Suddenly the slot banged open. Door Stormer stuck her chubby head to
the opening with a scowl. "Are you two sleeping like that?" she demanded
curtly. It all looked suspicious to her.

"No. We're just relaxing," I replied.

"Oh!" The slot clicked shut. I soon realized that she was suspicious and
afraid of me because I was a bold foreigner. She seldom dared to cross me.

Ursula had already been severely reproached by Bowlegs when she was
sprawled out in her chair with her legs propped up on the bed. Bowlegs ordered her to "sit like a lady." That was the spark that set off an explosion.

Furious, I had blurted out, "And these regimented hags who prance
around in uniforms try to tell us how a lady is to behave. How dare they!"
Most of the warders chose to ignore us after that, because we both lost our
temper when reproached by the guards. Another method we used to fend
off the guards was threatening to report any incident to the director. They
were more afraid of their own authority than we.

Sometimes it was easier to take the verbal attacks from an interrogator
than to accept the petty injustices of guards. One morning Ursula and I had
requested a table knife for our Kaffeeklatsch. Ursula, who was always so
generous as to give me half of all her edibles, had just received a package
from home. We were looking forward to having pound cake, which had
just arrived, with our coffee.

Scratch Brush was on duty that day, and she never made exceptions or
granted favors to any prisoners, unless, of course, they were male. The
duty shift changed after breakfast, and if the breakfast shift failed to note
our wishes, the following troop had no way of knowing. The incident
might not have created such an explosion if it had not occurred repeatedly.

More than once the morning shift had forgotten to note our requests, and as a result, we had to do without a knife if Scratch Brush was on duty.

When our coffee arrived without a knife, we politely repeated our request, stating that we had already ordered it at the proper time. Scratch Brush responded with a deep scowl and refused to bring the knife, slamming the slot shut.

We would not admit defeat. We stationed ourselves directly in front of the peephole, and when the bold eye appeared to scan the cell, we repeated our wish. The lid to the tiny aperture quickly slid shut. She ignored us. We began to sing "On Top of Old Smoky" as loud as our voices would reach. It took only seconds for steps to scurry to our door and the slot fell open.

"Were you two singing so loud?" Scratch Brush asked sheepishly. Of course she knew we were.

"Yes. We want a knife!" She grumbled something about finding one and scurried away like a wet hen.

In a few seconds she returned with a broad smile and a knife. Scratch Brush was always like that.

Since we had had a struggle to get our knife, we were not letting go of it that easily. Normally the regulations demanded that a knife be returned as soon as the prisoner had finished using it, but most of the guards had given us permission to make an exception.

We were startled when the slot fell open and a male guard, whom we called "the Bird," ordered us to give him our knife.

"We have permission to keep it in the cell till evening," I answered.

"Who are you kidding? Nobody has that permission!" he growled.

"Oh yes, we do," I returned.

"Yes, that's right," Ursula agreed.

"Give me that knife!" he demanded, unconvinced.

"No, I shall not!" I defied him. "We always ask for one and never get it. The other guards have given us permission to keep it."

"That's not the truth!" he contradicted.

"It most certainly is," I exclaimed angrily.

"Give it to him," Ursula said, "it doesn't matter."

"No," I answered stubbornly, "it's a matter of principle! He has no right to do that—just because we are prisoners." Finally I handed him the knife, furious. It was all so insignificant. But somehow the pettiness of an injustice the guards could get away with was directly related to the extent of one's humiliation and indignation.

The more I thought about it the angrier I got. This in itself was more upsetting than the incident. I reached the point where I could no longer contain myself and went to the door and started shouting. What I shouted I cannot recall. I called them Nazis, criminals, abusers of humanity! A flood of tears broke loose and Ursula joined me. I pressed the button. I would demand the director.

I know how prison riots are started now, because my outburst worked as a spark to set off a chain reaction. The trio across from us began pounding on the door, too. There were signs of rumbling at the other end of the corridor, when keys clinked in the lock of our door.

A huge blond officer with a serious face stepped into our cell. His stature, Germanic features, stiff black boots, and high-collared uniform all reminded me of the perfect SS man. I was too upset to get to my feet when he entered, and I remained on the bed. He approached the bed, sat down next to me, and placed his arm around my shoulder. He found the softest words possible in an attempt to console me.

"Why don't you tell me what the matter is?" he coaxed. The gentle tone sounded awkward coming from the big, burly fellow.

"They have no right to treat us like that!" I sobbed.

"Like what?"

Ursula and I attempted to explain all the difficulties we encountered with certain guards. It seemed ridiculous when we related it to him. They were little things, but somehow representative.

Finally he stammered, "You can have a knife any time you want one. Do you have any more complaints?"

I hesitated. "Yes . . . some things have been taken from our cell."

"What?" he inquired.

"Oh . . . little things." It all appeared to be utterly insignificant. But it was the principle—we were helpless prisoners, and they had no right to take advantage of us.

"What has been removed from your cell?"

"Hairpins and hand cream." Any other place in the world those nothings would not have mattered, but in prison, they were our only valuables.

I was ashamed that we had caused so much disturbance over the knife, which had provided the trigger for the outburst of all our pent-up resentments. When he had calmed both of us sufficiently, the brawny officer left our cell with the reassurance that we should report any complaint in the future. We agreed we would.

The first few weeks of imprisonment had been characterized by a heavy dread of the unlocking of the door, which meant some unexpected ordeal with an uncertain outcome. The latter weeks, however, had been filled with hopeful anticipation that the silent door would swing open—that some change would enter the cell, some alteration of events interrupt the long, monotonous hours of waiting for an indefinite future. November, December, January, February. We etched another week into the wood of the table. It was our best calendar.

No, the painful interrogations had not been the worst. Nor had that hideous invasion of one's last privacy through the eye in the door been the most unbearable. Nor the cage-like cell that locked one off from his freedom. It was the torture of a gnawing uncertainty, of not knowing one's future and not being able to raise one finger in determining it.

I found myself longing for some sign, any sign that would be evidence of what course my life would take. To know bad news was better than to be kept in the dark. That was the severest punishment they could give a man. Strip him of his freedom and deny him certainty about his future. This gave rise to another tendency—that of losing myself in the hopeless present.

The door was flung open. *"Eins."* Ursula was being taken for a visit with her mother. I tried not to envy her, because I was really glad for the welcome change in our lives. But the cell seemed lonelier than usual, and the tears of nostalgia I had kept suppressed rolled down my cheeks.

It was certain that no one would visit me. With Ursula's absence, thoughts of utter abandonment crept into the quiet loneliness. In those moments of solitude, the exchange of a warm word with anyone would have taken on a cherished meaning, and a new depth of significance for my life.

My thoughts wandered across a wall, into West Berlin, and rested momentarily in my dormitory home, a tiny international community of friends. What were they doing now? Had I just faded out of their lives when I disappeared in the East? Evenings many of them would gather in a small circle in the dormitory, laugh, drink, and celebrate any cause that might come to mind. Or they would discuss politics, religion, or philosophy over foamy beer mugs, and solve world problems. But did they know of this other world? A world full of suffering, which was only a few miles away in their own city? Did they even realize how precious their freedom was?

Thousands of their own countrymen were imprisoned in the same city, and for them life rolled on in irresponsible unawareness. Most of them were burdened with the problem of too much freedom—without orientation or direction they floated in the main stream, incongruous with life surrounding them.

Ursula had already made me more aware that East and West were worlds apart. I had had a chance to observe for myself on numerous visits to East Berlin that the youth there seemed to have more of a sense of responsibility and orientation toward the future than those in the West. They were forced to meet the challenge that their society afforded them. And no one remained neutral, indifferent, or disengaged. They were confronted with a state that demanded their energies and talents and one that presented them with a definite explanation and goal of history. They accepted it passionately or rejected it violently—but they did not remain indifferent.

On the other hand, the youth in the West were preoccupied excessively with the pursuit of pleasure or empty diversion. They were the passive products of a consumer society, ever seeking and taking in new forms of entertainment. They were the outcasts of their state. No wonder they gave evidence of the decadence of a lost generation, a generation that rejects the past, but has no goal for the future.

When Ursula returned from her visit, her eyes were red and swollen. Possibly a visit was worse than no visit. There was the pain of separation, the humiliation of seeing a loved one in pain and having to look on in helplessness. There were the silent reproaches to oneself. . . .

After lunch Ursula and I had stretched out across the bed for our afternoon siesta when the door swung open. It was the chubby, round-faced little man from the administration. We had nicknamed him "Gummi Ball" because of the snappy way he always seemed to bounce into our cell, and after a while we had also learned to appreciate his sense of humor, which was bouncy, too.

"Get your shoes on," he stuttered as he always did when he was passing on an order. "You are going to see your lawyer."

I had no time to arrange my hair or smooth out the creases in my clothes, and I was too dazed even to bother about it. Perhaps the visit meant some new development in my case. So many weeks had elapsed since my arrest, and the questionings had tapered off to an occasional interrogation.

I followed Gummi Ball into a new section of the building and to an exit which led to the inner court. The passageway was lined with curious gazing eyes of the guards who stood waiting. Their uniformed stares made me stiffen with a proud stature as I paraded past them.

Outside stood what looked like a bright green delivery truck with its motor chugging impatiently. I wondered what was being delivered, until I realized that it must be me. I had already heard about the awful vehicle, and I was meeting it for the first time. It was the East German version of the paddy wagon, and the Berliners had dubbed it with the lovely title of the "Green Minna."

Inside, it was sectioned off into boxlike cells, just large enough for a person to squeeze into. "Claustrophobia chambers" they might be called. Although I had never suffered from the malady, I was overcome with a strong sense of suffocation when the guard locked me in the black hole.

Initially, the stale air did not want to pass through my throat, and I panicked. I forced myself to swallow deep gulps of air and inhale deeply. In a few minutes I was able to adjust to my new cage. I discovered two narrow slits in the door which enabled a bit of air to enter—the only glimmering of light in the box. Then I heard the heavy sounds of other prisoners being loaded into the awful green monster, and within seconds we were rolling.

The ride itself had all the aspects of a nightmare, rolling in a dark cage which bounced to an unknown destination. After some fifteen minutes, which seemed immeasurably longer, we screeched to a halt. From Ursula

I had already learned that I was most likely being taken to the Magdalenenstrasse prison, an older building that belonged to the Security Police—the same one in which I had passed my terrible first night. The Hohenschoenhausen prison was top security, and no one, not even a lawyer, was allowed entrance for a visit. Only the employees of the Ministry of State Security had access to that protected fortress.

I was locked in an empty cell, where I was to wait until I was sent for. Musty and dingy, it was about half the size of my other cell, and the only bed was a slatted wooden cot. The bucket toilet in the corner effused a penetrating odor. I glanced at the filthy walls, where curls of paint were chipping off, examined the rusty bucket with its pungent chlorine, the scratched slats of the wooden cot, and for the first time I was grateful for Hohenschoenhausen. I felt sorry for the others who were forced to live in such cells. I could hear their steps echoing in the corridor, or their distant tapping in the walls, and examined their signatures which had been etched deeply in the concrete.

J began pacing nervously. A cold eye appeared in the door, and a key clanked in the lock. A young guard led the way through the noisy corridor and two sets of locked doors, then stopped before a large padded door. It was identical with the one I had entered on my first night. I discovered that I was in the same room.

Two friendly eyes assuaged my fears with a warm welcome, and Wolfgang Vogel extended his hand in introduction. He nodded for me to be seated and offered me a thick bar of chocolate when I refused a cigarette. For the first time in weeks, I relaxed and felt that I was a person, instead of just a number.

My first question to him was whether he spoke English. It was not that my German was leaving me, but I would have welcomed the change. I learned that he spoke little English, but had been a student of Greek and Latin in a Jesuit school. I pounced upon him with all the questions I had stored up for the first visit, but before I had gotten very far, he warned me.

"We cannot talk about your case. The investigation is not closed yet. Normally, I am not allowed to see a prisoner until his case is closed, but I received special permission in your case. But it was only granted under the condition that I promise not to discuss the case with you."

I was sick with bitter disappointment. I longed to know where I stood. What would happen to me? I had only conducted some conversations pertaining to escape, I assured him. I had helped no one escape. Could that be so serious?

He turned all my intense questions away with, "I have no idea until I have read your file. I wouldn't want to give you any false hopes."

I assured him that my interrogator had continually implied that I might be released without a trial, for the prosecutor did not necessarily have to press charges. I had been living in that hope.

His answer slapped me with a stinging shock. "Your trial is scheduled for some time next month."

"Trial." I fought to hold back the tears. The veil of uncertainty that lay over my future was ripped apart—at least its first layer. The outcome of the trial still awaited me. A naïve optimism that had fed my hopes until then was shattered. My actions were considered far more serious than even my most earnest imaginings had conceived. Yes, they would be keeping me for a while.

"Don't lose heart," Mr. Vogel encouraged, "I have something else in mind—negotiations. I have already tried to get something done for you and the other Americans here. There are four others beside you."

"What?" I wondered aloud. "What kind of negotiations?"

A quick frown wrinkled his brow. I picked up the cue and changed the subject.

"What have they done?"

"Two Negroes have already been sentenced to eight years for escape help. . . ."

"Eight years!" I exclaimed, appalled. "They might as well *hang me* as rob me of eight precious years of my life!"

"Don't get upset. They have done a lot more than you." His tone was unconvincing. "I am sure that you won't get eight years."

"But, still . . . I'll get a high sentence. . . ."

"They've helped five or six persons escape. There was money involved. The case is much more complicated than yours. Another American here was involved in a car accident where a bus load of children were injured. I'm working on a plan to get you all out at once."

Once more the idea of negotiations turned over in my mind. "What are the possibilities of the negotiations?" I inquired.

Again a scowl. "I'm not allowed to talk about it."

"Oh, all right. But I can imagine. I've seen films . . . could it be something like an exchange?"

His lips spread in a faint smile. "It might be." Getting up from his chair, he said, "I cannot talk any longer. I have an appointment. Your family is very worried about you. Why don't you write them a quick letter, telling them you are all right." He handed me a sheet of paper and a pen. This letter would circumvent the prison censorship and reach my parents.

"Do you need anything?" he continued as a routine inquiry.

"Oh yes. Could I have some clothes and toilet articles from my room in West Berlin? I've been wearing this same suit for weeks. I would also like to have my German and English Bibles."

He shrugged and wrinkled his brow in doubt. "It is forbidden to receive books from the outside, but I'll see what can be arranged. I'll be back at the end of next week." He lifted the receiver to request a guard.

He reached into his coat pocket and handed me a small plastic bag of hard candy and a couple of pieces of fruit. I shook his hand in parting and followed the guard outside into the cold corridor.

A feeling of lostness swept through me as I followed the clicking heels of the guard down the passageway. None of my legal questions had been cleared up. I was only one detail wiser. I would have to face a trial, and that would be without any idea of the nature or gravity of my crime. It was certain that I would try to defend myself, too. I would tell the court exactly what humane motivations led me to act as I did. Although they had their laws, they must understand. I was an American. . . .

Waiting in the dirty cell seemed an eternity of doubts, fears, anxieties. I was impatient to return and share my worries with Ursula.

I boarded the horrid Minna to be carted off once more in a boxlike cage. In the darkness within, my thoughts returned to the news of the setback with a heavy dread. Trial . . . judgment. . . .

Then it struck me. I had pronounced a judgment myself when I got involved in escape activity. Yes, I had set myself up as a judge, judging the laws of another country. And I had condemned them with my decision to violate them. Now I was to be judged for it. But this was more. I sensed that my entire life was being tried and tested during all the ordeal, for I had acted as a whole person. All my weaknesses and strengths had brought me to that decision that sprang into action. My rebellious disrespect for authority and avid appetite for adventure, a self-assured heedlessness to warning signs had certainly been mingled in my motivations. But was it not a passionate idealism, the absolute conviction that freedom is a basic human right, or the dedicated commitment to helping a brother realize his notch on the rung of life that were stronger? Or was it just Sammy and Hellen, the plea of one young person to another, the matter of course to be followed without questioning?

There was no scale to balance out all my motivations. My response would determine. The judgment would be pronounced on my life and not just a lone, isolated act. I had not reckoned with this judgment when I got involved, nor that I should be called into account for all my actions. A trial!

8

THE COURAGE TO BE

WITH A HAIRPIN, I scratched the third week of February into the table calendar. The door was flung open. The runner appeared in the doorway to take me for questioning. The questions had become routine and general in the past weeks. This time I had to write out a comprehensive curriculum vitae, pages of detailed descriptions of all the people involved in my case, and presumably all the Americans I knew in West Berlin. I selected a couple I was sure were harmless, and fortunately I was only superficially acquainted with a few. Even though I lived right in the middle of what might be considered the American colony of West Berlin, Dahlem, I had met only a handful of compatriots.

Head shapes, eye colors, height, weight, nose shapes, hair lines. . . . The Weasel greedily sought all the details he could get, no matter how insignificant or irrelevant. Not to supply them meant that I was not cooperating, and he informed me that my release was dependent on my cooperation.

I was also required to write out a "voluntary" detailed statement about my crime, beginning from the time I had met Sammy in East Berlin. Although the Weasel assured me it was strictly voluntary, when I decided I had rather leave off writing it, he apologetically explained that it was impossible. I guess the "voluntary" aspect depended on the will of the interrogator and not the prisoner! Somehow he convinced me that the prosecutor would not understand if I failed to do it. I was not enthusiastic about doing such a task in German, but I had all the time I needed and he already had all the information.

The Weasel probed into my political background with special intensity. Had I belonged to any political party in the West? Taken any part in a political demonstration or rally, or attended any political lectures in West Berlin? Had I toured the Wall? Who had sponsored the tour? Had I been shown the memorial markers of people killed along the Wall for trying to escape? What newspaper did I read? Thousands of questions.

Of course no matter how I replied to the questions, he concluded that I had been influenced by the harmful Western propaganda to act against his state. He crowned his report with asking me for my opinion of the Wall. Without forethought I blurted out, "It is inhumane!"

The Weasel proceeded to point out that many persons around the world had welcomed the building of the Wall. I noticed that instead of writing my statement in the records, he softened it to, "The Wall is a humanly hard step to take."

There was absolutely nothing that the Weasel's probing left untouched. All of the interrogations were in the seclusion of his private office, and the air had become charged with intimacy. More and more he was exploring the utmost corners of my private life, and I sensed that it was his own personal curiosity. Nevertheless, I was powerless to oppose him, and he knew it. The interrogator was king and commander in prison. All rules were arbitrary, subject to change just at the breath of his word. A prisoner's treatment depended on his will, and he bought and sold privileges for information. I was uncertain what he was really after when I found him testing the fiber of my morality one day.

"And why didn't you have sexual relations with him?" the Weasel challenged with a smirk. He was referring to an evening Sammy and I had spent alone in conversation at the Brauns' apartment. "He is a real Casanova, you know."

I was irritated by this latest invasion of my privacy. Besides, I resented his tone and feared what he was leading up to.

"I'm not that kind of girl!" I answered at once, before the insinuation in his expression was carried any further.

"Well, he did kiss you, didn't he? *Na,* come on and tell me just how intimate he was with you?"

I could almost feel the Weasel smacking his lips over the details of my relationship to Sammy. I was infuriated and no longer able to suppress it. "It's none of your business!" I blurted. "Your verbal probing is just as indecent as the physical examination I was forced to undergo! Both are perverse!"

The Weasel did not flinch. He merely continued his examination. "I thought all Americans were . . . uh . . . 'freer' in this respect." He raised his eyebrows questioningly. Then he proceeded to expound on his image of American sexuality. We were all promiscuous, and orgies were as routine on the agenda as Cadillacs on the expressways.

I wasted no time in setting him straight that the "sexual revolution" might be a tendency in America, but I had grown up in the sheltered hills of Tennessee, where traditional morality was still in force. The Weasel's shock that I did not correspond with his image of a promiscuous American was superseded only by his disappointment. When the little man had satisfied his curiosity, he at once hid behind the fanatic inquirer again, and I felt out of danger.

The Weasel closed our session with a bit of news. The next interrogation was to be a cross-examination of Sammy and me together. I could not withhold my delight at the prospect of being able to see Sammy again.

I spent a sleepless night awaiting the following interrogation. I had never looked forward to an interrogation, but this was an exception. I would see Sammy! Before I was taken to the Weasel's office, Ursula commented that she had never seen me so radiant.

When I walked into the Weasel's room, my heart fell. No Sammy. Perhaps my enthusiastic response had discouraged the move. I was choked with disappointment, and the Weasel's questions and my responses seemed to roll by in a rote cadence. Then the little man surprised me with some new questions.

"I want to hear about the other methods of escape that were discussed!"

That struck me as a trick. "I've already told you about all of them!"

"What about the bus of American soldiers?" A sly grin spread his lips.

I thought a moment. "The only thing I remember is that Harold mentioned that he knew a girl who had escaped in a bus full of French soldiers. She was so petite that the men slipped her into their midst while boarding the bus."

He accepted the explanation. Then he reached into his desk drawer and handed me a photograph. "Do you recognize him?"

I examined the man's face carefully. "No."

"Well, he knows you quite well," the Weasel grinned wryly.

I gulped. It *was* a trick, and I decided to play along. "Oh, he must be one of your agents then," I replied.

He hesitated a moment and caught on. With an amused smile he asked, "You mean you don't even recognize Allen Dulles?"

"Who's that?" I joked.

"Don't try to tell me you don't know your own boss?"

Finally he laid the picture aside. I had no idea who it was supposed to be, but the Weasel loved to get me into tight corners. Of course by now he knew that I had no connection with the CIA, but he loved to see me sweat it out. I had seen through this game of his and I played along, since he enjoyed seeing me squirm.

One day a surprise occurred. I did not know what I should anticipate when I arrived for an interrogation session. The Weasel had ordered the usual coffee, which already stood on the table. At once he handed me a long sheet of paper. A letter from home! It brought an instant rush of tears.

All that was so long ago and far away was brought so near. I was allowed to take it to the cell with me, where I read it again and again and again.

It was the first day of March. I knew because Ursula had counted off the last scratch for February. As the runner led the way through the interrogation wing I wondered what I would be questioned about this time. It seemed quite a while since the Weasel and I had had a session together. I was taken by surprise when the runner stopped before the door across from the Weasel's. I was told to wait.

When I stepped into the office I was met by the stern eyes of a familiar face. This time it was not the Weasel; it was my prosecutor. He scrutinized me carefully from his erect position behind a large desk. Before him lay a thick file with my name and a number across its blue cover. My heart pounded away in anticipation.

"Take a seat over there in the corner." He motioned to a hard-backed chair in the farthest nook of the room, although another chair was standing immediately across from him. The gesture was to humiliate me. I was to sit in the corner like a disobedient child.

"Do you remember me?" he inquired icily.

How could I forget him? "Yes . . . I want to apologize for the awful scene I caused at our meeting. . . ."

He interrupted sharply, "Your interrogator has already done that for you."

Then changing the subject, "I have called you down here today in order to inform you that the investigation of your case is closed. I would like to ask you a few questions myself."

He proceeded to question me about my meeting Sammy and how it came about that we discussed the topic of escape. Then he posed other questions about the case. Obviously, he knew few of the details of my case.

"That's sufficient," he signaled me to stop. "Well," he continued, "your attitude certainly has changed. Your openness and sincerity manifest that. Why couldn't you have behaved like this when I first met you?"

"I was too upset. . . ."

"What about?" he asked dryly. "Did your interrogator mistreat you?"

"I guess it was my own conscience, because . . . because I had not been telling the truth!"

"You've told me the truth now, haven't you?" He raised his eyebrows.

"Yes."

"Is there anything else you want to tell me? Do you know of anyone else who wants to escape?" His eyes peered into mine with penetrating scrutiny.

"No." Beads of perspiration collected on my brow, and my heart was racing viciously.

"You know if you lie to me and we find out later, the consequences for you are very severe."

"I'm telling you the truth!" What did he want from me? I had written pages of statements, answered thousands of questions, and I still had no peace from interrogation.

"Why don't you come over here and sit on this chair so that we can talk to each other better." His tone introduced a friendly note.

I moved to the chair directly across from him.

"Now," he continued deliberately, "I want to explain to you that I am not allowed to press charges, since I am from the General Attorney's Office and your case is not so . . . uh . . . [there was an embarrassed pause in which he groped for the appropriate words] . . . not . . . of such importance that it has to be tried in the Supreme Court. It will be handled in a lower court. I will inform your prosecutor about your behavior, which, incidentally plays a very important part! I am glad to see that you were wise enough to cooperate. It certainly is better for you, Miss Battle."

I detected heavy overtones of irony in his voice, and his words were weighted with insinuations.

"When will I have my trial. . . ."

"Wait until I have finished. Then if you have any questions, you may ask them. I will advise the prosecutor about your case. He will make the charges, and you already have a defense attorney. But you should defend yourself, too, Miss Battle."

I wondered how that was possible.

"You see, if you had not cooperated . . . well, I'm the one who decided how long this investigation would be carried on. . . . It could have gone on for months and months. . . ."

So that was the size of things. No negotiation could take place until I had been tried. If I had chosen not to cooperate, a long and weary investigation would have been dangled over my head.

"It isn't the investigators who have kept your case open. I was responsible for it. Perhaps if you had cooperated sooner, it might have been closed even a month earlier. . . . But you realize you *have* to cooperate with us."

He was satisfied that he had proved his power to me.

"Do you have any questions?" A nicer tone was apparent in his chilly voice, now that the reproaches had been released.

"When will I have my trial?"

"The normal procedure is four to five weeks after a case is closed. Sometimes it is sooner, or sometimes it takes longer. Your lawyer will notify you in advance. Do you have any complaints to make about the treatment you have received?"

I paused in recollection. His question was obviously a mere technicality. I could not bemoan the fact that I considered the affair a gross injustice. He only referred to prison procedures. Should I dare tell him my complaint? "No . . . uh . . . yes, I do."

"What?" The thick eyebrows rose at my sincerity. He was a man who was unaccustomed to having anyone cross him.

"Well, I was absolutely humiliated by the physical examination I had to undergo when I entered this prison!"

He glanced at the floor. "You were examined by a woman, weren't you?" He feigned ignorance about the procedure.

"Yes, it wasn't that. . . ."

"It is routine to get undressed."

I stammered, "That didn't bother me. It was the way the guard conducted the examination. It was perverse!"

"What do you mean?"

"I'm afraid I cannot explain."

"Well, if you cannot explain, I cannot do anything about it." Abruptly changing the subject, he asked, "Do you have any other complaints? Is the food all right? What about medical care? Are you healthy?"

"Yes. I have never kept such a regular schedule in my life," I replied ironically. "Yes, I guess under the circumstances everything is all right."

"Well, if you have any complaints or questions in the future, just ask to report to me. I usually stop in here a few minutes every afternoon." He picked up the telephone receiver and requested a guard to pick me up.

Some days later I was nervously pacing back and forth when Gummi Ball's round face appeared in the open slot. "Be ready for transport at 3:00 P.M. You are going to see your lawyer."

I immediately thought of my trial. He was sure to have the news I had been dreading for so long.

I welcomed Mr. Vogel's friendly smile. Somehow I felt shabby when I gazed at his meticulous grooming.

I responded to his inquiry about my state with the formula that most prisoners learned to accept: "I'm fine under the circumstances." No one, least of all the lawyers, was interested in the bitter complaints of the prisoners.

"I just informed the client who was here before you, a French girl, that she will be released on Friday. She's a student, too."

A spark of envy flashed and then was gone. No, I was happy to hear of her good fortune. But I wondered just how many foreigners were sharing my lot. I had already heard about an Englishman, too.

"I've come to tell you that you are to be tried in April, but not here. It will be in Neubrandenburg." He paused, deliberating his next words. "I don't know whether I can defend you at the trial, since I am involved in a three-week trial of a Nazi war criminal, an ex-doctor at Auschwitz." His lips curved downward in an expression of disgust. "It's a messy case. However, if I can't, I'll have to send an assistant."

Both pieces of news hit me with a sharp and crushing disappointment. "Why in Neubrandenburg? I do hope that you can come."

"I don't know why it has been assigned to that district. If you would like, we can have the trial postponed if I am unable to attend."

"Well, I would like to get it over with as soon as possible. But if it is better to postpone it. . . . Oh, have you read my file yet? I have some questions. What kind of sentence can I. . . ."

"We'll see how it works out with the trial," he interrupted. "In any case

I am allowed to talk to you a few minutes before the trial. We can discuss it all then. There is no need to talk about the case now. I am in a hurry. If there is nothing else, I have brought you some coffee, oranges, and a couple of things from West Berlin."

I was more than displeased with his putting me off. He carefully avoided discussing my case, which made me frantic. I had so many questions, and I wanted to defend myself, but I had no way of knowing where I stood legally. A guard appeared to lead me away.

Toward the end of March the Weasel requested my presence once more. I had no idea what was on his heart, unless he just wanted me for an afternoon coffee chat.

I entered his office, where the coffee, which was now as routine as the questions, stood steaming on the table. As I made myself comfortable in the corner easy chair, he looked at me with curious eyes.

"You will be going to Neubrandenburg tomorrow."

I swallowed a thick lump. My hour had come. "When is my trial?" I asked.

"I don't know yet."

"Do you know why I am to be tried in Neubrandenburg?" The question was still bothering me, and I felt that it must have some significant answer; there must be some mysterious reason for sending me so far away from Berlin.

"No . . . that is, unless it is because that is where Sammy has to be tried.

"You will return right after the trial, but you have to be there on the first day of the calendar month in which the indictment is made. For that reason it is necessary for you to leave tomorrow."

He fumbled with a cigarette and apologetically began, "One thing, though, the prison in Neustrelitz where you will be staying is not so modern as this one. It was not built by our state, you see, and the conditions are not so favorable. . . ." His voice trailed.

When I had finished my coffee, he jumped from his chair. "I'll probably be coming up for your trial."

A knot in my stomach twisted, but to cover my fright I asked, "Why? Just to make certain that I tell the truth?"

His eyes widened. "Aren't you planning on telling the truth?" His gaze questioned penetratingly.

"Of course."

"It is routine that someone from the Security Police go along. Since the trial is closed to the general public for security reasons." The Weasel apologized for having to interrupt our session. He had work to do. As he squeezed my hand, he wished me *"Alles Gute."*

Yes, "good luck" or "the best of everything." It seemed so ironical coming from him. Especially since he had pressed out all the information that would convict me.

When I returned to the cell I was struck with the thought of never seeing Ursula again. A cloud of depression hung over us, and we both wore our longest faces. We were companions of crisis, and therefore a unique bond existed between us. It was about to be broken.

When I had entered cell 182 I had found a frightened, withdrawn girl. Deep scars on her face were the lingering shadow of the ordeal she had suffered at her arrest when a violent skin reaction erupted. A sudden panic, which she described as an "anxiety attack," overcame her on occasion and in that moment she felt death hover over her. She confided that these attacks had been initiated when the Wall went up.

Convinced that she was suffering from a fatal heart disease, Ursula had run from one medical doctor to another. Each one had the same story. There was no organic difficulty. She refused to believe them and attempted to doctor herself with every sort of pill and preparation her aged grandmother suggested.

Ursula had been on the verge of a heart neurosis, and I had seen an opportunity to share the product of my limited training in psychotherapy. We had begun spontaneous counseling sessions.

I proceeded to teach Ursula not to fear her emotions. When she was upset, I encouraged her to cry. She was afraid to—she had been taught it was immature. It may have been immature, but it was healthy. It cleansed the emotions and purged the soul. Besides, I did not consider crying immature. Ancient cultures had recognized its significance. They even had strange rites and rituals which our modern civilization would deem hysterical. When a woman's husband died, she sat at her husband's tomb for days, weeping passionately and clawing her face. Perhaps our civilization was sick because of telling people it was more noble not to cry. After all, there is a time to weep and a time to refrain from weeping.

After a while Ursula began to cry whenever she was afflicted, and she was delightfully surprised at the relief it brought her. Then I showed her a breathing exercise. Daily after lunch we reclined for our siesta and practiced a deep breathing exercise together. Ursula was overjoyed at the discovery of the new feeling—one of complete relaxation. Afterwards, whenever the death panic crept up to threaten her, she stretched out and drank deeply of the free food of all life.

Finally, Ursula and I worked on forming new attitudes and building a new relationship to herself. Ursula was dominated by a deep lack of self-acceptance which she had inherited from her unhappy family situation. We analyzed her relationship to her parents and theirs to each other. The locked gates of her understanding broke open to a new independence.

After some weeks, the taut, strained lines left her expression, and the jittery nervousness disappeared from her gestures. A certain still growth became evident in her, and together we could laugh and cry, become indignant at man's inhumanity to man, or even meet our God in the darkest halls of suffering together. And now, as abruptly as we had been brought together, we were to be separated.

9

UNWILLING JOURNEY

THE EARLY MORNING hours of the first day of April were the harbinger of another misty gray continental day. Bleak and depressing as the weather might be, it was still a beautiful day for me—at least in one respect. I was riding to Neustrelitz in a car. As the drizzling rain gently patted the metallic roof, I inhaled the fresh air, which tasted of freedom outside stone walls.

Spring popped up all around me in vivid colors. I peered through the blurry windows at the moist color outside. The rich green world was a soothing contrast to the sad gray that had surrounded me for so many weeks. It whispered a promise, for in Germany green was the color of hope.

Bowlegs sat on my left and exchanged lively conversation with the two male guards in the front seat. All of them appeared to ignore me, and I had difficulty understanding the swallowed syllables of their dialect. They were real foreigners. East Berlin had been invaded by foreigners. No, not by Russians, but by Saxons. Nowhere in Germany, with the exception of Saxony, had I run across anyone who looked upon the Saxons with any amount of affection. They were the lazy, backwoods Germans, who butchered the language. The Communist indoctrination had best succeeded with them, owing to their ignorance, and they had migrated to Berlin, taking over the best apartments and jobs. There was widespread resentment against them.

The driver, who could no longer suppress his curiosity, turned to me with a question.

"Wasn't I driving on the night you were arrested?"

"I don't remember." The guards were not supposed to make conversation with the prisoners, and I was hesitant to say more.

He and his companion were both garrulous, each trying to outdo the other. They were not discouraged by my brief answer. "Yes, I am sure I did. I remember that the tears were pouring down your cheeks. Now, it is not really so bad after all, is it?"

When I remained silent, it was because I was offended by his question. He probed further. "What are the charges against you?"

"*Fluchthilfe.*"

"How did you happen to get caught? You ought to be more careful, you know." His tone and words were free of any moralizing about my crime. He accepted it as a matter of course, with only the admonition to be more careful.

"I was arrested when I came to East Berlin, the *Hauptstadt,*" I was accustomed to saying already. "I met a young man who had deserted the army, but I was not able to help him. I had told him some months before how he might be able to escape by himself, but the method proved to be impossible."

Bowlegs frowned in shock and pity. The guards laughed, as if I had made a great blunder. "Which organization sent you to East Berlin?" the driver inquired.

"Nobody sent me. That's the irony of it all. We had just talked about how he could escape by himself. Or, at least, how we thought he could."

"What were you doing in West Berlin?"

I volunteered the answers to his inquiry, because his manner was open and friendly. Besides, I welcomed the opportunity to point out what I felt was the injustice of the whole affair. I was sure that these simple guards were unaware of what their state was really doing.

"I was teaching English and studying theology."

"Theology?" His tone manifested disbelief.

"Yes."

"Then you must believe in Christianity. How can you accept such an antiquated *Weltanschauung?* Marxism is more modern. You know, the only difference between Marxism and Christianity is that Marxism is more scientific and in tune with progress. Christianity is an outdated old myth. No rationally enlightened person could accept it today."

That opinion did not originate with the Communists!

"Of course, I disagree, or I wouldn't be studying theology," I answered. "The trouble with those who claim there is nothing to Christianity is that they are usually uninformed about it, or they are rejecting their own childish notions and conceptions about God and the universe. When they are children, they are taught in childlike words about God, but when they become older, they fail 'to put away childish things.' Have you ever bothered to pursue Christianity more deeply? I mean on an adult level?"

"Well, . . . uh . . . actually no," he stammered.

Without bothering to explain the discrepancy between theory and practice in the socialistic countries, I began by explaining the basic limitations of the Marxist ideology as a real solution to man's problems. I knew he had been schooled and brainwashed in the subject.

"The trouble with Marxism is that it offers no real solution to the *human condition.* It hopes to remove evil from the world by changing society. And you even try to go about that with force. But do you think that a change in the social structure will change human hearts? Would such a change give man meaning for his life? Or would it prepare him for death? You see, you may chain a man to a stake and thereby prevent him from committing evil. Thus, you think you have overcome evil. He is good only because he does not have the freedom to be bad. But loosen his bonds and what happens? When the fetters fall away what does he do? Yes, man is a free agent, but still stuck with his own selfish interests."

Both guards entered into the lively conversation, and Bowlegs listened with keen interest.

"You must not forget that society is not that advanced yet. We have not attained the perfect state. Then every man will have his portion and there will be no more evil exploitation of men," the driver interjected.

"There is where you are mistaken. Anyway, economic exploitation is just one of man's sins. It stems from his greed and selfishness, but it is not the only one. There are many more that have nothing to do with materialism. You know something, already in America we have all of those things which you are striving for under Communism, but are people happy? I find that they are not! Now that their material needs are taken care of, they are discovering that these are just the most basic and primitive ones. They have spiritual needs. Although America is the richest nation in the world materially, she is still a poverty-stricken child spiritually. Suicide, mental illness, alcoholism, drugs, are only symptoms of her illness. . . . Yes, when the high standard of living is attained, that is only the beginning of man's problems. You Communists seem to think that they are then solved. Now let me ask you what you propose to do when your earthly paradise is established, where all people are filled and possess everything they want?"

I was excited that I was evoking an active response that showed no sign of belligerence.

The driver, who seldom gave his companion opportunity to squeeze in a reply, burst forth with the formulas he had learned. "Then people will have time for culture. They can further their education and enjoy the arts."

"Do you really believe that? I know many who have this golden opportunity in my own country, and they are indifferent to its challenge," I responded. "I think the real limitations of Communism lie elsewhere, though. It is based on a purely material explanation of the universe and history. It offers no solution to three basic problems of human existence: guilt, death, and the meaning of human existence. Oh, it tries to answer the third. It attempts to give man a meaning in life, a temporal goal to strive for. But it is only a temporary one. As I mentioned, when history is done with the business of social reform and justice, where do you go from there? Culture? The self-complacency and indifference that a high standard of living breeds do not encourage the flourishing of culture."

"What about guilt?" he asked eagerly.

"All men have consciences to live with, and they are often acting against them. They are often the victims of misjudgment or selfish abuse of others to achieve their own aims. Where does one then expend his feelings of guilt? Or expiate his real guilt? What about the Nazi war criminals? A whole nation was proved wrong, and how many really believed themselves to be doing the right? I know of literally hundreds of persons who retreat from life, who stop growing, who stop progressing, who become sick physically or mentally just because they carry a heavy burden of guilt with them throughout life. They are unable to purge themselves inwardly of the sins they may have committed, and it is only Christianity that offers the ultimate answer to the problem of guilt. It is only Christianity that offers the cross with its forgiveness. . . ."

Before I finished my explanation, I was interrupted by the guard's colleague who had been awaiting his turn. "It is impossible for a group of people with a common goal in history to err!" He was referring to the Communists' doctrine of the infallibility of the party. They assured the people that they could not err.

"Wait a minute!" I could not refrain from exclaiming. "Weren't the Nazis a group of people with a common goal they believed to be right?"

Perplexity clouded his brow, and after a pause, he answered, "The Nazis persecuted the Jews and Christians, but Communists don't."

That seemed to suffice for him. It was the only point of differentiation he could find between the Nazis and the Communists.

I had become so engrossed in our lively debate that I hardly noticed the landscape that rolled softly by on the outside. My attention was only briefly diverted when we passed a Russian military installation. I had wondered where all the Russians kept themselves hidden, and our speeding car afforded a hasty examination of where some were stationed. Afterwards I noticed numerous vehicles with Russian plates in the area, and I attempted with every approaching one to make a quick inspection of the driver's face. I was obsessed by an insatiable curiosity about what manner of man could burden the world with such a heavy yoke. But I detected no sign in the passing visages that distinguished them from a German *Bauer,* a Texas rancher, or a Spanish *obrero.*

We picked up the threads of the conversation that had been briefly broken. "And what about His Majesty, Death?" I queried. "How are you Communists prepared to face him? To meet him when he comes riding in on a black horse to take you away? Yes, what about death? There is no way of offering proof of a life after death—that is, unless one accepts the testimony of one who experienced it and was resurrected to tell us that the grave is not life's end station. . . . Yes, life is a big gamble. If Christianity is the truth. . . ."

The noisy Wartburg bounced up a drive and came to an abrupt halt. We had arrived at the prison. A small, yellow three-story stucco stared silently as the driver climbed out of the vehicle. The rusty bars at the windows and the barbed wire that fringed the high walls of the court were all coated with layers of age. The prison had been built by the Nazis; the Weasel had made that clear to me.

The fact that I was dressed in a tweed costume with a frilly green blouse and nylons, that I had ridden in a car, and had just enjoyed an intense discussion with the guards made me transcend prisonership to ladyhood. It was no wonder that I forgot to jump to my feet when I was introduced to the director of the prison. I remained seated and greeted him with a soft smile, which must have been highly irregular. No one seemed to hold it against me, though. When a handsome young guard was to lead me to my new cell, he hesitated before starting up the stairway. "I guess we can make an exception this time. I'll carry your suitcase up the stairs."

The two guards who had driven me to Neustrelitz took leave, wishing me "all the best" and an especially light sentence. Bowlegs had put in a good word for me with the prison authorities, for I had overheard their conversation outside the door. They appeared proud of their American prisoner.

The young guard led the way, grinning ironically all the while. He appeared embarrassed that he was carrying a prisoner's things. Perhaps the whole picture struck him as it did me. The chic of my apparel, my feminine helplessness, the fact I was a foreigner—it all seemed incongruous with prison. I could imagine the toughies, the hoods, the antisocial elements, the stereotypes of convicts, but not an American young lady. Although I was sure that East German prisons had housed all types of individuals within their fortified walls, I was in doubt about the kinds who had passed through this tiny prison in the north of East Germany. Perhaps it was also for this reason that I was treated with a certain air of respect, in spite of my lowly status.

My new cage was the hospital cell. I am certain that it was the best in the house. It differed from the other cells in size, and it was furnished with a hospital bed, instead of a wooden cot. One major adjustment was demanded from me, however. The luxury of a toilet was replaced by a huge black chlorine bucket with a round seat on top.

The meals were not as good as they had been in Berlin. Sometimes I had two free periods outdoors a day instead of one. Otherwise prison life was the same. With one exception: loneliness became my greatest enemy. I no longer had the friendly and consoling presence of Ursula. My anxiety was too severe to concentrate on reading, and I passed the long hours in nervous pacing. Once again I was confronted with a period of uncertainty, of eternal waiting. . . .

On the third morning after I arrived at the Neustrelitz prison, my cell door swung open. A tall dark officer of the Security Police entered my cell with a woman who appeared to be in her early fifties. She was a bleached blonde, rather attractive, and her rusty suede jacket gave her the appearance of a Westerner. I was surprised by the visitors and hopped to my feet as they entered with solemn faces.

"Your name and crime?" the officer demanded.

"Battle, and my crime is *alleged Fluchthilfe*." I do not know why I emphasized the "alleged" so strongly. It must have been something about his cold manner that incited my resistance.

122 · Every Wall Shall Fall

"In our state there is no such thing as 'alleged.' If the police have seen fit to arrest you, then you are guilty." He corrected me with an icy reproach.

The self-righteousness in his tone disgusted me. I had not had a trial, and he dared pronounce me guilty. Then I was overcome with self-pity and indignation. I was still unable to grasp the fact that I had really done anything worthy of being punished for so long. But I was annoyed with myself for having acted so arrogantly toward him. No matter whether my sense of justice accepted it, I had already come to the recognition that by their laws I was guilty. Nevertheless, his tone had rubbed me the wrong way.

"It is unjust! It is inhumane! What have I done?"

The woman carefully scrutinized me with a sneer. "Your government is not any more humane! You have no right to talk about humaneness. Just look at the dirty war in Vietnam!"

There it was again. Every single official I had met seized the opportunity to attack me on the war.

"I don't advocate any war, but one thing is certain. If Western Germany attacked you tomorrow with the help of the United States and in the name of German unity and democracy, wouldn't you call in the Soviet Union to help you fight them?" I demanded of them. "What is the difference?"

"Yes, of course," she replied, missing the significance of my comparison.

As I expected, the rest of the party line followed.

She sneered at me again, and the officer interrupted us. "This is your prosecuting attorney," he introduced his companion.

I had started off on the wrong foot, getting carried away in the first meeting with my prosecutor. To cover my surprised reaction, I collected myself and asked, "When am I to have my trial?"

"A date is not scheduled yet," she replied coldly.

"What? Not yet? They told me in Berlin that it would be at the beginning of April." I was unable to hide the disappointment.

"Oh, the people in Berlin. They have no idea of how we run things here." Her tone conveyed her resentment of the Berliners. "Your trial will probably be in the latter part of the month."

The tension between us was mounting. I recalled Ursula's words: "The women in the DDR are more fanatic than the men when they get involved in politics!" The fact that we had gotten off to the wrong start with each other and that I was to be prosecuted by a fanatic woman was beginning to shatter all my hopes of a favorable outcome. She struck me as one of the cold "paragraph people," a phrase the Germans use to denote their sticklers for the letter of the law. They were legal automatons that responded only to laws or rules, never giving birth to a free decision or reacting with any sign of spontaneous humanity. The Germans were famous for producing these mechanized bureaucrats. It was unknown to me at the time that the hard woman who was to be my prosecutor had been trained in the Soviet Union.

When the two walked out of my cell, I broke down. I was not only terrified about the coming trial, but crushed that I would have to remain in the dinky prison so long by myself. Besides, I had been deeply offended by the condescending manner of the two. I lay on the bed and began crying loudly. Once the tears began, they flowed ceaselessly as if the floodgates of a great dam had been released.

In some minutes the two re-entered.

The major gazed helplessly at the prosecuting attorney. "I didn't realize it, but women take prison much harder than men!"

This grown man, responsible for prisoners, was obviously naïve as to the suffering that people were being subjected to. That was the reason he could piously justify his state. How many prosecutors, judges, and even prison officials knew what they really condemned people to? I was convinced that he had been totally unaware of my dejected state and, being exposed to it, he wanted to alleviate my immediate suffering. It was not in his power. It was in her power, though. But then again, perhaps she was just another small tool of a greater apparatus.

"It is evident that you must have a chance to go over the charges of your written accusation before your trial. If you don't I'm afraid that something like today's outburst could happen. I'll have a law book sent up to your cell, too," the prosecutor announced. She had been greatly disturbed by my eruption, and was obviously worried about my causing a scene in the courtroom. The two departed, leaving me alone again.

I immediately flung myself across the bed and prayed my most earnest prayer. I prayed for death.

Another crisis had come, and this time I was unsure how I would surmount it. I refused to eat, and after supper I lay sobbing on my pillow. It was the time the guards always disappeared for their evening break, and the stillness of the corridors was suddenly enlivened with shouted greetings between the men's cells. From the sound of their German, I decided they were *Halbstarks,* the German hoods. I was probably the only woman in the midst of them, but I longed for an amiable contact with anyone. I sought any sign of life that would break the monotony of the sad solitude. I began knocking on the wall.

To my amazement immediate taps responded. When my neighbor learned he was knocking with an American woman his gruff voice announced it to the silent corridor. The reaction was hilarious laughter.

"That's a good one. Tell me another one," a voice roared in disbelief.

"Says she's in the jug for escape help," came the chuckling reply.

"Man, this is great. Someone can really spin 'em!"

They were convinced that some prisoner was amusing himself with a yarn. A favorite pastime was relating fantastic stories through the prison grapevine. Of course, to them it was absurd to believe that any American woman would be stuck up in the dumpy jailhouse in Neustrelitz in the middle of a group of rowdies. They were getting such a bang out of the whole affair, I could not withstand the temptation to shout back to them. I was afraid of the consequences of getting caught, but I yelled out, "Yes, I am an Ami!"

The loud guffaws ceased. A reverent pause followed.

"What's your name?" A note of shock was present in the inquiring voice.

"Hellen."

"Ach, Helene!"

"No," the gruff voice contradicted, "Helen, without an *e*."

"Where you from?"

"Tennessee."

A couple of guffaws pealed out. Then the melody of the "Tennessee Waltz" with German overtones echoed through the hollow corridor. The empty corner became enlivened with shouting conversation and enraptured singing. My cell was situated at the top of a tiny stairwell and I was first to detect the heavy footsteps of approaching guards. I became quiet, but the men did not notice.

An angry voice bellowed, "Don't ever let me catch you doing that again!" A slot slid shut and silence followed the retreating footsteps that waited some minutes before disappearing. The guard had not heard me.

The following morning after breakfast the director stood in the doorway of my cell. "Pack your things together. You are returning to Berlin." It was the unexpected answer to a prayer. I had never thought I would welcome with open arms a return to the Hohenschoenhausen prison in Berlin, but I did.

Ursula and I whispered up into the wee hours of the quiet morning. We were both overjoyed to be together once again. I was to remain in Berlin until my trial.

10

GUILTY AS CHARGED

I LAY ON A THIN BLANKET on the floor, naked. Ursula stood above me with a horror-filled face, and in her eyes were welled-up tears. The guard's eyes revealed fright as she asked me the cause of the sudden fainting spell that had brought me to the floor. I did not know.

As I had stood in the steaming shower a wave of nausea swelled up and when I stepped out, I was unable to put on my clothes. I stumbled to a scrub basin in the shower room and tried to vomit. I only coughed up empty air, and unable to remain on my feet I dropped to the floor.

When I was able to pull up to my feet, Ursula and the guard slipped a nightshirt over my head and led me back to the cell. All the men guards gazed at me curiously as I stumbled past them. The medical officer appeared after some minutes and told me to get dressed for an examination.

The spells did not recur, but I found myself swallowing two silver round pills three times a day. What they were for I had no inkling. I could only assume that it had been the emotional strain of the anticipation of my coming ordeal—the trial.

The latter part of April had arrived. The Weasel sent for me. I was greeted by him and his colleague. I immediately sniffed something irregular, since the Weasel was always alone at our sessions. His companion was the same individual with whom I had found such great rapport at our Christmas celebration. Both men wore forced smiles which attempted to conceal a certain perplexity.

After asking the routine questions about how I was getting along, there was a weighty hesitation. The Weasel's colleague suspended the silence. "Uh . . ." he groped for words, ". . . your interrogator has sent for you today . . . to inform you about your trial." I wondered at the stuttering difficulty. What new turn of events could cause such deliberation on his part?

"You are to be tried tomorrow. We will drive up to Neubrandenburg early in the morning," the Weasel announced solemnly.

"How early?"

"Oh, very early," he laughed. He seemed to welcome the question that diverted his attention from a weightier matter. "Say four o'clock. Do you think you can make it out of bed so early?"

"Of course I can! But what about you?" I asked. "I have to get up at five o'clock every morning. One hour earlier makes no difference."

In spite of our casual jesting which bounced back and forth, I still had the sensation of something terrible about to happen. The two men knew, and I did not. The Weasel's companion revealed the cause of the heavy atmosphere. He presented me with a thick document, half apologetically, and stated bluntly, "Here is your written accusation."

My heart raced and pounded. Even after months of questioning, I was still unable to relax, to have the inner security of knowing exactly what my position was. At an interrogation it was as if I was put in the pillory, exposed, to be ripped apart verbally. I was at the mercy of the examiner. No corner of my consciousness remained unprobed. My soul was scathed.

Somehow, though, the two interrogators were compliant and yielding in their manner when they handed me the document.

My eyes raced across the words. "The First Workers' and Farmers' State of the German Democratic Republic. . . ." That was unimportant. "The defendant is accused of *Verleiten zum Verlassen der DDR,* according to Paragraph 21, Section I." I was unsure what the word *verleiten* meant, so the first statement of the charges did not register. It was when I began the first sentence of the fifteen-page accusation that I reacted. "The accused Battle is charged with having been a member of a group that fights against the German Democratic Republic. . . ."

I flung the paper on the table. "This is a filthy lie! It is absolutely preposterous! I was afraid that you would distort my statements. That is exactly what you have done! There was no group! I had a series of conversations with different people. There was no organization to it at all! Only unrelated conversations!" I exerted no effort to suppress my anger. When I paused to gasp for breath, the stocky interrogator interrupted.

"Just calm down a minute. There is no sense in getting so upset. You mustn't take this language literally. It is legal language!" Obviously the Weasel had called in his companion, because the latter was better able to handle my outbursts. "Go on and read the rest of it. We are here to explain it to you."

Although my blood was boiling, I forced myself to try to comprehend the words that followed. My German seemed to leave me. The accusation was written in such a high flung, stilted, and twisted language. It struck me as being unreal, and I knew that I had met the Communist ideology in the raw in the charges.

My eyes stumbled over the words: "One of the tactics of the *Bonner Ultras* in undermining and attempting to destroy the First Workers' and Farmers' State of the DDR is the organization of small groups which employ methods detrimental to the security of our state. These groups direct their activity to the solicitation of citizens of our state, plan, organize, and execute methods of smuggling our citizens illegally out of the state. The accused Battle had identified herself with these methods. . . ."

I felt like ripping the pages apart. It was all so incongruous with the reality of my actions, that I should not have bothered to take it seriously. I tried to choke back the tears. Finally, I shouted, "The prosecutor is psychotic! A schizophrene! This is not the truth! This accusation is just an expression of all your hatred and aggression against Western Germany!"

Wild with rage and indignation, I proceeded to put them on the accusation bench. "This is a crime against humanity. . . ."

I was cut short.

"You are reacting violently because the charges are directed against you. Our officials feel that they have rightly evaluated your crime before making the accusation. They cannot be wrong. Your interrogator and I both feel that your crime has been given the correct paragraph. Nevertheless, you mustn't take this legal language so seriously."

I peered at him and then at the Weasel. The Weasel knew my crime. He could convince his colleague of the harmlessness of my involvement. But the Weasel dared not answer my scrutiny. His gaze focused on the carpet, and his pallid expression appeared to be one of shame. He cowardly let his companion continue.

"I know the prosecuting attorney personally, and I am sure that she is not schizophrenic. . . ."

"Then your whole ideology is! A whole state! It is madness! What do I have to do with the *Bonner Ultras?* I have always been one of their severest critics. I have tried to encourage West Germans to approach the East with understanding and reconciliation. This is just your ideology superimposed on my case! The real facts have been distorted to fit your doctrine! I simply felt obligated to help another person attain the most basic right of humanity—his freedom. I believe in this freedom! Yes, I could even accept the charge now if you said I had made myself guilty of breaking your laws. Your economy needs all the manpower it can get, and to remove someone from East Germany is a loss to the economy. Of course, it is necessary to protect your state by making such laws, preventing your citizens from leaving. But—" and that was a decisive *but,* "what you have written in the charges is an absolute lie! A complete distortion! I don't care whether it is legal language or not. It's the truth that matters!"

Truth. From how many viewpoints could one examine it and not pervert it? The interests of the state stood supreme, and these men had deluded themselves into believing a certain amount of the state's distorted ideology. Nevertheless, with an honest reservation they could make concessions and call it "legal language." Both men tried to soften the effect. But the fact that they found it necessary to do just that was evidence that something was rotten. A guilty person knows his guilt. He does not need the charges explained to him. They could have masked their efforts with the explanation that they understood my sensitivity, or that I was a foreigner and might have language difficulties and that therefore, they had to clarify the charges.

It became clear why the prosecutor had advised me to read over the accusation with someone before the trial. She knew that I would have reacted violently if I had seen it for the first time in the courtroom! I would have, too!

"Most of the persons who are tried for what you call escape help are tried under this paragraph. You mustn't get disturbed if the prosecutor calls you a 'manhandler.' This paragraph is called the 'manhandle' paragraph." The Weasel sat passively in his chair as his companion paced across the tiny room. "You see, the Bonn Government is responsible for soliciting our citizens. At present the Wall is the biggest business in the world—second only to the war in Vietnam."

I was amazed by the fact that he really believed that all the blame lay on West Germany for all the thousands who attempted escape. The floods of escapees who risked death and imprisonment to attain their freedom had only been enticed and seduced by the Western propaganda, according to him. The image of the golden West caused East Germans to become dissatisfied with their own state. Of course, many were greedy and willing to risk everything to have what their Western brothers proudly boasted. The German soil had been ravaged by numerous wars, giving birth to one of the greediest materialisms in existence. But that was not the only motivation.

How many in the East had abandoned all of their accumulated possessions to launch out in the face of an uncertain future? The innate longing for freedom was still urgently alive, and now a portion of Germans were enclosed within a penal colony. Perhaps the hope of Germany lay with them. They knew what freedom was about—even the humblest worker!

The more articulate of the interrogators continued his lecture. "What would you say if I told you how our citizens are used? For example, an organization from the West gives seven people false documents and dispatches them on the stretch to Denmark. All of them are arrested at the border, and we know that someone was awaiting their arrival in Western Germany. Now, the following day five more are sent out from the same organization along the same route. They, too, are arrested.

"If you think that isn't sufficient, I'll continue. The next day nine more persons, who received their false papers from the same group, take off with the same destination. Of course, you can guess their fate, too. This organization received enormous sums of money for the passports. That's how these people work. They solicit our citizens and then exploit them. That organization knew that those people would land in prison. Yet, they let them go through with it anyway. What do you have to say to that? Isn't that 'manhandling'?"

He spoke with conviction, certain of the justice of the laws of his state.

"I would say that the people who sent your citizens are certainly guilty of 'manhandling' and deserve to be punished. I understand, though, that the West German and especially the West Berliner police are taking action against deception and exploitation of this sort. I agree that it is a crime, but, again, what does it have to do with me? I am not one of those persons! Why can't you differentiate?" I pleaded helplessly.

He ignored my question, disclosing his inability to answer it. I felt that *he* did differentiate, but he did not dare express it. It was the public prosecutors who did not! But to them I was just another number, another file, another case that had to be processed through the procedures of law. An examination of my file could not be substituted for an immediate encounter. For it was the whole person who was on trial, not just a detached act. People were products of the sum total of their experience—all of their motives led them up to their involvement in a single crime. One had to comprehend that to attain real justice, not just the appearance of it.

It sickened me to realize that the fate of individuals was determined from the isolation of an office desk, utilizing books of paragraphs as guides. The prosecutors were not the ones who spent long probing hours of interrogation with the criminals, and even if they had been, their eyes were only open to see what they had been taught to see. It all brought to mind the dreadful realization that it is the politicians who make the wars from the bunkers of bureaus, but it is the common people who bleed to death on the battlefields.

I would not give up, though. I was still determined to break through the barrier of ideological prejudice, the real wall separating East and West. Arguments and words were insignificant. Decisive was my person. My accuser was not just one woman, nor a group of public prosecutors, nor even the laws of a state, but a human condition!

Back in the cell I was still fuming with indignation. They dared speak of humanism. Any real humanism meant that *law was made for man and not man for law*. Was it only through Christianity that one could arrive at this realization? It was Jesus Christ who had first flouted the old established authority when He healed on the Sabbath. He had violated a law to help an individual! After two thousand years, lawmakers still had not comprehended that truth.

I slipped into the corner, out of the range of the peephole, and began to copy down the charges. I decided to hide them somewhere and smuggle them out. I felt the urgent need to answer that hideous distortion which was indicative of their ideological approach. My eyes scanned the charges, page after page of a twisted summary of all that I had confessed to and signed in my interrogations. The accusation chose to ignore my real motives, my desire to help Sammy and Barbara. Instead, my motives were reduced to "political reasons." I had been influenced by the Western news media to act against the state.

When Ursula explained that *verleiten* meant "suborning" or "inducing," I was outraged. They had made the preposterous charge that I had enticed Sammy to leave the state. How absurd! After two previous escape attempts on his part! The Weasel had said, "We believe that our citizens cannot escape by themselves. By offering assistance you induce them." Those were his words, but what was the truth? I was the one who had been induced!

That night sleep was a prisoner in a ghetto of obsessive thoughts. My mind raced around in vicious circles of reproaches. "Judge not, that ye be not judged!" Yes, I had set myself up as a judge—condemning the laws of another country. Now, I was to be judged for it. But it was really my entire life that was on trial. Since I was merely the product of the past—a chain of experiences that brought me to the immediate engagement of the present. I had not heeded all warnings, or had I? Yes! I had distanced myself from this judgment shortly before my arrest, when I decided that I should leave off assisting Sammy. . . . Then it was the telegram. . . . My arrest was the unavoidable! If the telegram had not arrived, nothing else would have happened. I would have returned to America. The telegram—fate's snare or the arm of Providence?

The last four years of my life had produced many irresponsible decisions. Could it have been the careless ones that brought me into bondage and not the genuine desire to help, or an interaction of both? I had sometimes fled before the responsibility of resolutions or wasted energy and talents to selfish and destructive causes. I had committed what only the Christian knows as sin before God. Now my freedom was removed—freedom that had often been abused, and I had been forced to give an account of all my activities, to confess.

Confession . . . one sees the ugliness of one's own nakedness. Nothing secret remains hidden. Every soul must face a trial one day, a revelation of all the past, a responsibility for every decision, every act . . . must face a judgment . . . *the Judgment.*

I was already awake at four o'clock when the light flashed on, and I stretched my tired limbs as I climbed out of bed. I had chosen my black suit to wear to the trial with a specific purpose. Black was the color of doomsday.

As I descended the narrow stairway to meet the sputtering vehicle which was awaiting me, the Weasel beamed silent approval at the change in my appearance. His approving gaze imparted that I was still a woman and not entirely a number. But it all seemed so ironical to me—getting dressed up to get condemned.

I felt no anxiety before the impending ordeal. Only numbness—a state of shock that went beyond feeling. When the guard asked me whether I wanted a tranquilizer, I refused.

The woman guard who accompanied me introduced a new cheerful face. She was petite, warm, lively, and carried on active conversation in the native dialect with the other guards. The Weasel sat in silent withdrawal and his pale face was clouded with doom.

I hardly understood a word of the rapid discourse. But it irritated me when the guards cracked jokes, quoted the latest ball scores, or exchanged tidbits of prattling gossip. It was so irrelevant and out of place. Did they not perceive the oppressive cloud that hung over the day? Or were they trying to divert my attention? It was a pitiful attempt.

I looked at the Weasel's solemn face. He was so seldom given to jest and he wore all the traits of fanaticism. He was a "believer," as I called them. The Weasel always corrected me when I said that and claimed that the proper word was "convinced." A "believer" sounded too much like religion for him. One is "convinced" of the Communist ideology—one does not believe in it, he had told me. But I always disagreed with him. To be a Communist one had to accept by faith a certain interpretation and goal of history. One had to believe in Marx's interpretation of history before one became convinced, and one had to accept matter as the only god of the universe.

When the vehicle halted before the courthouse, my eyes widened in astonishment. My expectations had envisioned an old massive stone building with gigantic stairs leading up to an arch, under which *Justitia* resided. What I found was a postwar, provisional looking, army-type barracks. We had plowed through mudholes and parked at the backdoor, next to what appeared to be large garbage-disposal units, in order to reach it. I immediately recalled the irony of all the posters and placards pasted in the tiny towns and villages along the way: *Sozialismus Siegt!* (Socialism is victorious!)

There was no evidence of it at the Neubrandenburg courthouse. All of those advertisements throughout the land which assured people of the victory of socialism smelled like sour grapes to me.

We passed through neither stony portals nor wide archways to enter the shabby building. We squeezed through rows of stacked chairs and bumped against the stickiness of freshly painted walls. We stationed ourselves in the "witness" room to await the approaching inquisition.

The petite guard convinced me I should swallow coffee and a couple of tranquilizers. I did not know what I took them for, because I was already stunned to numb unawareness of my surroundings. My attorney, who was supposed to consult with me before the trial, had not appeared. I had conditioned myself to the superfluity of legal advice and had come to consider it one of the few luxuries of the system.

The guards continued their chattering and pretended to ignore me. I noticed that they stole occasional glances to observe my reactions. I was sure they had been warned that I had a tendency to get hysterical. From time to time they attempted to draw me into conversation, but I only responded in single-word replies.

Ten minutes before trial time, my attorney, who had assured me of consultation before the tribunal, had not arrived. The guards became concerned, too, and a husky young guard who spoke with a lisp arose from his chair and informed me he would look for my defense attorney.

After some seconds the guard returned and assured us that Mr. Vogel's powder blue Mercedes was parked at the front of the building. Mr. Vogel then appeared in person, wearing a friendly nonchalant smile. He gave me his hand and appeared unconcerned about discussing my case or courtroom procedure. Fortunately, the two interrogators had prepared me for it all.

A clerk popped in the doorway of the witness room to inform us that the judge and prosecuting attorney would be late. He then sauntered off down the corridor, the wooden floor creaking under his heavy steps.

My attention was diverted to the corner of the small room, where a radiator dripped. The leaking drops had already formed a puddle on the floor. Drip . . . drip . . . drip . . . drip . . . drip . . . ticked away with the seconds of time. Each drop was an eternity that invaded the present . . . now . . . now . . . now . . . now. . . . Eternity was making decisions.

I walked down the corridor that led into the courtroom, and the busy repairmen dropped their work and stared at me inquisitively. "So that's the criminal," they probably thought, "wonder what she's done."

The renovated courtroom was an improvement over the rear of the building. The odor of fresh paint permeated the stale atmosphere within the aging walls. I found my position on a bench behind my lawyer just opposite the prosecutor's station.

When the young judge entered the courtroom, I was immediately struck with the impression of a mathematician. He must have been in his early thirties and was substituting for the judge who usually presided over the district court in Neubrandenburg. His dark-rimmed spectacles seemed to enhance the seriousness of his countenance.

On either side of the judge sat a juror with a starched stiffness. These were not citizens who were selected at random to determine the innocence or guilt of a defendant. They were laymen who were politically schooled in the laws of the state and who served in the position for a certain period of time. One was a provincial looking woman in her fifties, with all the facial features of the submissive peasant. The other juror was her male counterpart and appeared to be ten to fifteen years older. His wrinkled face was expressionless and his hollow eyes were fixed on some point in the distance. His slow movements and passive manner did not fit his lanky body, only his age.

The judge opened the tribunal in the name of the people of the First German Workers' and Farmers' State. How he proceeded to conduct the inquest, I cannot remember. He presided from his podium with a thick book before him, which appeared to be the size of a *Webster's Collegiate Dictionary*. I knew it was my file, all those pages of statements I had spent months recording. He had marked certain sections and requested me to relate the incidents. No witnesses were present, although I had noticed that Sammy, Harold, and Sammy's mother had all been listed as witnesses against me on the formal accusation. I was my only witness. I would be convicted by my own testimony against myself.

Both the prosecutor and defense attorney appeared uninterested and the Weasel sat at the back of the courtroom, rapidly jotting down notes. The guards who were stationed either side of the exit, stared out into space. No other persons were present, because the standard operating procedure on political cases dictated the regulation that "for security reasons, the trial is closed to the public."

Of course it was necessary to prevent such trials from reaching the ears of the public. The state could not afford to expose to the people what was really going on in their courtrooms. The people might learn the truth. The thousands of political cases that passed through the tribunals of East Germany would disprove that the state was winning a popularity contest as it claimed to the people.

It all had the atmosphere of a kangaroo court. The officials' minds were made up already. They even knew the sentence that I would receive. No one was listening to my explanation. But when I stated that Sammy had a legitimate reason for escaping, the eyebrows went up, as if I had committed blasphemy against the state. To them there was no "reason" for anyone to leave their state.

The whole affair lasted only a couple of long hours which I passed standing before the judge. When it reached the time for the prosecution to present a summation of the charges, the same hate-filled psychotic distortions were poured out against me. Although the prosecutor addressed the tribunal, she fixed her cold eyes on me, not casting them away for one instant.

I shut my mind to the meaning of her hateful utterances and returned a gaze that demanded what manner of woman was able to commit the crime against mankind she was in the process of committing. What coldness and insensitivity to rights and feelings could bring one to make such preposterous charges? What callousness to truth? What adulteration of justice? I told her in a soul-piercing gaze that she, too, would be on trial one day, that she would have to face a judgment. But as my eyes spoke, she became more hysterical in her attack. Never had I seen so much hatred poured out against me. Finally, the tirade culminated.

"Five and a half years hard labor!" The shrill voice of the prosecution pierced the hollow emptiness of the courtroom. It was as if the few scattered occupants heaved a gasp and the walls echoed in a responsive sigh as she requested the sentence.

The judge glanced at the jurors with slightly raised eyebrows. They, in turn, quickly exchanged furtive expressions of amazement with the interrogator. The heretofore uninterested eyes of the guards stationed at the exit darted looks of unbelief at one another. But it was the defense attorney who assumed the most open demonstration against the severe pronouncement. The lines of his face were drawn in the shock of incredulity, and half springing from his chair, he turned and motioned me to remain calm. He had not spoken his *Plaedoyer* for the defense.

In reality the only gasping heard was my own. The sentence the prosecutor was demanding was extraordinarily harsh and completely out of proportion to my crime. The utterance had stunned me with the smack of a sudden, unexpected blow, and even as my lawyer addressed the tribunal, I slowly began to recover my senses. His words were faint and distant to my ears, and my thoughts rushed away to deliberate my own answer to the hostile charges that had been poured out against me. In those racing seconds after the pronouncement, the fire of conflicting passions tore through me, almost blinding me in unconsciousness. Rage, fear, hate, doubt, self-pity, indignation!

The "last word" was mine. Before the trial I had spent long and serious consideration, searching for some statement of justification for myself that would answer the distorted charges with an impact, something that would place the whole tribunal on the accusation bench with the injustice of their laws. I had the grandiose idea of presenting some eulogy on freedom, courageously bemoaning the abuses of a regime that ignored rights and prostituted justice. They forced individuals to violate the law. They were the criminals, not I. I was guilty only of breaking an evil law. Their guilt was heavier with the weight of responsibility for having made and enforced laws against mankind.

No, I had decided I would not rehearse my lines before going on stage. I would rely on my spontaneity—it usually brought me through better than any carefully planned speech. But standing in the courtroom I had been made aware that any idealistic oratory would have no effect on the hardened hearts and closed minds of the tribunal. I was overcome with the recognition of my helplessness. The state was *ALL;* the individual, *NOTHING.*

The faint words of my attorney became stronger as he approached his conclusion. He contended that the prosecution had falsely accused the defendant of having committed the crime as a part of an organized group. The initial act of involvement was the sole action of the defendant. Therefore, a less severe paragraph should come into question. Moreover, he maintained that the defendant had courageously confessed to her crime in great detail and recognized the necessity of respecting the laws of another state. If the prosecutor had requested such a high sentence to frighten others from committing the same crime, the trial should be open to the public. For as long as the trial remained closed to the public, the people could not receive the impact of the unduly harsh sentence.

When Herr Vogel had finished his plea for my defense, the judge motioned for me to rise. I came to my feet and addressed the judge and the jurors. The tears I had fought to withhold flooded my cheeks. I was totally unable to cope with the hate that had been advanced against me, or with the shock of the extremely high sentence.

"Yes, I realize that I have no right to violate the laws of this state, or of any other foreign country which has admitted me to its territory." This was the answer to their claim that I had defied the authority of their state and misused my privilege of entry as a foreigner. "But I ask you to consider my motivation. I was not acting with the malicious intent of harming the state, but with the strong desire of *helping* an individual. He was not able to realize his future in this state, and I acted out of the ethical conviction that I should help him to do so." I tried to imply that what the Marxists called the "law of chance or inevitability"—what I understood under Providence—had prompted me to make the decision that involved me.

The woman juror had a faint glimmering of sympathy in her eyes. Although the man's features remained expressionless, there was something in his attentiveness that indicated he had a slight inkling of what I was trying to say. If only the court had permitted entry to the people, who were unschooled in the doctrine of the state, I knew I could have won them over!

The judge rolled off a jumble of words which I failed to catch and concluded by addressing the defense with the possibility that the other law would be taken into consideration. The court adjourned. The sentence would be read the following day.

Herr Vogel handed me his handkerchief and accompanied me out of the courtroom. The Weasel followed us with the guards. "It's absolutely unbelievable!" I sobbed. "It cannot be true."

"They will never give you that sentence," the tall handsome guard assured me. The petite guard offered me another tranquilizer, which I gladly accepted.

Herr Vogel addressed the Weasel. "It is an unusually high sentence," he said. "We cannot get away with giving defendants such sentences when the trial is closed to the public."

"Yes," the Weasel agreed, somewhere else in thought. The pallid color of his face had faded into whiteness. "I don't think they'll give her that sentence, anyway." He turned to me. "Don't worry. They won't give you that sentence."

Herr Vogel excused himself and informed me that he was unable to attend the reading of the sentence on the following day. I should not place my signature on the sentence until I had conferred with him. Then we would decide whether to appeal. As he departed, he announced, "The prosecutor didn't even give me her hand after the trial, and it is customary to do so."

"How could she?" I thought to myself, "the prosecution is asking for five and a half years! She might as well ask for life. . . ."

11

NO OTHER EXIT

THE WEASEL had not escorted me, nor would my lawyer be coming. I was left to face the tribunal alone. The prosecuting attorney stalked into the room in winter boots and her long suede jacket, as if she had stopped in briefly on the way home from her morning shopping. The judge and jurors ambled in leisurely some minutes later and took their places.

The judge opened the session and rattled off the words of a long document at a rate of speed that not even a German professor could have comprehended. Apparently he was in a hurry. He swallowed most of the words until he neared the conclusion. Then his voice became more deliberate and he articulated distinctly. "The court had decided on a sentence of four years of hard labor, with category one, because of the seriousness of the crime!"

I held my breath until the trio had marched out of the courtroom. Wild with rage I whirled around. There was no place to go with my violent indignation. There was only one way out—to destroy myself! I rushed to the wall and began beating my head against it as hard as I could. Immediately the two men guards jumped to my side, grabbing me and pulling me away. I struggled with them to break their hold on me, but in vain. The two men held my arms tightly in theirs.

"Let me go!" I cried.

I burst out in hysterical sobbing. "No, no, no, no, no, no, no, no, . . . they can't do it to me! It's inhumane! It's unjust!" I cried out, still struggling to free myself from the guards. I fell to the floor.

"Get hold of yourself! Stop it! Stop it!" the petite guard shouted as the men dragged me out of the courtroom. "You can appeal . . . you can tell your lawyer tomorrow . . . you don't have to accept the sentence! Now, then, just calm down! Everything will be all right." Her matronly instinct responded to the need. She took me in her arms and stroked my head, attempting to console me. She appeared not to sense the awkwardness I felt —she was an East German security guard, consoling me as a mother comforts her child. She did not notice that I was an American, nor that I was a criminal in her state. I pulled away, and although I resisted in that instant, a wall had been broken down.

My body was trembling and I was still sobbing with a volume that must have penetrated the whole building. Somehow I found myself back in the witness room, and one of the guards held on to my arm while the others unpacked the lunch basket.

This time no one forced me to eat, as they had tried to do before. When I refused to touch the food, there was no urging or coaxing. The guards quickly munched on crisp chicken and gulped down steaming coffee, while I sat hunched over in the corner with a tear-soaked face. One guard never got out of grabbing distance from me. After the three had swallowed their last bites and packed away the utensils in a large basket, the guard in charge turned to me abruptly. "Do you think you can contain yourself enough to go now? We must stop and get gas and we can't do it if you are going to cause such commotion." There was a firmness in his admonition, in spite of the apparent attempt at gentleness.

"Yes . . . yes, I'll be quiet. Just get out of here—away from this dreadful place." A salty flow continued streaming down my cheeks, but it had ebbed into silent weeping. My body shook from the violent indignation that rebelled within.

When we piled into the Wartburg, I found myself wedged between the highest ranking guard and my feminine escort in the rear of the car. Workers, whose attention had been diverted from their labor by a woman's cries, stood gaping at the departing vehicle. They stared with solemn masks, and as the sputtering car rushed past them, I saw their faces. I knew they understood.

The driver intended to gas up some distance away from the city and he raced away impatiently to get away from the curious onlookers on the city streets. The petite matron stroked my head, which she had cradled on her shoulder, and pleaded with me to sleep. Soft and consoling words left her lips. "You can appeal," she repeated. "Don't worry. Herr Vogel said he would contact you tomorrow."

"But," I choked, "what is an appeal? Even a year for what I've done is unjust!"

All three guards reacted at once. "Wait a minute! Just think about the crime you have committed!" the driver interjected.

"Of course you deserve to be punished," the others chorused.

Their words were enough to release the pressure valve. "Ahhhhhhhhh-hhhh . . ." I screamed as loud as I could, "how can you be so blind to justice? You're just like the Nazis!" As I released my desperate cry there was one intent on my mind: to break away and throw myself out of the speeding car—to destroy myself. Wild with fury, I struggled to jump. They locked their arms through mine. I fought to break their hold. There was a scramble.

"She's gone mad!" the driver shouted.

"Shut up! Shut up!" the other guard bellowed angrily. "We'll have to stop right here!"

While struggling to pull away from the two guards, I had cut my right foot under the car seat. I felt a painful throbbing and when I was able to examine it, a blotch of blood was visible. I had ripped a hole in my stocking and torn my suede shoe apart.

The car screeched to a halt. "We're not budging from this spot until you calm down!"

The guards' tight grip was hindering the circulation in my arms, so I finally agreed to be quiet if they promised to let me alone. The two arms that held fast to mine relaxed their hold, but did not slip out of their locked position.

The remainder of the journey was passed in a sulky silence. Something within me was overwhelmed by the discovery that people could become so insensitive to justice that they could really believe I had committed a serious crime. Of course I knew how far this insensitivity had gone with the Nazis, but it all lay beyond my comprehension until I had confronted the reality of it myself. These were simple people, but they had certainly been seduced by an evil doctrine which had blinded them to truth.

It was the corrupting influence of that evil which caused every sane and healthy individual to react with violent indignation. Some swallowed it out of fear and let it eat away on their insides in bitterness or hate. However, my outbursts purged me of those bitter grapes of wrath, and months of imprisonment had produced indifference to what others might think about my uncontrolled reactions.

It was merely a question of releasing the dam within or without, and since their authority did not cause me to shrink back in fear, I chose the outward channel. I was met with reproaches from their rigid sense of self-control and discipline, a rigid training so harsh that it stifled and perverted all spontaneous life that welled up within. Unfortunately, that training imposed the exercise of control only toward one's superiors. The subordinates became the scapegoats! It was the Jews who had provided a collective scapegoat for all the hostility, violence, and aggression that had been bred and stored up. One had all the *Spielraum* one needed to trample in rebellion on the inferior underdog. That was how the concept of a *superman* and the *will to power* could be born on the German cultural soil.

The massive Hohenschoenhausen prison loomed up on the bleak horizon. We arrived soberly and I was dismissed without a word. Another guard led me to an empty cell in the midst of administration offices. It appeared to be one used for disciplinary measures, since the wall was coated with dingy smudges from fists and the door displayed all evidence of having been pounded and beaten.

The heavy door creaked shut. The clanging key revolved in the lock, and I was left alone with one of the warders. Ursula and I had christened her "Bunny." She hid the pity in her eyes behind a cloud of fear as she stared at me. I wondered whether she was thinking that a child of hers might be in the same position one day.

I threw myself across the slatted wooden cot and opened up the floodgates to a river of tears.

When the medic arrived with a tranquilizer, I stubbornly refused to take it, mainly because I knew they were trying to restore calm in the prison. I do not know how long my obstinacy would have resisted, if the Weasel had not appeared in the doorway with his companion.

With a sweep of the hand, he motioned the guard to leave. The Weasel's face was downcast and he said nothing. It was the colleague, who always commanded the situation, who addressed me. "Do you want to come along with us where we can speak reasonably with each other?"

I lay across the cot, hesitating. My lungs were aching from overexertion. "Yes," I said, as I rose to my feet.

The way through the long corridors, up flights of stairs, and finally through the dim, secluded wing of the interrogation rooms seemed longer than usual. We passed the Weasel's office and stopped before his companion's door.

The words of our conversation are but a void in my memory. I can recall that the Weasel silently faded into the twilight of the room and the conversation flowed between his companion and myself. He implied that no foreigner was kept in prison for the entire sentence, and that other possibilities for an earlier release existed. It was all just a matter of time, he assured me. But as he spoke words of reassurance, I sensed that *he* did not know, that *he* could not say what would happen to me. The decision lay in the hands of superiors.

I wanted to believe the man who spoke so sincerely. Was it just counterfeited consolation? Was he merely interested in tranquilizing me to keep me from creating a scene? There was a note of genuineness in his voice and his words seemed spoken with a sincere wish to soothe a suffering soul. After a couple of hours discussing everything from politics to psychology, I returned to my old cell.

Ursula met me with open arms and took on my burden. She had not expected the outcome of the trial either.

I curled up on my hard bed, which provided the only sanctuary in a great house of suffering, propped my head upon my blanket-pillow, and began to think. The opium of unresolved inner struggles and vicious circles of questions overcame me.

Justice, seen through the looking glass . . . kangaroo court . . . guilty until proved innocent . . . the omnipotent state versus the impotent individual . . . "There is no innocence in our courts!"

I wanted to spring from my bed and scream out, "Where did the state get the right? From where? Who authorized them to wield this power? Who vested them with the fate of individual lives? A band of revolutionaries? An interpretation of history? How could they know that it was the right interpretation of history?"

But it was the paragraph people of every country who rationalized away these evils. Every state had its laws, which were naturally in the interest of the state. To disobey the law brought consequences. Every despot had his laws, too. Hitler had his laws!

Yes, it was an age-old story. Political injustices were almost synonymous with the history of European government. Perhaps that was the reason individuals were able to become indifferent to them. Why didn't they rebel? Throw off their yoke of bondage? Were the people really too politically immature?

It was the files of machine guns at the borders, the rows of trenches filled with mines, the gauzy webs of barbed wire, or the sudden appearance of tanks, as when the agitation of June 17, 1953, stirred the people to demonstrate in the streets, that quelled incipient rebellion. But none of that stopped the Viet Cong! It only unified them. Maybe it was the full bellies that lulled "the People" into indifference and complacency. Or the internalized fear of authority. Or perhaps it was the hangover of a bloody battlefield, the soot and ashes of bombed ruins, the hideous confrontation with the ugliness of death . . . *war!*

I tossed about in my bed. The flashing light appeared more often, casting eerie shadows across the cell. The guards knew I was awake and they had surely been warned that I might do something foolish. In spite of the strong tranquilizer I had been persuaded to take, sleep would not come.

Against my better judgment, I accepted the four-year sentence. My lawyer felt that an appeal would be useless, since the court had given me a lower sentence than the prosecutor had requested. At the request of my lawyer, I apologized for calling the government officials Nazis—the strongest possible insult to the East German regime. The Nazis hated the Communists, and the Communists hated the Nazis.

A week or so after my trial, an unexpected event occurred. I was to receive a visitor. I had been informed that a colleague of Mr. Vogel's was coming. I suspected who it might be when the news was announced. A letter from home had already imparted the information that a Washington attorney, Mr. New, was working on my case. The two men, along with a West Berlin attorney, Mr. Stange, were all working on the possibility of negotiations.

I allowed myself no particle of hope. However, if there was nothing they could do I was left to face up to four years. Four years! No, I could not think in those terms. . . .

To my wonder, I was not hauled to the Magdalenenstrasse prison in the old green Minna on the day of the visit. Even the prison had its protocol, and it called for a better vehicle for the reception of a visitor from Washington. The Weasel and other officials escorted me in a car.

I momentarily forgot I was a prisoner, as I pinned my French twist in place and dabbed Ursula's sweetly scented cream behind my ears. Gummi Ball had brought me a new pair of stockings for the occasion, since mine were full of runs. I realized that the prison direction wanted me to look my best for the visit. If I exemplified good health and looked attractive, that was evidence to any visitor—especially to a foreign guest from Washington—that I was being well treated.

When the door swung open, I was impressed with the stately stature of a grand Southern gentleman. When Mr. New spoke in his gentle drawl, he only confirmed my impression. His black, wavy hair was sprinkled with gray at the temples and his face glowed with a smile that could only be American. Both men greeted me heartily, and we seated ourselves around the small table which displayed a freshly starched cloth.

I was filled with excitement at the hope of some item of good news. I did not wait for the attorneys to say a word, but burst forth with a myriad of questions. "Well, do you have any good news for me? Is there the possibility of successful negotiations? Will I be released soon?"

When Mr. New responded with a blank expression, I realized that I had been speaking German, a language foreign to him, but one that had become more facile for me. I awkwardly groped for words in English, and they usually came out in a German accent. This was the very first occasion I had had to speak my native language since my imprisonment. The extent of my English in prison had been the few songs I had taught Ursula.

Mr. New was reserved in his utterances, which seemed to run against his nature. He must have been aware of the hidden microphone. All of my inquisitive remarks about release or negotiations were referred back to Mr. Vogel, who, in turn, told me to consult Mr. New. We played cat and mouse a few minutes, and then the men eased into a less dangerous subject.

The Washington attorney conveyed the concern of the State Department and the interest of my countrymen. He also delivered a message of encouragement from my parents. The real issue, however, that of my release, was cautiously avoided. The only note of encouragement I received was the news that those on the other side were doing all they could for me. I should not give up hope. When I could no longer contain one question, I blurted it out. "Can I be out by September?"

The two men exchanged glances. Each indicated that the other should answer. It was already May, and only four months remained until September. As far as I was concerned, that was more than time enough to make decisions or to arrange negotiations. It was Mr. New who chose to answer the question, but inconclusively, "I think something might be arranged by then."

I read more certainty into his statement than was there. For me it was still an inconceivably long time till September, but if it had to be . . . I could wait. I had no other choice, but it made waiting bearable just to have the hope that I would not have to lose another year of my studies. Everything hung somehow on that date.

The guards entered with a tray of coffee—another of the items of protocol for foreign visitors. As I sat conversing with the two handsome attorneys, sipping coffee and speaking English, I was once more removed from the reality of stone walls and iron bars.

I became deeply engrossed in the social hour and would have loved to continue it indefinitely. It was Herr Vogel, as usual, who brought it to a close when he informed us he had another engagement.

As I passed through the door to follow the uniformed guard down the corridor, I returned to my old status of being a prisoner. I was locked in a dingy cell to await the return to Hohenschoenhausen.

Mr. New, who had just arrived from Paris via Madrid, bestowed on me a stack of fashion magazines and a bottle of perfume. Both were the most exquisite luxuries imaginable for prison life, but for that reason they were coveted. I resolved not to open my perfume until my release. It would be the champagne that christened the ship before embarking on a new life of freedom.

Ursula went wild over the American magazines. They were the first she had ever seen. Although I had also been detached from the cult of the fashion world, I was infected with her enthusiasm, and we spent long hours poring over the pages of *Glamour, Vogue, Mademoiselle* as Jesuits might have their volumes of philosophy. Not even the most insignificant advertisement was left unexamined.

My high spirits were squelched a couple of weeks later when I received depressing news from the Weasel. "You are to be sent to *Strafvollzug* within a few days," he announced gravely. That meant "execution of sentence," which was just a sophisticated way of saying penitentiary.

The Weasel's words were the voice of doom. I had already been around long enough to learn the ropes of prison life. I knew that most foreigners were retained in the investigative prison in Berlin, as long as any hope of near negotiations existed. The Hohenschoenhausen prison was the best of its kind, and foreigners were even sometimes catered to, as far as prisoners were ever given special privileges. The American officials in West Berlin generally assumed that prisoners were receiving relatively good care as long as they remained there. I had reckoned with remaining there until my release, and apparently the Weasel had, too.

"There is a new law which determines what is done with prisoners who have already been sentenced. If no negotiations are in progress, prisoners are sent away for the execution of their sentence. Previously, sometimes prisoners were allowed to remain here in Berlin."

His tone carried a tacit apology. Even as he spoke, I sought to interpret the move. It could only mean a turn for the worse, a penitentiary! Then it dawned on me.

"You're just trying to pressure the Americans into making a decision about the proposed negotiations!" I exclaimed with sudden insight. Negotiations had been impossible until after my trial. An attorney had just made a visit for that purpose, and Mr. Vogel had informed me that the General Attorney's office in East Germany had agreed to a proposal he had made. The decision rested with the American side. Obviously, they had not responded one way or another. It was an impossibility, since they did not recognize the East German regime. Although the attorneys did not inform me of their proposed plan, I sensed that they were shooting for some sort of prisoner exchange.

Amazement covered the Weasel's face and then a wry smile crept over his lips. "You're not so dumb as you look!"

"Do I look that dumb?" I had more than caught the significance of his words.

"Oh no, that is just an expression. It means that you are very clever!"

Nothing could have convinced me that the law which had just been passed or the decision to send foreigners away to the penitentiary was not made for my benefit. It was the East Germans' response to the Americans' ignoring them. They would force recognition: "All right, if you aren't going to let us know something by recognizing us, then we'll make it rough on your citizens."

Indeed I was the most vulnerable of all the American prisoners, since I was a woman, and since I had innocently wandered into my predicament and not become involved as a result of underground activity. My case was a clear-cut one of idealistic motives. But I had been incarcerated without any preparation for what to expect.

As the Weasel spoke of the penitentiary, I read certain qualms in his colorless face. It frightened me, and I was again seized with awareness of my own helplessness to act. I was at the mercy of lawyers, prosecutors, and politicians, and the prospect of reaching an agreement looked very pessimistic! The Weasel knew that the state did not need to retain me any longer as a punishment. They knew I had learned my lesson. But that was not the issue at stake. It was now a question of what advantage could be gained in exchange for me—economic or political or preferably both. There was not even the faintest trace of justice in the whole affair. I hated being used as the object of barter, and something in me rebelled against it.

Contemplating my next move, I asked the Weasel, "Can I talk to my lawyer before going away?"

"Yes, I think it can be arranged," he replied. "Is there anything else?"

When I indicated there was nothing, he dismissed me with grave sympathy. He squeezed my hand for the last time and wished me "Alles Gute," which seemed out of place for someone who was leaving for the penitentiary. An outspoken warmth was written in his eyes.

That was the last I really saw of the small, consumptive-looking Weasel. I had come to the realization that perhaps a man really did dwell behind the ideological façade. Perhaps a heart did thump within his breast and not a heavy stone. At least we had come to handle each other with respect. No, with more—with feeling. Nevertheless, pity surged within me for him. There was stern conviction in the mission of his work. But he was wrong.

I could even forgive him for all the mental torture he had subjected me to, but I was bothered by the question of how he could morally accept the responsibility for torturing people to the confession of preposterous political crimes? That was something he would be called to account for himself, in his conscience, if he still had one. I felt he did.

On the following day I met Mr. Vogel. I desperately related the news of the penitentiary. I knew that I would not be able to bear it. When I implied that the move had been undertaken in order to pressure the Americans into a response to the negotiations, he became violent and aggressive. "Who told you that?" he demanded angrily.

"It is my own opinion, but my interrogator has confirmed it!" The Weasel kept me better informed than my lawyer, and I felt more confidence in him than in Mr. Vogel.

"That's not true! I can't help it if your government isn't willing to make concessions. They don't recognize your action as a crime, and they don't recognize this government, but concessions must be made if their citizens are to be helped. You are being sent to the penitentiary because a law has just been passed. . . ."

"I already know," I interrupted. I was irritated that even he attempted to hide behind law. "But if something isn't done soon . . ." I could not withhold the tears any longer. "I'm thinking of . . ." I was unable to pronounce the rest. It was so desperate and final.

"I'll see what I can do." His angry tone softened. He picked up the receiver and requested a guard to take me away.

The brief encounter failed to relieve my fears. In fact, Mr. Vogel's aggressive response upset me even more. When he had asked which penitentiary I was being sent to, and I had replied Bautzen, an expression of horror clouded his face. Ursula had responded in the same manner. Bautzen seemed to evoke the same reaction from a German that Alcatraz would have from an American. The meeting had only served to confirm my misgivings.

After the hostile misunderstanding with my attorney and the fear of a penitentiary hanging over my head like a cloud of doom, my mind dwelt on desperate thoughts. I would also be taken away from Ursula. I could expect no help from my countrymen. Something had to be done, and right away. The penitentiary meant a long term, or they would not bother to send me. It was all final. I wouldn't go! I couldn't go! But all rebellion was to no avail. Unless . . . unless . . . the very last act of rebellion. . . . It would prove they could not get away with it. . . .

I flung myself across the bed. Ursula had been gone all afternoon for a visit with her mother. Why was she away so long when I needed her?

Somewhere I had read that a woman who had been arrested by the Nazis had bitten her wrists and bled to death. Suicide! It was the only way out!

I bit into my wrist and began gnawing away. The pain was excruciating.

Drops of blood oozed forth. I was committing the very last sin against life
—against God. It was called despair.

"My God, my God, why have You forsaken me?"

12

A NEW CAGE

I LOOKED DOWN at the crusty scab on my wrist. I was going to the penitentiary, after all. The absurdity of my desperate behavior struck me as I
had watched the sticky redness ooze from a punctured vein. I had not even
reached an artery, for the pain had been unsupportable. My despair had
not been that great. Still I had nothing to look forward to, even though I
lacked the courage to take my life.

The Minna bounced and sputtered down the highway. It was one of
those surprisingly sunny, so-seldom-seen-in-the-season days in Saxony.
Summer offered itself in full expression, a phenomenon rare for June. The
temperature had reached a high for the year and had interrupted the moody
altercations between pouring rain and violent wind. The guards had
opened the window and the vent in the roof, so that a strong breeze venti-
lated the noisy vehicle. They sat without jackets and with rolled shirt-
sleeves. We were moving southwards.

I sat in the outer section, which was designated for the guards. They
had not shut me up in one of the stuffy boxes, but had allowed me to sit
with them. It was a three-hour drive to Bautzen, and they knew I would
have rebelled. There was something about being caged up in a traveling
box, mingled with the fear of the destination, that produced a frightful
choking sensation. It could be endured for the fifteen-minute ride to the
Magdalenenstrasse prison, but I refused to endure the torture for two hundred kilometers. I would have pounded on the door.

All of the five-guard escort were men. When a woman prisoner was transported, there was usually one woman guard along. This time it was different, and I suspected the reason. Four Americans were being delivered to the penitentiary in Bautzen. Three of them were men. As they had been loaded into the prison conveyance, I thought I heard the clinking of chains or handcuffs.

The guards were at first shy about addressing me, but when the ranking guard broke the silence, they all joined him. We had to shout to be heard above the roar of the motor.

Bautzen was the last station in the German Democratic Republic. It was situated in a nook that bordered on Czechoslovakia and Poland, which made it more feared. As long as I was in Berlin, I could feel the proximity of the West. Of course, it was the security of self-deception, but perhaps it was not without basis. In East Berlin the strong ties with the West had exposed the prison personnel to life on the other side. They knew something of how Westerners thought, dressed, ate, and behaved. But the farther away from Berlin one traveled . . . I would just have to wait and see. Nevertheless, I had a strong apprehension about the encounter with the rural population of East Germany. The farmers and workers who had been highly indoctrinated were likely to be the most fanatic.

As the Minna joggled along over a country road, I had a strong yearning to try to communicate with the other Americans in the vehicle. We were all strangers to each other, and yet brothers in misfortune. I spoke as loudly as I could to the guards with the hope that the others would realize I was present.

I envied the men, because I knew that they would be together. The Weasel had said, "It's a pity that you're not a man, because you could be with your countrymen." Shared suffering meant allayed suffering. That was especially true in a foreign country. But now I had to bear my burden alone.

Not too far from our destination, I dared to mention a subject which must have been taboo with the guards. "Is Bautzen a town or just the name of a penitentiary?" I inquired innocently. The guard's face flushed crimson. The men darted hurried glances at one another.

The more gregarious of the guards replied, "You'll find out soon enough." A delicate pause followed his statement. Guards were not to discuss such information with prisoners—not even the destination of the traveling cage-box.

A lovely medieval town appeared on the horizon. Remains of the ancient city and broken pieces of fortress towers could be seen nestled in the landscape of the hills. Narrow cobblestone alleys and picturesque old buildings made the town a haven for tourists. In spite of all its romantic appeal, the name "Bautzen" evoked a cloud of horror on the faces of all those I had mentioned it to. Perhaps it was because the name had been uttered in prison that it rang so grimly. Within the stone walls of prison, Bautzen was synonymous with penitentiary, as if the whole edifice of punishment hovered over the town like a medieval cathedral. I entered as a captive, not as a tourist.

The impatient Minna sped along through an arboreous residential section, and bucked to a halt before a wooden barrier. The guards had already pulled the curtains of the partition window closed, for I was not to be seen seated outside a cell. The vehicle threaded its way through a maze of narrow channels and rolled to rest in the back courtyard of a huge building. A guard climbed out and entered the prison. He motioned for me to follow.

Bright green uniforms immediately caught my eye, and let me know I was no longer with the blue-uniformed Security Police. Peering eyes in expressionless faces followed my movements.

"Behave yourself well. Then you'll get out early. You are no longer with the Security Police. You are now in the hands of the *Volkspolizei,*" the head guard advised me with a friendly dismissal. "Good luck." Then he left me with the notorious Vopos, the People's Police.

The hostile welcoming committee filled me with fright. A frail policewoman with a hollow expression received me. She wasted no time in leading me to a door in a large glass partition wall and pointed the way up steep steps. "All the way to the top," she informed me. I was panting for breath when I reached the top of six long flights of stairs. That was the most exercise I had had for months, and I was weak from inactivity. A heavyset matron met me and opened the door to a large storage room.

Another younger policewoman stood sorting clothing and piling it on a heavy stack. The matron commanded me to get undressed.

Once again a flood of humiliation flowed through me. I commenced to remove my clothing and realized that I was now graduated to wearing an ugly uniform, one of the most degrading signs of prison life. Big drops rolled down my cheeks as I stood nude, awaiting the next order.

"Try these on," the matron ordered, handing me a pair of baggy cotton underpants. I slipped them on, and they hung to my knees like long bloomers. She rummaged through a neat pile of underwear until she arrived at what should be the right size. The bloomers were not cut after fashion, but they fitted.

The fitting of a brassiere provided a greater difficulty. They were hand sewn and sized only according to number one, two, three, four, for the measurement around the chest, not the breast. Nor were they made with elastic. We finally settled for a tight uncomfortable fit, but I was delighted that I was even able to receive a bra. Ursula had not gotten one in her imprisonment in Czechoslovakia.

A medium blue wool skirt was handed me. It displayed broad yellow stripes on either side. When I decided that it fitted as well as could be expected, I was told to keep it on. To wear with it I received a faded blue blouse, which also had a glaring yellow stripe down the middle of the back. That was symbolic. Red and black sandals with white socks completed the shabby uniform. An unmated jacket went along with the skirt, and it, too, boasted broad yellow stripes.

After I was outfitted in my blue weekday uniform, I had to try on my Sunday outfit. It consisted of the same articles, only in khaki. All had the appearance of being old war or postwar military uniforms. I presumed that economy or humiliation, or both, dictated that prisoners wear the shabby, faded garments.

We descended the stairs to the fifth floor and went down a long corridor, which was lined with white wooden cell doors. The glossy narrow doors were not the heavy broad metal ones of Berlin's investigative prison, but they, too, displayed an ugly black eye in their center.

The matron took a large metal key and unlocked the door to cell number three. I was met with the stale atmosphere of a dingy little hole, which was about half the size of my Berlin cell. A thick coat of dust lay on everything. A bed stood crosswise at the end of the cell, reaching the entire width of the room. A built-in table and bench projected from the right wall, and directly before them in the corner was the toilet, which had not the luxury of running water. The window, which was high above the bed, was paned with frosted glass.

The key clinked in the lock, and I was left alone. I lifted a blanket that covered the stained mattress, and a cloud of dust rose. I choked on the dense air, mingled with wet tears, and set about bringing order to the chaotic heap of clothes on the floor. I stacked them neatly in the small cabinet I had lugged from the attic. When I had tidied everything as best I could, I sat down on the hard bench and waited. Here, there was no permission to lie down.

One thing frightened me. I was alone in a single cell. How would I ever adjust to so many months by myself? Alone. An absolute aloneness. Without a single friendly soul. In a hostile country. Everything was so strange and different from Berlin. Even the guards. No trace of warmth. Cold. Dirty. The humiliating uniform. The stench of the toilet. Musty and hollow. No Ursula to confide in. The food would be different, too.

My heart pounded when the door opened. I sprang to my feet, assumed an awkward stance, and waited for the command.

"You are to go and get your lunch," the attractive policewoman ordered indirectly. Instead of saying, "Go and get your lunch," she evaded a direct command.

Part of the initial punishment was fetching my food.

I marched down the long corridor, descended a flight of steps and found a bowl of soup awaiting me on a table. It did not look appetizing, but I carried it back to my cell. Actually, the soup could have been placed outside my cell, but there was a certain humiliation, which tested my subordination, in having to fetch it from such a distance. This became evident as the bowl was brought nearer to my cell every day, and finally stood outside my door.

In the midafternoon my door swung open. A stocky, masculine-looking woman of medium stature stood in the doorway. Jet-dyed hair stood out wildly on her head, and she stared at me with hard eyes. She stood erect, inspecting me as if she were awaiting something from me. After some seconds the long pause became embarrassing. I did not know what I was supposed to do. Finally, her deep voice broke the silence with a serious tone, "Why didn't you report?"

"Report? What is that?" I asked, puzzled.

"Haven't you read the house regulations?" she inquired sternly, raising her eyebrows.

"Yes, I have read them over," I stammered, "but I don't understand what you mean by 'report'."

"Well, I guess you haven't had time to learn," she answered severely. I was unable to detect whether there was a sarcastic intonation in her voice or whether she was yielding. "Go up to the bed and turn around."

I moved to the bed and turned with my back to her. "Like this?" It struck me as being stupid.

"Now turn around and face me!" she ordered. By this time I was wondering whether I was getting the run around. Obviously she derived a keen satisfaction from giving orders and testing my obedience. It struck me as an amusing experiment with an American prisoner.

"Now you have to report," she ordered. "Say *Strafgefangene,* then your name and cell number. Then say *Alles in Ordnung.* You always address a guard with 'Frau' and then her rank."

How was I to know the rank of the guards, I wondered. Or all that bunk I was supposed to say. I was indignant. Nevertheless, order must be— *Ordnung muss sein!* That adage could only have originated in Germany, as did the stupid procedure in reporting.

I commenced to rattle off the information she had requested of me. I could not fake being dumb, because she was not going to budge from the spot until I got the rigamarole right. Now, what followed *Strafgefangene?* Oh yes, my name. I stumbled over my name with a German pronunciation— Oh, she got me so confused—then I attempted to recall my cell number. She had to tell me. Finally, I told her that everything was in order, *Alles in Ordnung.* But that was really a lie. Everything wasn't in order, as far as I was concerned. Somehow that ridiculous reporting irritated me more than the tacky uniform or the unsatisfying meal. It was there as a humiliating reminder of my role as a prisoner. The "manly" policewoman seemed satisfied and strutted out of the cell. This ritual was to take place every day.

Although my status had greatly fallen from that of Berlin, I did meet with a few improvements. I had a mirror in my cell. For the first time since I had been incarcerated I could look myself in the eye. And I did not like what I saw. My skin had withered and become pale, and deep new wrinkles crept out from around my eyes. I had never given the sign of aging any thought until Ursula had become upset about her wrinkles in Berlin.

My hair had lost its shine, and dull strands sometimes fell out in fistfuls as I combed through it. My eyes were dim and tired-looking and burned constantly. *"Na nu,"* I had told Ursula, "prison is no place for vanity!" Of course, now that I had a mirror . . . and no one was with me . . . after all, it was different. There is a difference between vanity and a healthy pride in one's appearance. Yes, it did boost the morale to practice grooming. . . .

Taps sounded at 9:00 P.M., but again I had to go through the silly ritual of reporting at eight o'clock, which was *Nachtverschluss,* the "locking of the cell" for the night. It, too, had to be done with ceremony, as good Germanic tradition dictated. This time, instead of saying that "everything was in order," you had to say that you were ready for the "locking-in." The whole scene was even more ridiculous, because it had to be performed in a long white nightshirt. My clothes had to be folded in a neat bundle and placed on the bench in a certain way. *Ordnung muss sein!*

The following morning I paced the floor wondering about breakfast. I spotted one of the newspapers that had been doled out for toilet paper and began reading. Still no breakfast.

Shortly before eight o'clock, the door swung open. "Put on your jacket and comb your hair." I was going to meet the Vice-warden in five minutes.

My heart raced wildly. I scarcely had time to get my jacket, when the matronly guard returned. I followed her to an office at the end of the corridor, where she left me standing. She returned and motioned me to enter.

The spacious bureau was brighter and cheerier than the others I had encountered during imprisonment. But the room offered no unique feature. Its simple furnishings spoke of the German middle-class taste, no different in East than West.

Seated at the desk, peering at me—through spectacles—with hard eyes, was a policeman. To his left, in one of the easy chairs, sat a hefty policewoman, half facing the man and half with her back turned to the door. Her sturdy frame and white blonde hair indicated her strong Germanic characteristics. She scarcely glanced in my direction when I entered, but the man scrutinized me coldly.

"Sit down," he ordered.

I obeyed, taking the empty chair next to the woman. He hardly waited until I was seated before he commenced to spout heated political phrases. His eyes were glowing with all the fire and hatred of fanaticism, and his words erupted with wrath against West Germany, against class enemies, against people who had been poisoned by Western propaganda. The poor worker in the West was exploited, unable to afford a vacation, while the fat rich capitalists leisurely whiled away their time in plush hotels on the Riviera.

He continued by explaining that all the abuses in the West were impossible in the First German Workers' and Farmers' State. Bonn was conducting an unrealistic policy against his State, because Bonn failed to recognize it. Of course, that was the reason his State had to make its existence *felt!* All the people in prison knew that the German Democratic Republic existed, had its own laws, and would go to any extent to enforce them! That was living proof. The politicians could ignore it if they chose, but the people felt and experienced their existence. I knew what he meant.

As he began his tyrannical tirades against West Germany, the *Bonner Ultras,* the class struggle, the exploitation of the worker, I was unable to suppress the tears. Here again I was confronted with the same kind of violent hatred I had met with in my accusation and in the courtroom. The same stilted ideological phrases. But so much hatred poured out against me was overpowering.

I kept asking myself, "Just what does all this have to do with me? Why is he telling me all this?"

The real issue lay somewhere else. Why didn't he talk to me about that —what I had done and why I had done it—instead of throwing around heated and loaded phrases that had nothing to do with me? The answer was not in all that ideological garbage he was rolling off, but in something more basic. The intrinsic rights of man—freedom. My desire to *help* . . . that was beyond his ideology. The fact that I was a victim of a German problem. . . .

He paused for breath. "And . . . I see that you are a student of theology. As far as that is concerned, there is no God! You Christians say that it is God who brings war upon men! But I say that it is man himself! All the evil on earth is man's doing—not God's. Men hate, kill, cause wars, exploit each other like savages! They then blame it on God's will. You mean to tell me that a God could live in such an evil universe?"

He gasped for breath and launched out again. "Christians are a heap of hypocrites, fleeing their responsibilities to their fellow-men, occupied with the hereafter and not with the present! Christianity is supposed to be a religion of love—Christians are supposed to love their enemies! How could they go to war against them or exploit them if they loved?"

He continued savagely ripping apart the Christian church. I was choking with nausea and impatience to answer his arguments. I knew that his violent attack was the severest part of the punishment I had received till then. Physical cruelty would have been more bearable. But what he was doing was inflicting the worst kind of pain, putting a helpless prisoner on the rack, torturing him by lashing into an assault against all he deemed precious, everything he believed in.

He finally concluded, "If there were a God . . ." and awaited my reaction. He had completed his verbal whiplashing, and a satanic smile appeared at the corners of his mouth.

I drew a deep breath. Suddenly, I was overcome with a profound peace. Instead of being provoked to an aggressive response, as he had expected, I answered calmly.

"Yes, I can agree with much of what you have said. Some of your attacks against the radicals in the West German Government may be true. I have always been a critic of some of the extreme policies of the Bonner government myself. But I simply cannot understand what that has to do with me. *I* am not a *Bonner Ultra*. My involvement in a crime against this state was upon my own moral conviction.

"In addition, I can only give you wholehearted agreement on some of your criticism of the Christian church! You are absolutely right when you say that God is not responsible for evil, wars, hatred—that men cause violence and warfare! But, do you know why? It is because they do not *believe* in God. Because they are selfish, disobedient. Men do not accept *goodness*. That is the only way that the earth will ever be rid of evil. But men choose to live by their own greedy desires instead.

"Yes, you are absolutely right. Christians have neglected their responsibilities. Many are awaking to this challenge, though. Many are taking their responsibilities seriously. That is, they really *believe,* instead of accepting the Christian church as an empty tradition."

I wanted to continue for I had not even touched upon some of his arguments. He had claimed that my crime was understandable, owing to my bourgeois background and training. I wanted to tell him that many farmers and workers were also included among my relatives and I was sympathetic with their grievances, with the underdog anywhere. But he interrupted before I got the chance.

"I see that we are not going to have any trouble out of you. We usually have little difficulty with the prisoners of the women's station." He smiled with satisfaction.

While the man had been talking, the policewoman had nodded her head with approval. There was blazing fanaticism in her eyes also. From the beginning of his tirades, the policeman's accent had given him away as the "self-made-man of the socialistic society." A certain type of fanaticism bred on ignorance, and I was reminded of some of the godless Southern religious revivals I had seen where the audience rocked in ecstatic affirmation of the fiery vituperations of the country preacher. When the harangue was over, I detected no sign of softening in the woman, and when I learned that she was in charge of the women prisoners, I was terrified.

"You may be dismissed," the policeman said. I rose and was turning to walk out when the policewoman snapped at me with a broad scowl.

"You must report!" The man immediately cut her short, excusing me from the responsibility. The prisoner would have plenty of time to learn that procedure, he informed her.

When I entered my cell I was shaking. I had been stunned. The initial words of the policeman had appalled me, and although I instinctively refused to believe them, doubt began gnawing at me.

He had said, "You have a four-year sentence. *You will be here for four years.* That means you won't be released until November 1969! You have to adjust to this fact!" His words were unconditional. He had made no reservations, no exceptions for foreigners, no ifs, buts, or ors. There was no word about getting out earlier for good behavior. All the encouragement I had received in Berlin was wiped away in a single stroke. I had believed it at the time, but the angry policeman had just tipped my world of trust topsy-turvy. What to believe and whom to trust? It was all a psychological nightmare. Oh, how much can a man take? Four years! Four years! Four years!

13

THE SEWING CIRCLE

THE STERN MATRON stood over me and examined each article I took in my hand. I had discovered that she was the highest ranking of the women guards, a *Meister,* which is the top noncommissioned officer. She was absolutely correct in her manner, very Prussian in her discipline, and commanded fear from everyone. I had to identify my toilet articles before receiving them. Moreover, when she demanded the removal of my ring and watch, I became furious. There was no ounce of generosity in the heartless policewoman.

As I was busy cramming the bottles and tubes into my shopping net, I noticed a bottle of *Sandorn* juice, a liquid vitamin preparation my lawyer had brought from West Berlin at my request. The authorities had not permitted me to receive it, since all medication from the West was strictly forbidden. There was no exception to this rule. Without giving it too much thought, I snatched up the bottle with the other things.

The Meisterin sent me up the stairs and followed several paces behind me. Since my cell was already open I rushed in and quickly hid the Sandorn bottle in my clothes cabinet. Fortunately I had made the move just in time, because the Meisterin, who had stopped to lock the iron bar gate which closed off the section, yelled for me to leave my things on the table outside the cell.

The stocky masculine-looking guard hurried with her companion to inspect all the objects before permitting me to take them into my cell. When I heard the clicking of the lock outside, and retreating footsteps, I commenced to clear away all my toilet articles.

I sighed with relief. It had been close. If the guard had discovered the bottle it would have gotten me off to the wrong start with the prison officials. I was sure that the matron would be wild if anyone was caught crossing her. Smuggling a forbidden article into my cell was a serious offense. Now I was burdened with another problem, that of concealing it.

There was no doubt that the guards would inspect my cell thoroughly every day. I examined every nook and cranny, but to no avail. I climbed up on the bedstead and reached out onto the window ledge. The niche appealed to me at first; then I decided that it would be the first place the guards would look.

I wandered over to the mattress and slipped the large bottle underneath. A small lump protruded. No, that was too likely a place.

I sat down and thought and thought. The more I thought the angrier I got with myself for having brought the bottle into the cell. There was no good hiding place, and I was sure to get caught. Two possibilities occurred to me after I realized that the big bottle could not be concealed on my body.

The first idea was drinking up the contents of the bottle right away. But that posed the problem of disposing of the bottle. I thought about smashing the bottle to bits and throwing them into the toilet. I was afraid that the noise would bring a guard running. No, I had to risk the only remaining possibility. It looked so innocent, and therein lay the promise of success.

I had a bottle of hair oil—I would peel off its label and stick it on the Sandorn bottle.

I proceeded to work on my project. I listened closely for the footsteps of the guards, in order to avoid getting surprised through the peephole. My heart pounded as I worked away on the bottles. It would have been a sin of excess to waste my hair oil, so I emptied the whole contents on my head and rubbed it in. I took both bottles and soaked them in water to remove their labels. The Sandorn sticker was stubborn, but after several minutes submerged in water, I could scratch it off.

There were two remaining difficulties with my little scheme. The hair oil was a product of East Germany. If the guards were familiar with the brand, all was lost. They would recognize that *Exlepang* hair oil did not come in *that* kind of bottle. In fact, no kind of hair oil came in *that* type of bottle. It was dark brown glass. Nevertheless, it was the self-assured innocence of it all that *might* outwit the guards. One had to pretend that nothing was strange and the guards would never suspect it. I began to feel like a real criminal in my efforts to dupe the police.

I gulped down a swig of the juice and my blood instantly became warm and giddy. I checked quickly to see whether there was any alcohol in the preparation, for if there were, then my offense was doubly serious. No, it was a high concentrate of grape sugar.

That evening I offered a strange sight to the guard who came to lock me in my cell for the night. Did she note the gay twinkle in my eyes as I stood in my nightshirt with long hair dripping oil and reported for the locking-in ceremony? I was intoxicated with victory.

One cheery Saturday morning, after about eight or nine days of isolation, I had a surprise. Outside my window the birds were twittering to the tune of summer and fluttering about excitedly. I was beginning to adjust to the fact that I would spend long, lonely days in solitude, with an occasional peek at my feathered companions. One thing had been preying on my mind, though. That was the question of work.

The prison appeared to be geared to German *Bequemlichkeit,* which was outright indolence! The guards even moved at a lethargic pace and spoke at a rate half as fast as their counterparts in Berlin. Their answers often consisted of short grunts or gestures. In some ways it proved advantageous.

I had only been called on to sweep the corridor one day, and that had been the extent of my labor. I could hear sounds of other prisoners whom I was never allowed to see, and I assumed that they were doing all the work. The guard who had assigned me to the sweeping detail had been inclined to do so only to test out her authority with me. She was the youngest of the guards.

Now the pretty young guard who had received me on my initiation to the penitentiary was on duty. She appeared in the door of my cell and requested me to follow her for a cleaning duty. She beamed with a broad smile, pleased by something, and I discovered her reason when I descended the stairs.

At first I thought she must have made a mistake when I saw four other women working on the floor. No, she assured me that I was meeting the others. All the scurrying and scuffing footsteps and shrill voices that had been active outside my cell door for days immediately took on personalities.

The other women busied themselves with scrub work in the corridor and bath. They all glanced away from their jobs when I arrived with the guard and then continued their work, as if I had always been a part of their clique. No one spoke to me.

I was told to relieve a shabby looking woman who was polishing the floor with a contraption I had never laid eyes on. It was a heavy metal floor buffer. When the woman had finished buffing her half of the corridor, I relieved her to finish the rest. I was unable to push the heavy device, and only after considerable effort I got the knack of swinging it back and forth.

When my chore was done, the guard led me into a large room at the end of the floor, where a plaque with "culture room" hung on the door. The huge room was about four times the size of the head matron's office and had two long windows which were paned in opaque glass. The windows were curtained with panels not unlike the matron's. As I scanned the room, I noted a television set, a radio, about eight red armchairs, all arranged to give the room a taste of cosiness. I marveled at such a room in prison. Although no real signs of culture were evident, the large room promised better days. However, I wondered whether "culture" really meant "indoctrination." I was immediately introduced to the "sewing circle."

The other women were seated around a table with their heads bent over needlework in their laps. When I shyly joined them at the table, the guard left us alone, locking the door to the room.

Curious scrutiny and probing questions immediately took place. We all exchanged names, crimes, and sentences, and the other women spent much time expressing their astonishment that I was an American. Most of them had never seen an American.

The liveliest of the lot introduced herself as "Lola," a nickname she had labeled herself with in prison. She was a clown and an absolute original for a German. Lola wore a flaming mane of red screwlocks which she kept in the style of Louis XIV. For that reason she had also been dubbed with the name Quatorze.

Lola had been charged with the very same crime as I and had received the same sentence. When a woman dentist had approached Lola for information about escaping to the West, she had begged for help in reaching her sick mother. Lola had sent her to "such and such a place" to ask for a certain person, and the dentist gave her a thousand marks for the information. The woman did succeed in escaping, and the penalty was more severe when scientists and doctors had been assisted in flight. The tragedy of the whole affair was that Lola had been arrested three years later. Lola, who was an East Berliner, was just as shocked with her high sentence as I was with mine.

As Lola chatted away, I noticed that she had taken Ingrid, the youngest of the group, under her wing as her protegée. Ingrid was a buxom twenty-three-year-old. She was just as reticent as Lola was garrulous, but her stillness had a strong maternal air about it. Perhaps it was because Ingrid had just brought her first child into the world in prison.

It was a sad story, perhaps the most heartbreaking of all. Ingrid had been sentenced to four and a half years for espionage. What had actually happened, though, was that she had attempted to escape with her boyfriend. The two had tried to tackle the Wall. Her friend had managed to break through the rows of barbed wire, but Ingrid had fallen and entangled herself in the snare. He had escaped to freedom and left her lying there bleeding. Worse, however, was the realization in prison that she was pregnant with his child. The father was in the West, and he would never see his child. She had to go on living in the East.

The charge of espionage had been brought against Ingrid because she had worked in a State Ministry and had confided secret information to her friend. The police claimed that the information had been passed on in the West. It had also weighed more heavily in her case, since she was a member of the East German Communist Party, the SED.

Ingrid was completely engrossed in the work of knitting—it was her first attempt. She was knitting her son a sweater. Mother and baby had been permitted to live with each other about a week, and then baby was sent away to a home until mother was released. I scrutinized her carefully, for I was fascinated by the aura of womanliness Ingrid evoked. So calmly composed, balanced, and set, she conveyed a warm maturity. She was not attractive, and was rather clumsy in her manner, but there seemed to be an impenetrable depth of femininity about her, rooted in her very nature—a soft, silent submission. However, Ingrid's equanimity was deceiving. She was deeply insecure, obsessed by irrational fears and anxieties which she gradually revealed.

Lise was the third member of our motley crew. Her full name was Liselotte, but we called her Lise. To me she provided the perfect image of a grandmother with her soft, squinting eyes and sallow, wrinkled visage. I was appalled to realize she was only thirty-four! Had prison altered the lines of a face already corrugated by nature and the struggle for survival? I was dismayed, for I had the same lot to await, if there were no possibility of getting released sooner.

Lise had served the longest stretch of the group. Two years of her five-year sentence had already elapsed. They were written in the crass lines of suffering on her face. She was the picture of a German peasant, with her stocky and broad matronlike frame and her long silky black hair twisted in a knot on her neck. Lise's squeaky voice spoke in the native dialect of the small Thuringian village she had come from.

Lise's husband was also in prison and with a sentence of ten years. But Lise did not talk about it. Whenever the subject was mentioned she withdrew from the conversation and pretended to busy herself with her needle-work. They both had been charged with attempting escape, but there was some question concerning his involvement in espionage for the West. How-ever, no one knew for sure; the information had traveled through the prison grapevine. Both of them had been snatched away from their two children, whom they had not seen since the arrest. Her peasant background made her especially fearful of the guards, even to an exaggerated extent. Lise had been a member of the party, too, and now there was a hint of bitterness and resignation in her.

The last member of the group was Margot, also an East Berliner. She was thirty-six, and all the attributes of a spinster were beginning to set in her personality. Nevertheless, she appeared ten years younger and never spoke of her age. It had also seeped out through the mysterious grapevine. She had recently cut her long bleached hair, which hung below her ears. The new hair that had grown in had left her with a two-tone mixture of color. Thick patches of gray revealed themselves where the new hair had appeared, and her physical appearance had suffered most from the imprisonment.

Margot was the most reserved of the prisoners, especially with the East Germans. She was stingy with her answers concerning her age, crime, and sentence. She attached herself to me immediately when she learned that I was an American, but even with me she kept herself veiled in an air of mystery.

Word had traveled around prison that Margot had been charged with "economic" crimes against the state and had received a three-year sentence. It was rumored that her crime had something to do with black marketcer-ing, which many in East Berlin indulged in.

Margot appeared to take imprisonment the hardest of all. She had led the best life before, which was wanting in nothing materially. But as the "rich man wilteth as the blossom in the heat of the day," Margot had lost every-thing to the state. The court had confiscated her car, apartment, precious jewels, and left her with a bare minimum to start life over from scratch. Margot had a deep mistrust of the other women and wanted to confide some black secret to me right away. My better instinct cautioned me to hold back until I had found my way into the group. The tragedy of Margot's story was that her father had denounced her to the Security Police.

Resting in a bent posture with her shoulders drooping, Margot appeared to be the most pitiful of the women. She had already been imprisoned a year, and one year had been enough to completely break her spirit. Her tired head was half-bowed in a nod and sagged from her curved neck. Her haggard face held lines of suffering and resignation.

From the very beginning of my encounter with the group, I sensed a rivalry for my loyalty. There was competition of two camps—Margot versus the others. I was hesitant about committing myself to either camp. I was determined to remain neutral, at least until I could discern the facts surrounding the dissension.

The first opportunity to be with others raised my spirits. After months of being closed off from people, I experienced a rebirth in enjoyment of the companionship of so many persons. I also felt a strong bond of sisterhood with the women, who were all victims of the same evil. Therefore, I bubbled over with enthusiastic accounts of my prison experience to that point. The women were overwhelmed by my candor. They were unaccustomed to it with each other, and least of all, to being sincere.

The political atmosphere of their state had instilled in them a deep distrust of each other; I knew that the fanaticism of the regime and the laws against even speaking out against the state were so severe that they had broken down trust and sincerity. Prison was the last place they could be cultivated. I did not realize that I had verbalized the undared when I openly spoke my opinion about my harsh sentence and the injustice of the cruel regime. I had only uttered what each one felt but did not dare say.

I recalled, as I often did in my imprisonment, Robert Frost's poem, "Mending Wall." There was a wall through Germany that divided a country; separated a people; alienated individuals from each other. But, worst of all, that wall estranged people from themselves! Yes, they all built up walls between each other, walls that were carefully guarded with the weapons of their personal defense mechanisms. They shut each other out. Fear. Who could be trusted in a political atmosphere that required imprisonment for speaking out against the state? Trust could not be learned. No wonder they longed for escape. It was not just the material advantages of the "golden West" that attracted them, as the state claimed. The state was missing the boat if it thought that was the only reason its citizens were fleeing by the thousands. Escape was much more. Oh, how I hated walls between human beings!

Margot took me aside and warned me to be careful about what I said. There was a squealer in our midst, she claimed. One of the women had denounced her to the matron, slandering her severely. That made her retreat from confiding in all the women, since she was unsure who had done it. She became irritable, touchy, and always on the defensive. She suspected "the red one," as she called Lola, in order to avoid pronouncing her name. Margot and I conversed in English and French when I learned that she had worked as an interpreter. I was hesitant to do so, since I already felt a thick cloud of jealousy in the group atmosphere and wanted to avoid a storm. I was still unsure just whom to believe. Lola also said that I had to watch out for someone's loose tongue. Everything Margot related seemed exaggerated, and Lola extended her friendship so willingly. . . . Only time would tell.

Lola informed me that the guard on duty was the prisoners' favorite. She had been endowed with a warm generosity and had been christened "Gisela." Gisela seemed to assume a pronounced serious expression when she ordered us to do something, but a smile always quivered on her lips to avoid breaking through. She got on extremely well with the other group of women prisoners, who were mysteriously kept apart from us. I was eager to hear about them.

Lola was able to supply every detail about the other women, although she had not been with them herself. Lise and Ingrid had spent several months with the others before Lola arrived. After her arrival, the women had been immediately divided into two groups. The other group consisted of a circle of spies. A tall gray woman, supposedly Russian born, had received a life sentence for espionage. She had been married to a German professor and had a doctor's title herself. The other women were not fond of Dr. Gruenfeld, because they were suspicious of too much intelligence.

Another prisoner, whom I was sure to see before long, was Helga, the women's trusty. She had served almost six years of her life sentence for treason. The story went that she had worked for the Ministry of Security, fled to the West before the Wall, and "unpacked" all of the East's security information. Later, she had allegedly repented of her crime and decided to return to the East. They arrested her at the border. At least, so the story goes. . . . Lola warned us all that prisoners had a tendency to spin yarns. The other women felt that there was some catch to Helga's story. Helga was a cordial, well-behaved, and obedient prisoner, but who wouldn't be with a life sentence hanging over his head? Since she commanded the respect of all the guards, I detected silent envy from the other women.

The other two women in the other group had sentences of eight and nine years for espionage. One of them, Ellen, an attractive woman in her early thirties, had been arrested with her husband in Czechoslovakia. It was rumored that Margret, a single woman in her fifties, was a Lesbian. None of the women was sure, but Lola claimed that Margret had made advances to her. I had already wondered about encountering that difficulty in prison, but fortunately Margret had no real contact with our group.

The excitement of our new encounter was interrupted when we all had lunch together. Moreover, Gisela switched on the television. I was amazed by the cosy atmosphere—first, lunch, then television. Although we were operating on a weekend schedule, the generosity was Gisela's.

Not all of the guards were as generous as Gisela, and it was not every weekend that the prisoners could eat lunch together. In addition, we had to clear out of the room immediately after lunch. The other group had to have their turn, and the two groups usually alternated in the use of the room.

Sunday was still a special day in a socialistic society, which surprised me. It was a holiday, even for prisoners. The Sunday meal provided the week's only piece of meat—unless you consider sausage meat; it was more often slabs of fat than lean. Its courses invariably comprised watery gravy, salted boiled potatoes, and some cold vegetable, usually red cabbage. In the evening, peppermint tea, a slab of real butter, and—every two weeks—sugar and jam were apportioned to the prisoners. The rest of the week, lunch was a one-course dish, containing carrots, potatoes, cabbage, or cauliflower. The second meal, in the evening, served as supper and breakfast. It consisted of a slab of either lard, margarine, or butter, a thick piece of sausage, and as many slices of bread as one wanted. To drink there was always the same dark bitter fluid, which was erroneously called coffee.

On Monday morning I was introduced to a new daily routine—work! The compulsory labor I had been sentenced to required eight and a half hours a day in the production of *"Stoessel,"* which best resembled "relay contacts" in English. The job consisted of assembling the not too intricate gadgets for use in an electrical switch system.

Sometimes we had to spend the day slipping two metal washers onto the necks of screws, literally thousands of them. Nevertheless, there was a method to it. Each day an order was sent up, requesting the needed material. Whether we mounted screws, or assembled the relay contacts, the trusty passed the word on to us.

It was slavish, mass-production, assembly work, which was performed with a monotonous routine. The only advantage it offered was that we could chat while accomplishing it. However, the enslavement was enhanced by the exigency of factory norms. A prisoner's behavior was evaluated according to his completed sum of contacts or screws each day; there was a minimum norm determining the quantity, and the earnings were also calculated from the output.

Although a prisoner earned the same wages he would have in the national economy and was subject to the same tax deductions, he received only about a sixth of his earnings. Half of this portion he could spend each month on supplementing his food from the prison canteen. Prisoners were allowed to spend about five dollars a month for cigarettes, chocolate, cheese, cake, sausage, eggs, and similar articles.

The eight-and-a-half-hour work day was only a part of the whole work plan. After work, the *Feierabend* of evening leisure did not really begin until household duties were taken care of. I was introduced to scrubbing details, washing, waxing, and polishing. It appeared that the officials had sought out the women's section to assign it special punishment—it was on the fourth and fifth floors of the building, and the steps reaching down to the cellar had to be cleaned several times a week. What was even worse, the German Hausfrau's intense obsession with cleanliness was carried to extremes in prison. In any other country of the world, the guards were sure not to be polishing pedants—but that's what they were in Germany! Nothing was overlooked, even the stone steps leading outside to the courtyard were scoured and scrubbed. Although it was more humiliating to be a charwoman than an unskilled factory laborer, the exercise provided an opportunity to uncoil and work off the tension built up during the day, and I found myself looking forward to the evening chores.

When our sewing circle met in the work cell, a series of complaints was on the daily agenda, and the atmosphere became a hell of pettiness. It was unhealthy.

If it wasn't the other group of women, it was the guards; if the guards hadn't their turn, the food was attacked. All of these items did supply stuff for grievance, but we were soon swallowed up in an ocean of grumbles. I was beginning to suffer the torment of depression. I was still unable to eat the tasteless meals and had already begun to take off pounds. I had made numerous attempts to get dental care, but without success. When I revealed this to the others, Lise had the same complaint—she usually did, no matter what the symptom was. She had been trying for months to get dental and medical attention, and several teeth had fallen out. Lola, who was unrelenting in inciting us to complaint, had provoked us to protesting the treatment.

One day I felt ill and, convinced I had a fever, I asked a guard for the thermometer. The other women had advised me to do so. What was worse on that particular day was the fact that we had to work on empty stomachs; we had had some sort of ugly preparation of tripe for lunch. Hairy pieces of stomach and other suspicious looking organs floated in the gooey sauce, and no one had bothered to touch his meal. My comment upon this specialty was that I wouldn't give that even to my dog! The others agreed.

After several minutes, the Meisterin returned and told me to come with her. She led the way to the medical station, which was at the end of the corridor. Three policewomen were standing in front of the door, gazing curiously at me. I was embarrassed to have to parade by them before entering the cell.

The matron handed me a thermometer, a rectal one, and told me to pull down my pants. Then, as if she were above administering to a prisoner, she called the trusty from her scrub work to come and insert the thermometer into my rectum! Her intention was obvious. She had wanted to humiliate me. The girls had said that the thermometer generally used was an oral one. The matron thought she would put an end to my complaints about not receiving medical attention.

The Meisterin detested me. She was suspicious, but it was a suspicion based on her own prejudices and not one I had given ground for. She was extremely reserved and cool with me, and I never could guess her thoughts or predict her moves. Her steel eyes never met mine when we spoke, and one of them crossed when she moved it in a certain way, leaving a self-conscious expression on her visage. I knew she was biased against me, because she had taken my wristwatch away, allowing the other prisoners to keep theirs. There were other intangible signs, too, the kind which women seem to sense instinctively. The others told me that she especially resented me.

I suffered on account of the matron's resentment, because I knew I had done nothing to deserve her attitude. I also knew what lay at the root of it, though. I was an American! The party progaganda had poisoned and prejudiced her against accepting me as an individual. I could best understand her reaction when I attempted to picture a similar circumstance in America. I imagined that it was much the same as being a Russian woman in a Texas state prison or maybe a Negro in an Arkansas prison.

Indeed, the first days of working together—five women in a small cell—were pervaded by an air akin to hysteria. All babbled at once, excited over the exchange with a new person, especially since the arrivée was a Westerner. The dingy work cell took on the cackling and clucking of a hen house. I was less interested in production and more interested in palaver, since I had accepted the fact that I was in a school of life. A keen inquisitiveness concerning my companions' political and religious attitudes dominated me. Although I was uncertain how much sincerity could be expressed, I sought to sense hidden meaning behind their utterances.

It was a rare encounter for me, being able to confer with two common members of the Communist Party. I had known ideological Communists in Western countries and had discussed and debated with them, but never had I engaged in a discourse with party members on an equal basis.

One day in our work circle the question I had long been expecting popped up. It was inevitable, since every television news broadcast and every newspaper published account of it daily. In fact, it was always in the headlines. The war in Vietnam! It was Lola who brought it up. If she was not posing a loaded question, then it was her streak of sadism seeking satisfaction. For it was a question I could only lose on in an East German prison. "What are the Amis doing in Vietnam, anyway? It is thousands of miles away from America."

I paused. It was a question I had asked myself many times, seeking assurance about the real motives. I couldn't say "fighting Communism," that was risking the undared. Besides, it was vague, indefinite, an empty phrase.

"Before I explain anything," I began hesitantly, "let me say that I, personally, cannot accept any war as a means of solving problems. I am definitely not an advocate of any war, but of peace. But, perhaps I could attempt to understand my government's involvement. That means starting at another point—let's say, with the two major world powers, the Soviet Union and the United States. They are deeply suspicious of each other. Each feels that the other is aggressive and power-hungry. Since after the end of World War II many countries came under Soviet domination, Americans tend to think that Russia seeks world domination, especially since the Marxist ideology is such . . . excuse me, do you know what dialectical materialism is?"

"What's that?" Lola asked. She had never heard of it. I was astounded. I asked the others whether they knew. Margot was the only one who knew anything about it.

"But you, in the Party, don't you know what it is?" There was no response. I, a Westerner, an American, was telling Communist Party members in East Germany about their own ideology! It was like being in the Christian church and not knowing about the doctrine of salvation. But then, I guess many Christians were just as ignorant of Christianity. It was really no different. They were simple women with little education. But what did the Party teach the people? Till now I only observed that everything had been reduced and simplified to the "class struggle." So I posed another question, testing their information before I proceeded with any more explanations. I addressed it to Lola, since she seemed to be the spokesman for the group. "What do you understand by capitalism?"

"Why . . . uh . . ." she stuttered with embarrassment, "exploitation."

"Is that all?"

"Yes. It's the same thing. There's no difference."

"In other words all private enterprise is bad? It exploits the worker?" I inquired.

"Yes, that's it!" By this time Margot was biting her lips to keep from smiling at the naïve impressions that had been propagated in the woman's thinking. But I wasn't amused, I was appalled. The poor people had been politically manipulated. Apparently, everything had been reduced to the ready syllogism for the folk. "Communism is good. Capitalism is bad. The East is communistic; therefore, good. The West is capitalistic; therefore, bad!" Something like that. It sounded familiar, though, for it was not too different on the other side of the Wall. It was just that the oversimplified premises were reversed. There was the same difficulty with the freedom of the press. It was a question whether the manipulation of the press by the party or its control by advertisers was worse. Both were evils and enemies of the genuine freedom of the press.

I continued, changing my approach. "Many Americans fear Communism. . . . No, take the divided country of Vietnam. Compare it with your own divided Germany. Let's say tomorrow West Germany decides to attack East Germany in the name of reunification and they call on the armed assistance of the United States, for they could not accomplish it alone since so many Russian troops occupy East Germany." Eyebrows flew up. That was another forbidden statement. I ignored the reaction and proceeded with my simplified explanation.

"Then, of course, the East German Government would call in the Soviet Union to help them. Don't you see—politically this is similar to the case in Vietnam. With the help of the Chinese and the Soviets, the North is conducting a campaign against the South for the reunification of the country. There is a question, however, as to the loyalty of the South . . . therein lies the difficulty. (I dared not say that there was also some question concerning the loyalty of the East Germans.) In any case, the 'Ami', as you say, has gone in because the South Vietnamese Government has requested it, in the same way as your government would request it if an attack was launched by West Germany."

Why wasn't the world still screaming of the injustice in Germany, as it was in Vietnam? I could not help observing marked parallels in the German question. There was a deep-seated fear among the officials of the East German Government that the same type of war could take place on their soil. Which was the legitimate Germany? For this reason the East Germans were especially hysterical in their violent condemnation of the Vietnamese war.

"But why are the Amis killing so many women and children? Bombing hospitals and schools? Bombing civilians and destroying the crops?" Lola probed viciously.

"Are they? I really don't know what's going on over there. There are always two sides to any question—and then, I guess, a right side, too. The media here cover it in their interest, just as the American media do. The truth lies somewhere in the middle!" I knew I had dared too much. My last statement was a direct criticism of the press in East Germany, but I had tried to soften it by pointing out the weakness of the other side. I had as much as said I didn't believe what I heard and saw in East Germany. Of course I didn't, but to announce it could hang me. That struck Ingrid as strong, for she was an avid and credulous reader of the East German newspapers. She religiously accepted everything she read.

The coverage of the war news was a preposterous distortion. There were seldom reports of troop casualties. No, daily there were pictures of mangled children, twisted faces of tearful mothers, devastated schools, and black ruins of hospitals. No wonder they could call Americans Nazis and have their people believe it! Were we really? From my cage I had no way of knowing.

Although I tried to watch and read the news with a strong critical mind, I invariably fled to my cell after a television program and cried my heart out to myself. I had to sit silently in their midst as the citizen of a country whose government was committing crimes worse than Hitler's against a brave, little people who only sought unity and prosperity.

What was *really* going on in Vietnam, I had no way of knowing, but when I saw the pictures of bombed hospitals and schools, of children with their faces blown off, or crippled mothers reaching out for their mangled babies with faces stained with tears and blood, it worked on me psychologically, too. There must be *some* truth in it I kept fearing. In the pit of my stomach a sickening knot twisted and never left me, and I kept explaining to myself, "But the American *people,* the people—they only want to help. They are generous, hospitable, peace loving. The world sees them now as butchers. Are they butchers? Then why doesn't someone stand up and tell the truth? Why doesn't someone answer all those angry, rebellious students who are protesting?"

Lola continued her inquest, in a vicious, bitter tone, almost reproaching me for being an American.

"You know, the Ami doesn't make a good soldier anyway. But, the Iwan —that's a real soldier! They were the real fighters in the last war, tough and hardened. The Ami had the weapons, but the Iwan can fight."

I interrupted her. "You may be right, but I'm not so sure that it is anything to be proud of. Americans just aren't taught to be warlike and aggressive, and if they aren't good fighters, it may have some advantage for peace." As she continued her probe, I perceived a deep prejudice against America, and finally she uncovered the root of it when she related an episode of her personal history.

"My father is extremely bitter against the Amis. He was a Communist in the last war and fought against the Nazis. We used to live in West Berlin, but the Amis forced us to come to the Eastern Sector. Yes, just chased us out! We were living in the American Sector just after the war. You know how it was—hunger, starvation. Well, Daddy saw an American jeep pass by one day, and it stopped at a light right near him. It was loaded with food. The soldiers had lots to eat, but they didn't give anything to the people. Well, he just thought it would be nice to get a couple of bananas for me and Mama, and he jumped onto the jeep and grabbed them. You know what happened? He was put into jail!

"Finally, the Amis forced him to go and live in the Eastern Sector because they said he was a Communist. Actually, he only fought with the Communists against the Nazis. He was never in the party. Now, he claims that what's going on in this state isn't communism—not real communism. A real Communist is a humanist. Yes, the Amis put him into the jug, and after he had spent nine years in a concentration camp. That's what I can't understand. The Amis and the Iwans fought side by side against Hitler, and now they fight each other. Didn't they understand? He just wanted to get something to eat. We were all starving. . . ."

Lola choked back the tears. She never cried, but she loved and admired her father with a real adolescent hero worship, and hardly a day passed without his entering the conversation. It had been a bitter blow. Nine years in a Nazi concentration camp and then jail with the American occupation troops. I did not know all the details; perhaps it was only her father's story. . . .

When a guard entered the work cell, our discussion broke off abruptly. Lola jumped to her feet and reported for the group. When all the prisoners were in a group, the group eldest was responsible for reporting. Lola was the youngest in time at Bautzen, but she had managed to develop a special relationship to the matron. She boasted that the matron and she got on exceptionally well with each other. Since she was the only one of us who bragged of that questionable honor, it aroused my suspicion when the matron decided to place Lola in charge of our little group. There was nothing tangible I could put my finger on. It was all in the realm of uneasy feelings, and they were not to be relied on.

"*Strafgefangene* Battle! *Kommen Sie Mit!*" the warder commanded. I was caught unaware by the sudden command and arose from my seat with a pounding heart. Of course, it might not be ground for unrest, but where was I being taken? Our assembly production was often interrupted in order to talk to the matron, to meet with officials from the administration, or to perform some special work detail in the building.

I followed with the weight of dread and the guard unlocked my cell door. "Get your things together for a couple of days. You are going on transport!"

14

REUNION

WHEN THE GUARD had locked the door, I immediately rummaged in the cabinet to collect all my cosmetic articles. I stuffed them into a shopping net, all the while reflecting on the destination of the sudden journey. I concluded that there was only one place to be sent from Bautzen—that was Berlin.

The reason for the trip gripped me with doubts. A release was out of the question, because I had not been told to pack all my things together. A prisoner was never informed about what was being done with him, where he was being dispatched, what would occur. They disposed of him as if he were a piece of livestock—loading him into a dark delivery truck, carting him off to an unknown destination, and penning him up in a cage on arrival. There was only one possibility for the trip that impressed me. It must be a visit. After I had written such a sad letter home, maybe . . . no, that was impossible. My parents did not have the financial resources for that. . . .

With a sort of sad anticipation I departed from Bautzen in a Wartburg, escorted by three security policemen who had driven down from Berlin to fetch me. The matron had given me a chance to change my clothes from the lumpy prison uniform to my wool tweed costume before leaving. I had stated deliberately to her that it felt marvelous being a *person* again. The matron had replied with a significant scowl, denoting her disapproval.

My conjecture had not been incorrect, and when the first signs of Berlin became visible on the horizon, a tinge of excitement and joy pricked me. Berlin, that was my second home, even though I was confined to the East.

When we reached the massive and fortified Hohenschoenhausen, its cold stone walls, covered with vines of prickly wire, and its vigilant watchmen with slung machine guns seemed to welcome me back. My first thoughts were of Ursula and a mist clouded my eyes. I wondered what Gevatterin One was up to.

I was received by Gummi Ball, who was still as bouncy as ever. He greeted me with a bold grin. "What, are you still our guest?"

"I'm afraid so," I complained with amusement, "but it sure is wonderful to be back in Berlin! This place is paradise in comparison to Bautzen."

He bounced off down the corridor to my old cell, and when the door was pushed back, I noticed someone's things stacked on a chair. When I examined them more closely, I discovered they were Ursula's. She was still around! I had been away a month, and her trial was scheduled for that same month. But, the things were packed together, and the bed was unmade. There was a fine layer of dust over everything that told me she had been gone for a while. The dust was my calendar. I lifted the jar of instant coffee

I had given her, and happy, shared coffee hours crossed my memory. I tucked it away in its niche, and Gummi Ball and I removed the last trace of Ursula from the cell.

Odd! How very strange! I felt a sense of security in my old cell. How could I ever consider a prison cell with any warmth? But returning to the same cell in which I had shared so much with Ursula also brought a taste of melancholy. Friends in fate. Partners in persecution! The precious paths that had crossed and intertwined had wound and twisted away. I was reminded of Ursula's encouraging words before I left. "You were a meaningful event in my life! A significant experience! One that has made prison have meaning and value for my life!"

That was the highest compliment I had ever received, and one that confirmed a mission, and yet, she was gone now, and with her traveled any sense of mission I might have found in our encounter.

On the following morning I was once more paid all the respects of protocol's regulations governing foreign guests. Again, being clad in fine clothes, the ride in a car instead of a Minna, and coffee with my visitors allowed me to consider myself a guest of the state. I had often joked about the East German "hospitality" with the Weasel and especially the fact that the police had provided me with an escorted tour of their state, having covered territory from the high north all the way down to the southern border as a prisoner. These "fun" remarks had always been clouded with overtones of tragic irony, though—laughing on the outside and crying on the inside.

I had to be taken to the dirty old Magdalenenstrasse prison as usual and wait the same eternity of time. When I was conducted to the visitation room, the door opened and at the first glimpse—"Daddy!" I rushed and embraced him, greeting him with a flood of tears. Mr. Vogel and Mr. New were his escorts. After exchanging greetings with the other men, I accepted my father's handkerchief which came to my immediate aid.

The guard assigned to protocol promptly brought a large tray of coffee. I advised the men to drink it all, because my interrogator had commented on Mr. New's leaving half a cup on his previous visit. Coffee was expensive in the DDR. The Weasel had taken it that Mr. New disliked the coffee. The men were amused by my sensitive admonition about not offending the prison personnel.

Although I was filled with a myriad of questions of utmost importance, they all fled my memory, leaving only insignificant utterances to exchange. Small talk. There was also the warning my father had spoken—"the walls sometimes have ears"—that chased away to forgetfulness all of the questions concerning negotiations. Thus, we were left with topics like "What do you eat?" "How is your health?" and "We all miss you." Not that these are insignificant to a parent, but I was burning to discuss issues of major importance.

My father had brought along a file of newspaper clippings concerning my imprisonment, with the idea of conveying the concern of my countrymen. Although it aroused my appreciation, I questioned its value as long as the "decisive" people were not interested in helping me. Of course they were, he assured me, but I had seen no evidence of it, and he could not give me any information that would verify it. Being interested in helping me and doing something about it were two different things.

I leafed through the newspaper clippings, they came from across the country, but the local papers had gone all out. I was suddenly hit with the importance of the whole matter! In a cell, isolated from the outside world, I had no way of knowing that anyone was concerned, that they even cared, although my father had conveyed some of their messages in his letters to me. Condemned to being isolated from the western world, too, I had become encased in a capsule somewhere in the corner of a hostile world.

America seemed so far away, and all of those realities which characterized her confronted me anew when I entered that visitation room in East Germany—the warm, broad smiles, which could be mistaken for no other nationality; the round-toed shoes or the closely cropped hair. Those were just some of the outward signs. It was the warm openheartedness, the simple sincerity, and the naïve optimism which I welcomed. American men. The big boys with broad smiles. A wholesomeness and freshness. Their manner was so foreign to the Prussian stiffness, the starched reserve, the cold distance, and long, brooding faces of the heavy-spirited, oppressed Germans.

I examined my father's new suit. Yes, this was a big visit for him. Europe for the first time! But under such conditions.

"Daddy, you have to take advantage of your trip over here. See as much as you can, for I know you'll love it! Especially West Berlin. You simply cannot leave without meeting it."

Mr. New spoke. "I wish we could take you with us now, and we'd all stop over in Paris for a gay soiree!"

Mr. Vogel interrupted. "I'd love to come along with you!"

The words stung. I heaved a sigh. *"Pareeee! Ach,* wouldn't I have a ball there with you three men! Wouldn't that be *wunderbar!"* I felt so oppressed by having my wings clipped. I was what the Germans called a *Wandervogel.* I was obsessed by the spirit of *Wanderlust*—the call of the open! Surely I suffered more in prison than all of those people who had entered prison from the villages and provinces. No one loved life more than I.

"Unfortunately, they won't let me go. But, Daddy, can you visit some people in West Berlin for me? Especially Dr. Sieg would appreciate knowing how I am getting along."

He wrinkled his brow, glancing at Mr. New. "I don't know," he answered, "this visit isn't supposed to be publicized! It is secret. You see, it is the first time an American parent has been allowed entry into the prison here. I don't know whether we can make this fact known."

"Oh yes," I exclaimed, "of course you can! Parents are allowed to visit their children! All the other prisoners I know get visits once a month. What have they been telling you?"

"Well, it has never been done by an American."

"I'm sure it's all right to let it be known." My suspicions were confirmed when I sensed that the information my father had been given was inaccurate. Apparently, the contact between the American authorities and the East German attorney was not as fully established as it might appear. I was distracted by a painful recognition as I noticed my father's hair.

"I see that you have added some gray hairs since I last saw you. I know I have caused them."

"Oh no," he denied with a warm smile, assuring me that nature had brought them along with increased age. He did appear older. Small lines of suffering marked an expression that was usually filled only with glowing good humor. All the wrinkles of his visage were signs of pleasantness that had carefully masked any difficulty life had brought, but the corners of his mouth revealed a drawn suffering that could not be hidden when he relaxed his smile.

Of course I had caused the gray hairs! It was obvious, though, that we were both trying cautiously to conceal the real pain and worry brought about by my imprisonment. Each wanted to alleviate the other's burden. The agonizing truth remained unspoken, hovering silently over the instant.

We flitted about from subject to subject, popping out with the first thing that came to mind. The ticking seconds were so precious, and I dreaded the instant when someone would intrude with a "halt."

"We brought you some lotion and the other stuff for your skin." My father pointed to a package on the desk. "Also some citrus fruit and instant coffee."

"What a delightful surprise!" I exclaimed as if I had just received a package of diamonds. All those objects were the real luxuries of prison life. In fact, any American products were coveted treasures. I had written home that my skin was suffering from the diet, because rough, dry blotches had popped out on my face. The absence of vitamins and fresh air, the heavy dust in the work cell—it all contributed to wither and dry the skin.

I peeked into the package. A glass of honey, grapefruit and oranges, Hershey kisses, a big box of Ritz crackers—dear Daddy, the Ritz crackers had traveled all the way from America and seemed so out of place on the list of necessities. Cleansing cream, skin lotion, moisture cream for my face —"It's my birthday and Christmas all at the same time!" I exclaimed.

My father reached into his vest pocket and pulled out a small notebook. After glancing over it a few seconds, notes that he had jotted down, he passed on a list of regards from America, concluding with "The four-legged dishwashers [that's how he always referred to our two dogs] send their canine greetings, too."

I was moved. He never forgot to mention the dogs. There was something in each letter about them.

"I hope I can make it home before the old dog dies. [He was seventeen years old and we had been the best of pals forever.] I'll never forgive the prison authorities if he dies while I am in this place!"

Mr. Vogel, who had been busy on the telephone, returned from the desk and announced the dreaded moment. "I'm afraid we are going to have to break the visit up. I am supposed to be out of here by 1:00 P.M."

The time had arrived. The visit had flown by in a short hour and a half, leaving all things of importance unsaid. Now it was too late. Pressed for time, I blurted out once more, as I had at Mr. New's visit, "Do you think that I can be out by September?"

Mr. New hesitated, looked at Mr. Vogel, and concluded, "I think we might have a *decision* by then."

A decision was not a release, though. Didn't they understand just how important the time was for me? I had wanted to convey that in the visit, but I had failed to. I had forgotten in the excitement. Besides, there had somehow slipped over me an awareness of not really experiencing—an absence of feeling. My state of shock was shattered, however, when my father embraced me to leave.

"Don't leave me, Daddy," I begged with the helplessness of a tiny toddler who needs its father's hand to take its first step. "Please don't go."

The clinging hug between father and daughter bridged thousands of miles of separation. There was a lifetime in that one embrace.

In the doorway the guard was waiting impatiently to take me away—yes, to lead a daughter away from the security and protection of her father. But my father's helplessness to act was greater than my own. He was a free man, unable to exercise his freedom. I was a prisoner, obeying!

"Goodbye!" I cried out as if it were the last time I would ever see him. I dared not glance back, for my face was flooded with tears.

In my cell in Hohenschoenhausen, I had time to register all the tiny details of the encounter of the morning. The first thing that aroused my nostalgic thoughts was my father's handkerchief. I still clutched it tightly in my hand. I examined it and laughed softly through the tears. It was an old, unpressed one with scattered tiny holes that years of use had worn through. That was Daddy! He had worn a crisp new suit, which spoke for the exterior. But tucked away in the pocket was a handkerchief that said more.

I pressed the handkerchief out on the bed with my fingers. I compared it with the one Mr. Vogel had given me after the trial. I still had it, too. It was the finest linen, intricately designed on the border, and carefully ironed in folds. These two hankies spoke for two different worlds—

the German's love of finery, his vanity, his concern with his appearance and his impression on others. An exactness. This was offset by the American's relaxed casualness, the Anglo-Saxon practicality, for after all, a handkerchief was an object of use. Much of what I had criticized before, now became a welcome sight. A precious discovery of the sweet naturalness of America was crumpled up in an outworn handkerchief. America, I love you!

When I returned to Bautzen there was not the warm reception awaiting me that I had received in Berlin. The matron regarded me coolly, as she accompanied me to doff my robes of freedom and femininity and return to the shabby garments of the workhouse, which really looked like those of a poorhouse. Back to the slavery of the production line, carried out in a cell with an ugly, raw, hundred-watt light bulb protruding from the side of the dingy, gritty wall. There was an air of shabbiness about it all, and the petty provincialism of the guards was more confining than the bars on the windows. Yes, I loathed this prison. It was so different from Berlin.

The following day our sewing circle was transformed into a social hour in the culture room. It was the customary Saturday morning relaxed atmosphere of chatter and needlework, and the women were eager to hear my account of the visit with my father.

"And he came all the way from America just to see you for an hour and a half!" Ingrid exclaimed. It was beyond her comprehension.

"You don't understand," I said. "My family has no conception of the conditions here, and after my last letter home. . . . My coming to Bautzen seemed so final. I don't think it is the usual procedure with foreigners. Nothing can convince me that I wasn't sent here to try to get a decision on the negotiations that are being discussed. I don't think my father would have come if I were about to be released. So, in one way, it is a bad sign. You see, in Berlin I had such good treatment, but here I am treated no differently. . . ."

"Yes," Lola remarked with cold envy, "we weren't treated as you were in Berlin! The meals were more horrible than here. You had to have permission from the doctor to lie down. We had no decent bed, but a wooden cot, slanted at the top, and covered with a thin mattress. There were no comfortable chairs in our cells, but hard, wooden stools!"

We had hashed out the subject many times before. Every time Lola ended up envying me for the treatment I had received in Berlin. I convinced them that not only foreigners received this, but some of the East Germans, too. Brigette, Ursula—they all had the same treatment as I. For these women Berlin had meant the time of the worst suffering. For me it had presented a vast improvement to the conditions I had at Bautzen. The other women had no Christmas celebration with their interrogators! They had had sausage on Christmas, when I had enjoyed roast goose. Envious resentment clouded the atmosphere. I had no idea myself what criterion was used to determine the treatment of prisoners in Berlin, but the others found it unfair and unjust.

I thought about my own countrymen in Bautzen and wondered about their treatment. I was eager with curiosity to catch a glimpse of them. I had already confided this information to the others. An idea occurred to me as we sat around our table of needlework, and I arose from my chair. I tiptoed over to the wide window in the door. I peeked outside to see whether the guard was within seeing range, and not discovering her, I crossed the room to the window that faced the back courtyard. It looked out on the courts where we had our free time in the fresh air.

Although Bautzen was a men's penitentiary, a tiny wing was set apart for the women prisoners. It was shut off from the main building and could house a maximum of twenty. The men had their thirty minutes outdoors in the morning, while ours was in the afternoon. Perhaps I could climb up on the window ledge and peer out of the transparent windows at the top. If I were lucky, I could catch a glimpse of the other Americans. Two I would recognize, because they were black, and I could be almost certain that the prison housed no other Negro prisoners.

The windows were long and paned with opaque glass in the bottom panels, but the upper windows were fitted with one transparent pane. One could see out only by climbing up on the ledge, and I stepped up on the radiator and reached the ledge. I commanded a tremendous, wide view of the entire courtyard.

All eyes were on me. Apparently, none of the women would have dared to do the forbidden thing that I was doing. *Verboten* was the strongest word of authority in the German language, and the one that commanded the most respect. This obedience was so ingrained that a German was appalled to see someone cross a street against a red light, even when the street was deserted of cars. It was all so arbitrary, and their exaggerated fears were foreign to me. It was absolutely *verboten* to look at the men prisoners or to look out the window! As long as the guard wasn't around, what did that matter?

"Oh, there are a couple of good-looking men down here!" I stated on making the discovery. Lola's mouth watered and Margot perked up her attention.

"There is an old man with gray hair, too, for you, Lise."

She responded with one of her peasant guffaws. I was thrilled to see the men for the first time, especially since it was forbidden fruit. My searching glance failed to find the other Americans. I quickly jumped down with a loud thud. Margot was splitting with curiosity and ventured over to the ledge to follow suit. She finally backed out with fear, postponing it until our next meeting in the culture room. The sport of window-peeking promised to provide a favorite pastime for us!

Half an hour later the stocky masculine guard appeared. She had been given the questionable name of Tosca. The only Tosca I knew about was Puccini's, and the two resembled each other as much as a Poland-China hog and a peacock. Lola requested permission to get a knitting needle from her cell. After some seconds she returned, and we continued with our needlework session. At least, *they* continued with *their* needlework, for I had not gotten involved in it. I was hoping that my prison stay would not be long enough to knit a sweater, since I was sure it would take me a couple of years to complete it.

When Lola returned, Tosca was wearing a venomous expression, and instead of locking the door as she usually did, she left it wide open. We all exchanged furtive looks of amazement. I listened to the waning sound of her footsteps, as she wandered out of range of the doorway and waited at the corner. She was parked outside to eavesdrop.

Shortly before lunchtime, she returned to tell us to get ready for lunch. She met us with a grim expression. "Somebody has looked out the window today!" she stated firmly, staring straight at Margot. "I don't want to hear about it happening again. If it does it will be reported to Frau Meister! You can be punished for that!" She marched out of the room in a huff.

We all looked at each other. Nobody said a word. Red blotches of rash appeared on Lola's neck, and her face became chalky white. Margot felt that she had been accused of the act, and I was the guilty culprit. How did Tosca know? We had all talked about a hidden microphone in the cells, but nobody really took it seriously. Lola had said that Margret from the other group knew there were hidden microphones in the work cells! My gaze began scrutinizing all the walls, traveling down the wires of the lighting, moving out along the floor boards, sweeping the entire expanse of the huge room. Nowhere was there evidence even of a faint possibility of a hiding place for such a device. The room was sparsely furnished and offered few nooks for secluding such an object.

Later in the day, when we had a chance to discuss the incident freely away from the guards, I said, "There is no way of her knowing about the window, unless one of us has told her!" I was setting up a trap to test the reaction.

Again splotchy red appeared on Lola's pale throat. "Oh, that is silly," Lola replied. "Who's had a chance to tell her? Nobody's been out of the room. She was probably standing outside the door—she's like that. Always sneaking and slipping around to swallow what information she can."

"No, that's impossible. I looked outside the door before I climbed up on the ledge." We dismissed the subject, and Margot and I confided that we were sure someone had told Tosca. The only other possibility was a concealed microphone, and it appeared unlikely.

15

A STRANGE REQUEST

TWO DAYS AFTER the window incident I was called out of the work cell after Ingrid had returned from an hour's conference with the matron. The matron had sent for me.

I went to her office and reported. While she told me to take a seat, I tried to penetrate her blank expression to detect her real mood. She scowled as she began to speak. I was terrified of her when she was in a bad mood, and I was leery of what to expect. "I've called you here, because I have some complaints against you. First of all, can you tell me where your German Bible is?"

"Yes," I answered innocently, not understanding the ground for anger. "I loaned it to prisoner Weisswald to read before I went to Berlin." Margot had asked to borrow it for a while.

The matron's pallid cheeks flushed in crimson fury. "I don't want that to happen again! The books you have in your cell are not to be shown to the other prisoners! Now, what about your soap? Some of it is missing?"

"I gave prisoner Stern a bar, because she was complaining about constant perspiration. My soap is good for checking it," I again answered, still wondering at the matron's outrageous response. Lise had been delighted to receive a bar of American soap.

"We'll have no blackmarketing in this prison! Profiteering is forbidden. The next time you give any prisoner anything, you must receive permission from me!" Her skin glowed with anger.

"The trusty told me it was permitted to give another prisoner something when she needed it, and I was just trying to help prisoner Stern. There was no profiteering," I answered emphatically. There was no cause for her exaggerated distrust of me.

189

"In the future you will ask me before you give anything away. Is that clear?" I nodded. She hesitated, avoiding my eyes, and started again. "Another thing, prisoner, you've been trying to influence the other prisoners to the bad, against our state, saying all kinds of things against it. If it happens again you'll be punished! You'll be put in solitary confinement!"

I gasped. I had never seen the matron so explosive. "What have I said?" I demanded. "That's not the truth! Someone has lied to you!"

"We know what you've said; we have our methods of finding out just what each prisoner *really* thinks and says. . . ."

I interrupted, "But I've already told you that I think there is a prisoner who reports on us, and she doesn't tell the truth!"

"We don't need to listen to prisoners to get our information!" she stated evasively. She glared at me again, her eyes filled with violent hatred. "You've been trying to get the other prisoners to strike, and making statements about the food. You said you wouldn't give the food to your dog. I'm sure that the dogs in America have a better life than many *people* around the world."

"My statements have been distorted!" I exclaimed, fighting back an outburst of tears. "What I said about a strike was in fun, in jest. Do you think I would seriously consider striking *here?* Besides, what I said about the food was on one certain day when we had tripe for lunch. All of the other prisoners said the same. Now I don't know whether you eat tripe or not, but I don't! And I don't know of anyone who gives it to his dog, either. I do not complain any more than any other prisoner!" I attempted to defend myself against her outrageous attack.

"I have reason to believe you are the instigator of it all! We have our ways of knowing. You've been trying to influence the others against the state."

"What have I said? Just tell me, so I can give my explanation of it! I haven't said anything I would not say here in your office," I demanded again, now sobbing.

"Don't try to put on an act for me! I know what you've said!" she went on, leaving no opportunity for defense. "The other prisoners have confirmed it."

"I demand a confrontation with those who've made that claim!" I said.

"There will be no confrontation! We know what you've said. In the future, if you have any complaints bring them to me and don't discuss them in front of the others! You are dismissed."

I reported coldly, and returned to the work cell. I sat stiffly at my place and began to shiver. I could not go on working. The outburst had been violent, and I started to cry profusely. Her accusation was unjust and distorted. I knew what had happened, though.

Before I had gone to Berlin, I had spoken only with Lola in front of the other women, warning her about informing on us. I became sure that she was the informer, and when the other women were constantly being called in for criticism of petty mistakes or statements that had been twisted, I decided to defend them.

Hardly a day had passed without Lise returning from the matron's office with a tear-soaked face. It had hurt me so much because no one tried any harder than Lise. She had only one wish for remaining alive. That was to get out and get to her children. Nothing else mattered. She had become the work horse of the group, exerting her last ounce of effort to accomplish her best, even taking on the worst jobs. Lise was the living example of the old adage: "The Italian works in order to live, but the German lives in order to work!" Lise was one of those live-in-order-to-work Germans to an extreme degree. Her only reward was constant criticism.

The same was true of Ingrid, who had returned on several occasions from the matron's office, also pouring her heart out. The criticism had completely destroyed the very last trace of her self-confidence, and she had become convinced that she was nothing but a blundering idiot.

Margot had been denounced and slandered. She already stood on the matron's black list. Even the guards detested Margot. They, too, had come in contact with Lola's poisonous tongue.

And what about Lola? She had never been called on the carpet for anything. She had only received verbal love pats of praise from the strict matron. In fact, the matron had relieved Ingrid of the responsibility for the group as eldest and had placed Lola in charge.

Now I was on the matron's black list. Lola had skillfully worked the matron into her paw. She prided herself on the fact that she was from a "worker's family" and continually played that up with the matron, telling her that she was eager to learn about the "teachings of the state." The matron's words to me had been "some of the prisoners want to learn more about the teachings of our state, but you are influencing them against them!" So that was it. Lola was the biggest hypocrite, but she was so adept at being one that the matron protected her blindly. Or, there was one other possibility—she was an informer planted by the prison officials!

The matron's angry outburst had been too much for my frayed nerves. I finally asked the guard for permission to return to my cell and lie down. I was in no condition to work. I also requested to report to the prison's liaison officer between the Security Police and the Vopos. I had spoken to him a couple of times already, and perhaps I would be able to bring my complaint to him!

I lay across the bed, furious with the hopeless injustice of the matter. Lola had created a hell in the prison. Where the corroding evil of lies reigned—where distrust entered through a back door and walled in each individual—where malicious pettiness ate away like a cankerous sore, the realization that this primitive woman had us all in her twisted clutch made me react violently.

A guard stood in the doorway. *"Kommen Sie Mit, Strafgefangene!"*

I arose from the bed and followed her down the stairs to the medical station. I entered and looked into the deep brown eyes of the doctor who was sitting behind a small desk that also served as a medicine cabinet.

"Take a seat," he said. "What's the matter?" He placed his hand gently on my shoulder, attempting a tender consolation. I was still shaken up from the matron's vehement injustice.

I darted a quick glance at the cold stare of the matron, who stood in the doorway and the curious scrutiny of the strange policeman who leaned against the wall. "I can't stand it here anymore!" I would have revealed the real cause had I not felt the matron would have made me out a liar to defend herself.

"Here, drink this," the doctor handed me a dark liquid. "It's a sedative. I want to get your medical history and make a blood test." This was not the same doctor who had examined me on entering the penitentiary. The first doctor had been very impersonal, and had made a thorough examination in a couple of seconds. If I had not been so outraged, I would have become dizzy, for a needle in the bend of my arm always made me squeamish. I ventured to ask the friendly doctor for some eye drops. The poor lighting and the concentration on the intricate work had inflamed my eyes and made it almost unbearable for me to wear my contact lenses.

"What's the matter with your eyes?" He lifted my chin in his hands and examined my eyelids.

"I wear contact lenses, and the strain from the work, the lighting, and the dust have irritated my eyes."

"How long do you wear them each day?" he asked with amazement.

"All day," I answered.

"What? That's terrible for your eyes! I know, because my father has had very bad experience with them. You can wear them an hour or two, but not all day!"

"I've had them for five years now, and I haven't had any trouble with them," I stated.

"Well, as long as you're with us, you shouldn't wear them at all. We are responsible for your health. I know cases of stars wearing them for an hour or two on the set, but all day. . . ."

"I'll take the responsibility," I argued, growing frightened that he would take them away from me.

"Here, we are responsible for you, especially in case anything happens. I don't think you should wear them at all!"

"I'll sign a statement that I assume the responsibility for them. Besides, there are various scientific opinions about their use." This time I was angry that he dared to forbid their use.

"I *know* that they are bad for your eyes!" He was insulted that I challenged his knowledge of science. "Well, if you insist on wearing them, I'll give you some eye drops until we can arrange for a visit to the eye doctor. Then the doctor can determine whether it is advisable to wear them!" he concluded, still perturbed that I had disagreed with him.

Later I was shocked to learn that he was a prisoner himself. He had said "we" have a concern for you, "we" are responsible for your welfare. He was a trusty, a lifer, and also an informer—the place was crawling with them!

I was brooding over the events of the afternoon, when I was told to report to the liaison officer downstairs. We had named him Max, and I approached the meeting with dread, for if the matron had gotten to him before I had, he was sure to have a closed mind.

Max was gruff and abrupt and tact was foreign to him. Everything about him was medium—his height, weight, stature, and his tone. One characteristic stood out on the otherwise plain man; he had a terrible scar across the right side of his face that twisted his mouth upward and caused him to speak strangely. He was noted for being more generous than the Vopos, since he was from the Security Police and assigned to Bautzen II with the rank of first lieutenant. Later old Max became a captain. He seldom addressed a prisoner with the title of "prisoner" before his name, as the policewomen did. He usually said "Fräulein" or nothing at all.

I entered Max's office and he curtly offered me the chair across from him. He usually asked me how I was getting along, but this time he only frowned and waited for me to start speaking. Max had difficulty in communicating, and he left the prisoner to bear the brunt of the conversation. My first meeting with him had alarmed me. In one of his embarrassed pauses, he had not known what to say, and he finally came out with "I guess you know you've ruined your life!" He had been referring to the imprisonment, and although I knew it was untrue, it struck me a harsh blow. I had retreated to my cell with a desperate flood of tears. Again the thought of four years' time came crashing down on me.

"I have requested to speak to you because I feel there is a problem in the women's section that needs discussing. The last time I spoke to you about it I implied that a woman prisoner was making life unbearable for the women's section by reporting false stories to Frau Meister. You told me to come to you if we couldn't solve it among ourselves."

He hardly gave me time to finish and jumped into an attack. "Prisoner Battle, we are very displeased with your behavior. Frau Meister told me that the other prisoners have said you were trying to influence them against our state, saying things about the war in Vietnam, trying to incite the prisoners to strike. Now we are very displeased. You must not forget where you are! This is no place to make propaganda for the western world, and we shall not stand for it!" He growled at me in ugly tones.

"I have already told you that there is a prisoner who is slandering all of us! It hasn't happened only to me, but to prisoner Weisswald, too! It is a preposterous lie that I tried to stir up a strike. I made a statement once in jest about striking! All of my remarks have been distorted! The atmosphere is unbearable! If I wasn't slandered by a prisoner, as the matron claimed, then it must have been a hidden microphone! And my statements have been taken out of context and distorted!" I exclaimed. After I observed his biased, thundering discharge, I knew he had closed the door to my side of the whole matter.

"What? We are not in *America!* We don't have to hide microphones in our prison cells to know how prisoners think or talk. We don't need to use the fascist tactics of your country!" He tore into me, hurling stormy insults.

"How do you know?" I practically screamed back. "Have you ever been in America? I am sick and tired of all these statements about America from people who have never been there. I think the best thing for me is to go into solitary confinement. At least, I have my peace from liars!"

"Well, you insulted me about our state, implying that there are hidden microphones. No, we have nothing against it if a prisoner *wants* to go into solitary confinement."

"What else should I think when Frau Meister denied that her information is from prisoners and quoted something I've said in the work cell? Besides, prisoner Baumgarten said that one of the prisoners stated that the work cells were tapped. The idea did not originate with me!"

"Hmmmmm." He scowled, doubting the truth of my words. It was useless to argue with him. He had already been prejudiced by the matron and was unwilling to listen to me. I was convinced that solitary confinement was the only solution to the dilemma of the work cell.

"Yes, I'll tell Frau Meister that from tomorrow you will be in solitary confinement." He lifted the phone receiver to inform the guards that I was returning. He dismissed me with irate brusqueness.

I trudged up the steps. They would never believe me. They could never believe me, when my word went against theirs. I was an American. I was convinced that Lola was a venomous spider who had caught the whole outfit in her web. Maybe she was even planted to inform the officials about the prisoners. It was certain that I would be better off in solitude than in an atmosphere of acute distrust and tormenting fear, constantly worrying that every word I uttered would be twisted, distorted, and reported. I was unable to cope with all the hate I encountered in their reproaches, and the fiery clashes made me ill. I wanted no trace of ill will, and they were sure to leave me alone if I were by myself. Yes, it was a strange request, but it was the most peaceful solution if . . . if I really had the strength to stick it out.

The guard stood waiting at the bars that closed off our section. She did not lead me to the work cell, but took me back to my cell. I threw myself across the bed and reflected on the new "adventure" that awaited me. In the evening when we all got our water from the faucet, I hurriedly whispered to Margot, "Tomorrow I'm going into solitary. Watch out for Lola! She's slandered me, too!"

Those were my last words with the group before I withdrew into my voluntary isolation. I thought about my attorney's words. If I can't even stand it an hour in my hotel room by myself, how would I be able to take months of it? Even years? Four years? Alone!

16

TO WALK ALONE

ANEAS, THE SLENDER, self-confident young guard stood at the door of my cell. She was wearing her usual scoffing smile which she tempered with a distant friendliness. I was amused to observe that her eyes always twinkled with a roguish gleam, especially when she flitted about and flirted with the policemen. She spoke to me in a cocky manner, "Pack your things together. . . ." She hesitated, eyeing me closely. She had spoken the cue for a release—it raced through my mind. She closed the cell door. My heart pounded. I crammed all my belongings into the shopping net in record time. Every prisoner lived to hear those words—"pack your things together!"

The cell door flew open. Aneas fought to suppress a grin. "You are moving downstairs," she said. Disappointment overwhelmed me, but I was too proud to show her that I had fallen for her trick.

"All right," I said, as if I had been expecting her conclusion. I left the work cell and returned with her to my cell.

"The house is being renovated," she explained. "You will have to put up with living and working in the same cell, but the renovation work shouldn't take too long. Dump everything into a blanket. You'll take cell number seven downstairs."

I began piling everything into the blanket. Cell 7—that was Lola's cell. Where was she going? There were not enough cells for everyone. Someone would have to double up. That, of course, would be Ingrid and Lola, because no other two prisoners could tolerate each other.

The new cell was a replica of the old one, only smaller. I decided that I preferred living upstairs, since downstairs the guard station was just two doors away from me. I could not dare so much as above, because I was unable to hear the guards approaching. As I hung my hand towels on the rack beneath the mirror, I noticed a box lid on the floor next to the toilet. "Lola left her polishing rag," I thought. There were old newspapers stacked under it. From some unknown motivation I reached down and picked up the rag. I noticed that Lola had used the lid as a trash basket and had failed to empty it. Discovering a crumpled paper wad, I took it in my hand. I was unaccustomed to rummaging in other people's trash, but something prompted me to explore. I unfolded the paper.

Lola had boasted that she was writing a book, and for that reason had often asked the matron for paper. I assumed that it must be a discarded page, and I began reading curiously.

"Report: I would like to report that the prisoner Winter [that was Helga!] informed the group that while she was an employee of the Ministry of State Security. . . ." There was no more. But I could guess the rest! It was a report. I had evidence that she was an informer! Oh, that was the proof I needed.

"The woman is an absolute demon!" I thought. She even had the markings and features of one: long, fiery red hair, a satanic gleam in her diabolically slanted eyes. When she had worn her hair pulled back one day, I had noticed the large pointed ears, and if it had not been for the long mane, she would have passed for any medieval painting of the devil! Her approach had always been sugar-coated with openness, sincerity, and trust. She had told Margot, as she had me, in the first few days, "When it all gets to be too much for you, you can confide in me. I would be careful what I said in front of the other girls, though. Word has a way of getting back to the wrong people."

Lola had tried to play us all against each other. She had attempted to strike up a cajoling friendship with Margot, but in Margot's absence, she spread hateful rumors about her. She was so sly and cunning, she could slip out of any snare with an explanation that she had been misunderstood. Besides, she gloated in unconditional confidence that the matron was on her side! Although I had the proof against her foul play, I did not know what to do with it. If it was only a relationship between the matron and Lola, the higher authorities would take action against it, but if she was planted to get information, it would all backfire against me. I would wait. I would hide the paper on my body, and save it until the time was right.

Poor Helga. She was the very last one who needed to be denounced. She had already served almost six years of a life sentence! How could anyone be so evil? Helga had entered prison, a slender young lady of twenty-six, who was about to be married. After six hard years of life in prison, living on a diet of too much bread and water, she had become bloated, fat, and unattractive. Her yellow skin revealed large, open pores, but her disposition was always pleasant and accommodating. She was cooperative, but too loose with her tongue. *Knast Klatsch*—jail gossip. She had rich resources in the prison grapevine and knew more about prison history than the guards. She was a real knastologist!

She had a solution for any problem prison existence afforded. It was from Helga that I learned how to polish the yellow canvas stripes on my skirt with sandstone, and she informed me that the stone was also good to polish the nails with. In her early prison days, it had been her only toothpaste. The only soap had been curd soap. She practically ran the whole show in Bautzen, because all the policewomen were too lazy and comfortable to do it themselves. Even the matron turned to Helga when she needed to find things in the house. Helga also had inside information on all the guards and the men prisoners. Where or how she got it remained veiled in mystery.

My first impression of Helga had been a negative one, for she had given a talk with slides in the culture room—one of the kind I had feared. Prisoners had the opportunity to do special projects to exhibit their willingness to cooperate and their change in attitude. Helga had given her cultural talk on Dresden, which was not too far from the prison. The emphasis of the slides was on the old prewar city with its art treasures. She concluded it politically, though, with pictures of British and American bombing raids on the city and their aftermath. They were the "terror" bombings, senseless raids, aimed at destroying the Soviet Zone, and preventing socialism from flourishing.

It was the first encounter with that brand of propaganda for me, and it was shortly after I had arrived at Bautzen. I had exploded afterwards in front of the women of my group. I was almost certain that Helga even withheld some of the pictures when she staged the showing for our group, because she knew I was an American. She had shown them to the other group of women first, and the slides were stacked in neat order on the table. When our group saw them, she carefully removed some of the last ones.

Afterwards, I was fuming. I poured out my anger against the Germans. "You Germans will sell your souls to save your necks! You don't care who comes along, you just hypocritically duck your tail and obey. Now, you are trying to claim that bombings that occurred against Hitler were unjust. Do you know how many English cities were destroyed? Do you know how many Jews were murdered? What about the Poles, the Czechs, all the Russians who were murdered by one man's madness? And you make the claim that the bombing of Dresden was unjust! Oh, I have never heard such arrogance, such self-righteousness, such a lack of humility on the part of a people who have no right! Twisting, distorting, perverting, you are trying to place the blame on the others!" My strong words had been pronounced in the intimacy of the circle of women. Perhaps that was the reason I was denounced later. Helga had not heard my remarks about her talk, but they were sure to have returned to her in time. I was furious, though, that a prisoner was playing their game!

One day Helga disappeared from the prison. I was seized with panic. Lola was appointed temporary trusty, and that meant she was responsible for me and my work again. Helga was due to return, because all her personal belongings were left in the cell, but when that would be, no one could say.

Exactly as I had expected, I was required to do the very thing Lola knew I hated most—mount the screws! She knew that my output was lowest with screws, and she also satisfied her sadistic streak in making me do what I liked least. I couldn't complain to the guards, because Lola would have said that the screws were needed for production, even though I knew they were not.

When I heard that I was compelled to make the screws, I feigned illness, something I had never done in my life. I took on intense cramps, too severe to permit me to work, and nausea. Normally, the guards would have waited a day or so before calling in a doctor; that was their usual way of taking care of any problem. I assured Aneas that I could get along without a doctor, I only needed to lie down. No, she sent for the matron, who felt it was an absolute necessity to call in the doctor. She was convinced that I was suffering from acute appendicitis! I tried to talk the women out of calling the doctor, and my protests only strengthened their conviction that I was seriously ill. I was unable to succeed, and the doctor arrived an hour later.

It was *der Piepse,* the prisoner-doctor. I was lying on the bed when he entered the cell. He came over to the bed with a strange gleam in his eyes. Indeed his eyes were burning with lust as I looked into them. He frightened me. I glanced at the door. I was grateful that Aneas stood there in supervision. *Der Piepse* was a lifer, and I knew he had been locked up a long time. Poor man.

After a brief examination I convinced him that I was already familiar with the symptoms, and I was sure it was nothing serious. My clever pretense had been in vain, only postponing my ordeal with the screws, because I had to tackle them on Monday morning.

I suffered silently for two days, but I examined the other women's work as it was placed outside in the evening. I was the only one who had to assemble the screws! I knew they were not needed. Still the guards would not have believed me if I had asserted that charge. Finally, on the third day, I threw a violent fit.

"I'm going crazy! I can't stand it any more! I just can't go on!" I broke down in a rage of sobs. I had reached my limit, but the fit had a purpose.

"What's the matter?" the matron demanded, upset at my reaction.

"I'll go crazy if I have to sit here hours on end, putting these washers on the screws! It isn't work for a human being! Especially, alone, having to count all these screws! I can't touch another screw!"

The matron stared solemnly for a minute and then replied, "Since you have to work by yourself, you are permitted to make the double contacts all the time. That is, when the other material isn't urgently needed. Lie down a few minutes, and calm down."

The matron had made her first concession to me. The work of assembling the double contacts was more varied, and counting by pieces was unnecessary. They were arranged on a board, and I only had to keep track of the number of boards and multiply at the end of the day. The victory over Lola was mine. But I hated the way I had been forced to go about it. However, these women knew no reasoning. I began to suffer from the rigors of solitary confinement. The same work, day after day. Alone, it became tedious. It was the worst kind of slavery, for the slavery to machines, methods, or routines was worse than the bondage to human beings. One could protest, rise up and rebel, or retreat in self-pity when one was doomed to servitude to man. But, bound to line-production type of slavery, one was forced to face a cold, apathetic, indifferent system. I felt a deep sympathy with all those workers who were condemned to a life on the assembly line. They were forced to become machines, too, mechanized in the process of production. I began to loathe my work—I hated being a machine, especially a dead cog in the depersonalized apparatus of Communism.

One afternoon I had a great surprise. A package from America!

The guard on duty, Inge we called her, was the simplest and sweetest of all. She was always correct, but natural and sincere. She did not strike me as being a policewoman. She was completely feminine in her manner, and certainly the most naïve of all the guards.

When she dropped my package on the table across from my cell, she peeled away the wrappings carefully and fingered each object before passing it on to me. She had to determine whether any forbidden articles were present. Not knowing American products, and not wanting to show her ignorance, she handed me all the contents of the package. She hesitated when she came to the five or six paperback books that were included. "Books aren't generally allowed," she deliberated aloud, "but I think technical or school books are permitted."

"Oh yes, these are all technical books for my studies," I quickly asserted, fearing she would not allow me to have them. If the matron had been on duty, she would have snatched them away and that would have been my last sight of them. She had even made me leave the magazines my father had brought in the personal effects. The books were all in English, a fact which made my keeping them even more questionable. I was willing to fight it out for them, though.

The biggest surprise, however, was the discovery of a plastic bottle of vitamin pills. They were strictly *verboten,* but Inge had not detected the container's contents.

I took my newly acquired possessions into my cell and began to examine them piece by piece. My books were gold mines that I would fight to defend. I was determined, but I knew that when the matron discovered them, there would be real *Krach*—a quarrel!

I examined the food—peanut butter, what I had craved most in my long imprisonment; some chocolate bars; miniature boxes of raisins, the health food I had requested; a small glass of instant coffee, which was really the most important, for my coffee hour was the most cherished time; some Fig Newtons, lotion, shampoo, soap. I was rich! And a small bottle of grape juice with the bread of oblation, which were to provide my Eucharist on Sunday morning.

Every Sunday I set aside some time for my own religious services, commemorating with Christians everywhere in the world the observance of the Lord's Day. Although I was isolated, it became meaningful for me to participate in a spiritual community. Then I knew I was not alone.

I was troubled with a new problem. Where was I to hide my vitamins that Inge had failed to detect? I had managed to pull the wool over the guards' eyes with the bottle of Sandorn juice, but fear of being discovered had finally driven me to drinking most of the bottle at once. I had been too new at the prison game at the time. So, I had not really solved my problem. But it would be easier with the vitamins, because they did not take up so much space.

Behind the toilet was a small niche, where the metal was fused to the wall. I folded some old newspapers together and crammed the bundle into the hole. I observed it from all sides. No, it was not visible, but if a guard did any serious examination of the cell, she was sure to come across it. I could probably count on the guards' avoidance of the toilet area. They never got near it, for they hated it even more than the prisoners. Besides, they became lax in their controls after a prisoner had been there so long. . . . It would be a safe place.

I emptied the contents of the plastic container into a Nivea can which had contained my bobby pins, dumping the pins into a leather pouch. I wrapped the tin in newspaper and tucked it away in the dark niche behind the toilet. I would defend the vitamins as I would the books. They were my only hope to rescue my health from the poor diet. I calculated: a hundred tablets; that is about a third of a year. Yes, it would make a great difference to my health! I anticipated the matron's return with trepidation, but at least, for the weekend, I could enjoy the excesses of prison prosperity with my food, vitamins, and books.

On Monday morning I was deeply engrossed in trying to assemble the relay contacts when I heard someone softly skulking along the corridor and unlocking my cell door. Obviously, "they" did not want me to hear. I stopped my work and listened. The books! Or my vitamins! I waited, and I heard the door to my cabinet bang shut. Then the cell door closed just as softly as it had opened, the heavy key revolving in the lock.

The blood rushed to my face. If they took my books, what could I do? I would have to wait until lunchtime to examine my cabinet and find out whether they were missing. When noon finally came, I rushed to my cell after I had filled my bowl with soup and headed straight for the cabinet. The books were gone! Then I sprang to the hiding place of my vitamins. They were still there, carefully concealed in their newspaper wrap. I hardly swallowed a bite of lunch for worrying about the next move. Tosca was on duty, and she was the least lenient. However, it had probably been the matron who had required her to remove them.

When Tosca unlocked my cell for me to return to work, she was scowling but she said nothing about my books. Almost immediately I announced, "I would like to report to the director of the prison." I had spoken deliberately, with an assurance of victory. Fear clouded her face and she grimaced, as she was in the habit of doing—a stern expression of distrust and authority.

"I'll tell the Meisterin!" she said. That was all, but I sensed an easy victory.

Back at work I began to fear discovery of my vitamins. It weighed on me, for if they found me breaking the rules, my precious books were jeopardized. Even if they granted permission for the books and the forbidden fruit was detected later on, I would receive some punishment. If I could only make it through the day without being caught, I would dig up another hiding place. Yes, I knew. I would carry them around with me. They were unusually large, being of the more potent kind.

It occurred to me that the East Germans had never seen vitamin pills before, because East Germany was not yet manufacturing them. Good. I would wrap them in a plastic bag, letting them pass for candy-coated nuts. I contemplated whether they should become candy or bath pellets, and I decided on the former. After all, I had eaten candy-coated almonds that were very similar in size and shape. There was no way of *proving* them to be anything else—unless, of course, a curious guard bit into one of them. That would be a tragedy! It was not unlikely, either, because American products had an attraction that aroused the curiosity of the East German women. One day they might come across the idea and try one out. I would risk it, though, and if I kept them with me at all times, they would not have the opportunity to try them.

In the afternoon when I returned to my cell, Tosca informed me that I would be allowed to keep my books, but on one condition. "You can keep them, but if you show them to anyone else, they will be taken away!"

"Whom could I show them to?" I asked. "I'm in solitary confinement."

So that case was closed. I was delighted to spend long, free hours tasting new tidbits of ideas in my own language.

The days ticked by with the same routine. Then they became weeks. A month. Two months. Finally I was lulled into a state of apathy, my greatest enemy. I found my life in prison to be a pendulum where one stroke swung between life and death. Between the strokes was a state of nullity—the nonexistence of terrible apathy. It was worse than despair. Despair meant that life was clinging to its last thread, suffering its most intense pain, abandoning its ultimate hope, only to be quickened and revived when it survived. Apathy was an unconditional nothing. One neither felt nor cared. It was the living death, being too dead to die. No suffering. No joy. Nothing. I knew that it was an artificial state, a sort of protective shell to keep me from the pangs of suffering. It was also because of the removal of all outer stimuli, the absence of people, the monotony of routine! Life went on and on and on. A ceaseless, immutable flow.

At first, I had traveled the inward roads, but they were now barricaded and I rested in a void, a bottomless vacuum. I continued my duties by rote, as if I were a human being, but not experiencing myself as one. An absolute emptiness possessed me and living or dying were matters of indifference. Even to approach a choice or a decision between the two was no matter of concern.

In my isolation my senses became keenly aware of their surroundings. At noon, long before lunch had been distributed, I could sniff out its content. I knew when the delivery trucks appeared, because I could hear them unloading under my window.

In isolation the senses are called upon to exercise their full powers, and in the absence of other distractions, such as people, they could have their full play. Besides musty smells of the old building, my nose had to put up with the toilet stench and cooking cabbage at noontime. Occasionally, I could inhale some scent of alcohol from the medical station, but that was rare.

It was my sense of hearing, though, that found the greatest opportunity to be called to utilization. I could paint myself a vivid picture of prison life from the sounds that floated into my lonely cell. After a while, I could even establish which prisoner was where, just from listening to the clanking keys and the unlocking of cell doors. I always knew when the matron arrived in the morning, because she had a characteristically heavy footstep, and unlocked her office with a certain twist of the key. I recognized which guards were on duty, long before they unlocked the cell, from their movements, or the way they peered into the peephole, or how often they came to check on me.

I ventured to climb up on my bed to peek out the window when I knew no guards were around. The sounds from the court in the evening always invited exploration. Men's boisterous voices shouted greetings across the yard; occasionally, a bottle was thrown from a cell window onto the concrete surface of the court, crashing into smithereens, but that usually occurred in the early hours of the morning. Most of all, I loved to hear the sad strains of music in the fading twilight—the melancholic harmonica, the chords of men's voices, and the lonely guitar—all telling the same story.

Every evening after supper the sonorous strains floated through my window from a distant cell. These expressions of suffering always filled me with a sense of solidarity. "Oh, guitar, we are brothers! I come from across the Atlantic. But I am here, too. Crying with you!"

The August sun was torrid. As I circled in my outdoor cell, my eye caught the presence of a male prisoner in the corner window. The window was tucked away out of the range of the huge watchtower, which stood hovering over the circle that radiated triangular cells. The centers of the triangles were filled with lush green lawns; shrubbery had been planted, with scattered carnations, asters, and chrysanthemums around the sand walkways.

Upper stories of neighboring houses and sounds of traffic and passers-by on the street reminded me that life went on—just over a wall. Captivity and freedom were divided by a layer of concrete; although the web of wire that fringed the wall was reduced to single strands, an electrically charged wire ran the extension of the wall. It warned anyone who might get impatient to leave his damnation and risk freedom on his own terms.

Now a young man stood in the open window and watched me with a sad sense of separation. We had exchanged glances almost daily for weeks, and even though he was able to signal me messages with his hands, I could only answer with a slight nod or with my eyes, for the guard in the watchtower could observe me. The prisoner appeared to be in his middle twenties, and two dark, expressive eyes observed me from his handsome face.

Yes, he reminded me of Sammy, and a passionate urge for life welled up in me. Sammy, so many hours wondering about you. . . . Where are you now? . . . Will we ever see each other again? . . . West Berlin, my second home. . . . Two and a half blissful years on a defended island of freedom. . . . Freedom, life! *Kudamm,* all aglow with the plush coffeehouses and the glaring lights of western "civilization," the sprawling Free University and the kids in the dorm in Gelfertstrasse, all the eager young faces of my English pupils in the old brick *Menzelschule,* which protruded itself as an ugly sore spot in the ultramodern *Hansaviertel,* and the fresh, free air of West Berlin and the exuberant optimism and impudent humor of its burghers. . . .

I stopped in the corner of the triangle, in full range of the window, to do my required round of gymnastics. Every time I rose from touching my toes, my eyes met the young man's, which smiled with sympathy and longing. When he was sure the guard in the tower was looking away, he took his chin and tilted his head backward. I answered with a nod. I knew what he meant: "Chin up!"

I had been staring at the ground and singing to myself:

When you walk through a storm, keep your chin up high,
And don't be afraid of the dark.
At the end of the storm is a golden sky,
And the sweet silver song of a lark.
Walk on, through the wind! Walk on, through the rain!
Though your dreams be tossed and blown.
Walk on, walk on, with hope in your heart,
And you'll never walk alone.
You'll never walk alone!

His encouraging gesture was the one word no one else could have spoken.

September was approaching. All my hopes hung on September. I knew that I had counted too much on attaining a release by then, but my inner state reflected a pause of anticipation. I was afraid to hope, and yet, more afraid not to hope. My whole future hung on my freedom at that time. At least, I thought it did. Anticipating an earlier release, I had set a date for it, and it would be crucial if it did not occur by that time.

September came. September went. And with it traveled the tepid days and warm optimism of summer. All my hopes withered and fell dead to the ground like the leaves of autumn. I was still behind bars.

I received an autumn letter from my family, telling me that all attempts at achieving an earlier release had failed—a plea for clemency had been refused. That was the cold voice of doom for me. I knew that I was there to stay. Oh, perhaps not for four years, but for a long, long time. Even two years would be too long! I could not last that long, I was certain. If they had allowed me my spiritual outlet or even visit with a chaplain, I could have made it over the hump, but even after my request, I was refused. They had no provision for it.

Unable to find succor in myself or any other person, once more my thoughts turned to self-destruction. The passionate urge for life was separated from a desire for death only by a thin membrane. Indeed, when life was blocked from its natural expression, it sought to destroy itself. Thus I lost myself in obsessive thoughts of suicide, and the more I did, the less I could lift my eyes toward heaven.

A day did not pass without my contemplating the final decision of self-destruction. The knife the trusty had given me for my work I kept hidden in my cabinet. Sometimes I removed it, fingered it, and tested its sharpness on my wrists. Or I conceived other ways—hanging from the bars on my window, throwing myself down the flight of stairs, or swallowing a detergent solution. Daily I engaged in a dialogue between life and death, which became a vicious circle of coldblooded obsessive thoughts.

I sat down and took up my pen. I would write, for I had to confide my state in someone. I began a letter to my parents.

The blackest night of my soul has broken through! The dark clouds of my spirit have gathered, as the heavy, black clouds before the storm! I am obsessed by thoughts of self-destruction, and every day I conduct a dialogue between life and death. Thus far, life is the victor. Nevertheless, I continue to ponder the words of the American patriot,

"Give me liberty or give me death!" That's my present plea! There is so much life in me that has to be stifled, choked, and suppressed, shut off from the world in the gloom of a living tomb. That is death itself. Everything in me cries for freedom—my temperament and my task in life, to give of myself.

Even the few minutes of fresh air I can drink in each day, my brief retreat in nature, impresses me with my captivity. I regard the birds, and I cannot help being envious of them. They can fly where they choose—soaring above walls, or just sit in the sunshine and enjoy an afternoon's coffee. Why can't I, too?

Today is Sunday. I am reminded of the Hungarian folk song, "Lonely Sunday." The song is said to be the cause of a suicide. No, I don't want to die! Sunday is also a day of resurrection, of hope, of new life! I want to live!

No, the letter would never get out—never get out of that prison! Nevertheless, I stuck it into the matron's box.

BOOK III

17

A JOURNEY INWARD

I SAT UP IN BED. It must have been after midnight, and the mournful howling of a hound had roused me. In an instant my mind flashed back to my childhood in Memphis. My cousin's superstitious grandmother had told me that when a hound bayed at the moon, someone was dying. An icy shudder rattled my spine. Death! Then I recalled Ingrid's obsessive fear of dying. Black ravens, flapping outside her window had awakened her. I listened for a while and discovered that it was the pitiful wailing of a man, the cries of some male prisoner sounding through the night.

"Help me! Help me! Somebody please help me!"

The dirge echoed momentarily, waned, and died. There was something about a man's cries that ripped into my heart. One expected to hear a woman weeping, but to listen to the helplessness of a man. . . . No! I had arrived at the end station of life.

Hell had taken on a new meaning! The total absence of human contact, the complete abandonment to oneself, and the slavish monotony of life in solitude were its torturing pangs.

I was shocked one afternoon when I was allowed to view a television program about the political education of children. All of the panelists felt that the first grade of school was the place to begin. A mother pointed out that she had been surprised when her six-year-old son came home from school one day and was frightened to learn that visitation permits had been issued to West Berliners to come and visit their relatives in the East. "Now all the bad people can come over here!" he said, fearfully. His teacher had told him that the Wall had been built to keep all the bad people out of the country! Then, I was enlightened with regard to the cold war.

213

Yes, I engaged in a struggle on the front lines of the battlefield in a war that was fought daily. Untruth. Unreason. Hatred. Hostility. I encountered them ceaselessly in my combat with newspapers, television, and books. They were the hidden persuaders that sought to win victory through brainwashing. I involved myself in the battle, for to ignore them would be to ignore the spirit and temper of the times that had brought them there. This evil spirit had oozed its way into people's consciousness, and unless someone accepted the challenge to confront it and combat it, it had all the promise of victory. So, I read the newspapers, watched the newscasts, and read novels that were designed to separate man from man.

I recalled that in one discussion the Weasel had informed me, "Our people have learned from Hitler that whoever controls the press, controls the people."

That was the justification for controlling the press—manipulating the masses into political involvement, dedicating them to the doctrine of the state. I had challenged the lack of the freedom of the press in my talk with the Weasel, and his only explanation was that Hitler had done the same.

The politicians also incorporated all the expressions of democracy into their through-the-looking-glass vocabulary, cleverly cloaking them with new meaning. "Democracy" meant the dictatorship of the proletariat—the farmers and workers. "Freedom" was economic independence—the freedom from exploitation and starvation and social security. "Justice" was the punishment of the "enemies" of the state who were always guilty and never proved innocent. But the people were reassured that justice, democracy, and freedom reigned, and the poor peasants swallowed the story.

Gradually, I discovered that the people's picture of the American government was even more distorted than the American people's picture of the Russian government. Many of the stereotypes, oversimplifications, and prejudices were the same, but blown up to enormous proportions. And I had to suffer because of their prejudice. They could not look at me and see a live person, but could see only an ugly image that had been superimposed on their brains. Imperialist, capitalist, exploiter—that was equivalent to "American." I was an enemy!

It was Sunday. Another lonely Sunday. I sat staring at the floor with my bent elbows resting on the wooden table. My eyes traveled upward to the open window. The view was obstructed by an outside blind, which was a panel of opaque glass. It was set at an angle and enabled a fragment of sky to peek in. *Himmel* in German meant both "sky" and "heaven." As I drank in the scene, I was struck with a realization. Yes! From outside my cell, a "touch of heaven" reached in, like a long finger of light.

Here, where a naked existence was forced on me; here, where all my possessions had been removed; here, into the loneliness and austerity of a prison cell, a fragment of sky, a "touch of heaven" reached in, penetrating the obscurity with a promise. As I reflected upon the ray of light that entered, it became a stream, swelled up into an ocean, and flooded my whole being. I was swallowed up and absorbed by a deep and encompassing insight. A thrilling discovery.

Its nature was *love!* Filled with an overflowing sensation, I perceived all the mystery of a paradox. All other subjects of concern were cleared away. I was absolutely free! Oh, my God, this love is perfect freedom. I am free to love! Yes, even to *love my enemy,* for in the presence of this love, no man is an enemy. Oh, my God, You are *alive!* You are *real!* Not merely a mental abstraction, nor a figment of my wishes, nor of my imagination, but—a power!

Love your enemy. It is possible! In the genuine expression of this love there is a power of understanding the other, an openness to a dialogue, a sincerity which breaks through all prejudices. And yet, it holds all the terrible mystery of a paradox. In the dark, austere, and grim reality of stone walls and iron bars, love could be born! The amazing revelation gave meaning to my immediate suffering.

Its intensity waned and I was challenged by another chain of probing thoughts. Had I been wrong in making my judgment to commit a crime, to get involved in helping someone escape?

It was certain that what I stood for and believed in when I made my judgment was right—but was the judgment itself right? Not just legally, but morally? I claimed to have been seriously interested in the approach of reconciliation between the two Germanys. Indeed, in peace. Had I acted against my concern? Peaceful and reconciliatory solutions to problems can only be effected when one works within the framework of laws.

I had violated a law. No matter how morally wrong that law might be, easing of tension and increase of understanding could not be attained by my judgment. Or could they? Could God have taken a poor judgment on my part and now be in the process of molding it into a good one? Only because of and through my imprisonment could I personally engage in a dialogue with these people. Just sensing this possibility filled me with a magnificent hope and a sense of responsibility.

My way would be a new way—the way of the people, through the people, to the people—to their hearts! Yes, the real people of any country can be spoken to. Time . . . patience . . . removal of prejudices . . . dialogue . . . a real sense of mission. I could *become* all of the things I wanted to say to these people, although it was forbidden to say them. I could attempt to translate a new way, the way of "love your enemy," into my whole person, into my encounter with them.

Another realization struck me. Perhaps Communism with its domination of a third of the world was God's judgment pronounced on history—pronounced on His people who had turned away from Him, neglecting their responsibilities. A disobedient people who had failed to love Him, and who had failed to love their neighbors, much less their enemies. Active love just could not exploit others, nor remain silent and inert when much of the world was dying of starvation. Yes, it was God's judgment spoken on the Apostate Church, which had turned to disobedience.

Communism was seeking much of what the church had turned away from. The early church had pooled its resources, establishing the first "socialistic society." Jesus himself had broken through all class barriers of His day. He was the champion of the little man. The very least in the world, including all the outcasts and rejected of society, received His boundless compassion and became first in the kingdom. Jesus, the King, had been the servant of man.

I trembled at the anticipation of the new world that would result if Christians really believed, really took their responsibility of *here* and *now* —*this life on earth*—in faith. Once Christians began, the way was paved for a new revolution!

And yet, I was just as guilty as all the rest. Four years was a judgment on my life. It corresponded to the time I had spent abroad. Away from the dictates of conformity to the American scene and from the protection of the nest, I had been forced to examine, evaluate, and exercise new decisions. Many had been wrong ones. Often the maturity I thought I possessed slipped away when the restraints society had imposed were removed. Yes. The four-year punishment struck me as a judgment on the past four years of my life. The same length of time I had stopped walking in faith and had wandered away rebelliously. The removal of four years of freedom I had abused or squandered. I asked myself, "Providence's punishment? Divine discipline? A magnificent mission? Or is it all of these?"

I would begin anew, acting from different motives. Morality, responsibility, my own personal freedom had to originate from within, not from without, as from fear of authority or criticism. That was the only way I could become genuine and be able to give anything to others, the role I had singled out as my own mission in life.

I picked up my German Bible, and it fell open to the second letter of Timothy.

"That's strange," I puzzled, "I've never noticed this underlining before."

Parts of the chapter were underscored in red. I began reading verse 8, the first underlined part:

"Do not be ashamed then of testifying to our Lord, nor of me his prisoner, but take your share of suffering for the gospel in the power of God. . . ."

Those words were written to me, the message was for me. The Bible had been brought from West Berlin, and it did not belong to me. I did not know where it came from, but the message was mine! How many times had my eyes rolled over those same words without perceiving their real significance.

New meaning penetrated me. I realized that the anticipation of this same love was the object of my ultimate concern and had somehow brought me to my immediate state. I thought back . . . I was alone at sea between two angry hurricanes, and not even aware of their presence. The very personal, unprejudiced acceptance of human beings, wherever and whoever they were—simply the love of people, the desire to help them—was in between the two raging storms and totally unaware of their existence. The Wall did not stop me; for me there was no wall. There is no wall between East and West, black and white, or any two human beings. They are all one!

All governments, institutions, and laws were subordinate to man, not man to them! I had not lost my orientation to the society that surrounded me and become oblivious of its rules! I had never belonged. Anywhere! Or, yes, everywhere! I was a part of the whole, of humanity, of all people everywhere! "I'm Lady Ulysses," I thought to myself, recalling my favorite lines of Tennyson's poem: "I am a part of all that I have met."

There is absolute power in this love—it is life! He who lives, passes life onward, and he who loves is more powerful than an atomic bomb! The chain reaction of love is more potent for the creation of life than the bomb for its destruction! Yes, love is a pebble dropped into the pool of life, causing ripples that travel to the farthest shores. Love is the light, set on the hill in a world of darkness. One light, one pebble, one life has the power to change the universe!

Love alone can reconcile, mend, repair, create anew. But love demands total surrender!

I was overcome with a yearning to write. Perhaps I would start a diary. I took up my pen and opened my Bible to I Corinthians 13.

"Love is patient and kind; love is not jealous or boastful; it is not arrogant or rude. Love does not insist on its own way; it is not irritable or resentful; it does not rejoice at wrong, but rejoices in the right. Love bears all things, believes all things, hopes all things, endures all things. Love never ends. . . ."

Yes, love is patient; it endures; never fails. The first page of a diary in a language that is not my own. Yet, I must write. I must capture and live this experience to the utmost! The pain, despair. . . . No! Love is patient! It conquers! The night of November 24th returns to my memory . . . the night of a snowstorm; the night of a birthday; the longest night in my life—the night of my arrest!

I laid my pen aside. What about the night of November 24, 1965? It was his birthday, three days after my own. What is a birthday? The day of a birth. It can also be the day of a rebirth! Yes, poor Sammy. Where was he now? Was he at Bautzen, too? The arrest was the unavoidable. It had to be! The telegram . . . they already knew. They had a letter he had already written me. But, oh, I couldn't help him. Now there is meaning. . . .

Now I must live it. Can I do that in isolation? I must find myself, too. Somehow I'll know when I should return to the others, if I am to return. Why must it all be so painful, though? Dear God, why is it all so painful? And at the same time, so beautiful? Yes, love, like a child, enters the world through pain. Birth takes place in suffering.

It was this love that opened the door to myself. In the stillness of solitude I could withdraw from the outer world, retreating to an inner refuge, as a medieval monk in his seclusion. Yes, that was it—the life of a monk or a mystic! It was then that I discovered real freedom, independence of the external world.

I had always wanted to wander down the inward roads, exploring all the mysteries of the depths of the soul, but endless activity in the outer world restrained me and bound me in fetters. Now, I was free to embark on the journey! I could create—power was mine! I had been one of those impoverished people who were afraid to be alone and who lost themselves in the empty pursuit of pleasure, seeking escape from themselves—a true child of the twentieth century. Poor, poor, lost twentieth-century man! He was such a foreigner in his own skin. He was out conquering the universe, but he was unable to make a home in his own soul. When he was forced to examine himself naked and alone, what did he find? Nothing.

How little modern, technical man knows of the inward universe! He spends money, effort, talent to discover and conquer the planets, but he is just a helpless babe, lost in the mysterious darkness of his own soul, so foreign to the inner forces of his being. That's why he stalks about in a heavy armored shell of protection—he is life's biggest tortoise! The outer coat is hardened to deflect all the stimuli from the outside, but inside is a soft, pliable, sensitive mass! Yes, all those explorers of the universe had not discovered the riches of their own soul. We were victims of our age, spiritually impoverished, split and foreign to the humanity and deity within.

Just don't confront yourself. That was the formula for security. Twentieth-century men were self-alienated strangers, lost on a sea of self-abandonment. Thus they turned to artificial means to force themselves to break through the guarded fortresses of the inner world. Everything was geared to the outer world, the objective world, the world that science could measure and discover, the world of the god, Matter. But, no one dared tell men to penetrate the inner world, the subjective world, the meditative world, the world of the spirit, of love. No wonder a generation could become sick, lost, desperate, alienated, hopeless, empty, wandering around in shells that threatened to break if anyone dared penetrate them. There is where you can find God, oh man. There you can know Love! In your own soul! But you don't believe in a soul, you say—you only believe in a brain, a consciousness—no wonder you are a noisy gong or a clanging cymbal. Oh, look within yourself I plead with you! There is a treasure there, and it is a creation of God.

I recalled a statement I had read from Pablo Casals: "I think if you have an awareness of what you are, you will find God." That was the key to the kingdom. Man, who had become so alienated from himself, was estranged from God! Avow that you are an atheist; I reply, know thyself! Protest that there is no proof of the Creator; I demand, discover thyself! That would be the next epoch of exploration—if the human race survived to embark on it.

"Stone walls do not a prison make, nor iron bars a cage; . . ." I had read the poem at one time in English class, way back when, but I could not recall the author—some Cavalier poet. Those were the only words that remained, not even the title. But they said all. One could soar above prison walls and enter a world of freedom, unknown outside. The discovery of freedom from the enclosure of a prison cell was exhilarating. Outside my cage, I had never been so free!

Oh, my God! Forgive them. "For they know not what they do." Do they really not know? No, of course not. But only Your love can break through all barriers and reach real, living human beings!

18

A VOICE IN THE WILDERNESS

ONE SATURDAY there was a national celebration for the birthday of the DDR. The guards were livelier than usual, and the matron relieved them of night duty. It was a grand holiday, compared to our July 4th. A colossal celebration had been arranged by the television network—a bag full of surprises; and weeks before the announcers had been encouraging everyone to *Spiel Mit,* to "play along." All of the audience participants were supposed to make some sort of small gift at home, and the whole game would take place in five different broadcasts during the day. The first broadcast began at 8:00 A.M., and the guards would never think of missing it. So, all the prisoners were permitted to view the program.

Since I had been in isolation the guards had not allowed me to view television with the other women. However, in this case an exception was made. I sat in the back of the room with one of the guards, and the other women sat at the front. In a thrilling and suspenseful manner, various citizens of the German Democratic Republic were surprised with awards for their faithful service in factories, schools, and even a railroader and a roadhouse cook received national recognition. Everyone enjoyed the show, and we returned to our cells in good spirits. All the people had been "little people," but genuine and deserving. Thousands of prizes had gone out to people all over the country, and the holiday festivities impressed me as really containing a national spirit, especially when thousands of Leipzigers turned out for the fireworks and show honoring citizens from the entire state. Something in the state was very much alive—some spirit that was national and uniting.

After the last broadcast in the evening, which was a gala ball in a grand hotel in Leipzig, the matron locked all the prisoners in the cells. Then, she returned to the cells, unlocked the door and chatted with each prisoner for a while. My cell was the last one, and I could overhear the conversations with the other prisoners. I began to dread her coming to my cell. What would I say to her? We always had difficulty talking, and if she had read my letter. . . . I had long since regretted having written it.

But there was something else on my mind, a decision wanting to be made, that had been hanging over my head since I had written the depressing letter, and especially since I had made the thrilling discovery. It was the *other* of two possible decisions remaining for me to transform the nature of my lot.

When the matron arrived at my cell, she remained in the doorway. I made an effort to rise, when she opened the door, but she immediately interrupted. "Remain seated." She was in a good mood, and there was a smile on her face. That relieved some of the tension of anticipating a talk with her. In the recent days her attitude toward me had improved remarkably. Of course, I offered no threat to her or the state by being closed off by myself, and it might have been for that reason, but I felt the cause must lie deeper.

The matron had slowly come to know me, through my work, which was now producing the highest output of all the prisoners; through my letters, that spoke in sincerity of my desire to do right and rise above the cancerous bitterness and accept my lot with courage; and through my person, which had attempted to translate the lightening revelations of love into action and a way of life. Genuine dialogues take time, patience, understanding. The stronger has to be willing to wait for these from his partner. My youthful impulsiveness and impatience had caused my violent outbreaks, but I continued to return to the recognition that these dialogues were a necessity of life—my real purpose for being in a Communist prison, in spite of all my weakness and resistance to that recognition.

"How did you enjoy the show?" she asked.

"Oh, I really enjoyed it. It was a wonderful experience," I answered.

"What impressed you most about it?" the matron inquired.

"The simple humanity it expressed. These very modest people have finally been rewarded for their good deeds. They were certainly deserving. Also, the solidarity of all the people. I think it is wonderful to experience a genuine community spirit—all those people in Leipzig, crowds coming out to honor citizens they didn't know, just because of their faithful service. One seldom finds that spirit any more—the common people, working and playing together."

Her eyes glowed at my reaction. "What did you think about the MC of the show?"

"I thought he was terrific! He seemed to be enjoying it all more than anyone else! In fact, all the announcers were excited. I think it was a grand day for the people. And, yes, the turnout was unbelievable. More than two million participated! I think that is unprecedented." The Germans seemed to blossom out in their expression of community spirit. "I enjoyed the surprise ending, too, when at ten o'clock everyone was told to take the present he had made or bought and give it to his neighbor. It was all so full of goodwill. It was more moving than Christmas!"

"Yes," she went on, "I really enjoyed it, too. This spirit doesn't exist in Western Germany. There the common people are exploited. The West German Government wants war, with their laws claiming the borders of 1939 as the legitimate ones. No, I'd rather die than see our little Republic turned over to the hands of a capitalistic government! I was here at the end of the war—soot and ashes, total destruction, a land completely on the bottom! Just because of greedy industrialists, wanting more power. We had to start over from scratch, building a state out of the ruins of nothing. The Soviet Union wasn't able to help us as much as the Americans helped West Germany. They were having a terrible time themselves. Do you know how many Russians died in the war? More than fifteen million! No wonder the Russian still hates the German! It is very hard for us to win the confidence of the Russian people and convince them that we really want peace and socialism. They are very reserved with Germans, even though they are a hospitable folk, and still bear a strong resentment against us. But our state is grateful for their help, and gradually we are developing a friendship with them. They saved us from the hands of the capitalists. Yes, the Russians are a great folk, a hard-working and disciplined people."

"Do you really believe that West Germany wants war?" I inquired.

"Yes!" she answered absolutely. "Of course, not the people, but the politicians."

"You know what bothers me," I went on, "is that I feel there is so much hate and distrust on the part of both governments. They both fear each other, and they have so many prejudices about each other that they don't dare recognize what they have in common. I lived in West Germany and West Berlin for more than three and a half years before I was arrested. I lived with the people, and I feel that they want peace just as strongly as the people of the DDR."

"But that's not the Bonner government!" she contradicted.

"But I feel that the people are stronger. There are already numerous groups that are pushing for a reconciliation with the DDR. Many are ready for recognition as the only realistic policy. That is the only reasonable solution in the genuine interest of the German people, of course, but it is the least pleasing to the politicians."

"They'll never take us, though! The Soviet Union won't let them! When are they going to realize that? Many of us have built this state with the sweat and blood of our toil. We suffered hardship for years, being denied many things. Now that our economy is stabilizing itself and flourishing for the first time, they want to swallow us up! Never! Never will that come about!"

"Aren't you concerned with uniting the German people, though?" I cautiously probed.

"Yes, but never under the rule of capitalism—that is what brought Hitler to power. Our state is concerned that a war never again arise from German soil; we will do all in our power to prevent that!"

I did not know what else to say without getting into an ideological argument. One had to start at the roots of the problem—determine whether the class struggle was a reality. She believed in it, and there was a "do or die" spirit in her words, and a deep involvement with the fate of her state. There were many others like her, too.

The party was full of them, those who would give up their lives to defend a state that had sprung into existence from the nothingness of soot and ashes, by itself, without American dollars, in just twenty years' time. The first line of their national anthem was "Resurrected from the ruins, and turned toward the future. . . ."

I admired their spirit, their commitment, their involvement, but I pitied them for the dilemma that resulted from their absolute pessimism concerning human nature. This pessimism had taken on psychotic proportions —fears, suspicions, and distrust of the other side developing into hatred, and an aggressive approach to counteract what they considered a real threat to their existence. I tried to understand the origin of such suspicion, and I could only conclude that since it found its stronghold on the Russian soil, the Russian peasant must have been terribly exploited by the ruling classes. The peasants had been in bondage for centuries and finally they had risen up in insurrection and demanded their own.

Yes, their unconditional pessimism concerning man was rooted in the godlessness of their ideology. God was dead for them, because they had destroyed His victory over evil!

My thoughts had wandered away from her words, and when they returned I heard her saying, "The German has difficulty making friends. He isn't hospitable at all. He can't get out of himself enough."

"Oh, I don't know," I responded. "I've met many warm, hospitable Germans in my stay in Western Germany. People have always been so kind to me. But, maybe you're right. Perhaps the German is the least hospitable and most reserved of all the peoples I have ever met." The matron had been referring to her own inability to open up in trust, attempting to explain her personal reaction to me.

Then I changed the subject. I had made a decision. "Frau Meister, I've been thinking about something for a while. I believe that solitary confinement is working on me in a bad way . . ." I groped for the right words. "I had fallen into a depression before because of my isolation . . . and . . . I thought it might be a good idea to return to the other women!" I waited for her reaction.

She hesitated. Her pallid cheeks became speckled with flecks of crimson. She directed her embarrassed gaze first at the floor and then to me. "I realize that the other women aren't so educated as you are. . . ."

"Oh," I interrupted with keen insight into what she meant, "that isn't the trouble at all; I never measure people by their education. It's the education of the heart that matters most to me—the *Herzensbildung!* I know so many intellectuals who don't know how to get along with people. People, that's the only thing that matters at all. I have greater difficulty getting along with educated people who are cold, stuffy, or reserved than I do with simple people who are natural and openhearted."

Her words were a revelation to me. All her suspicions had originated from her idea of class consciousness. Those were Lola's suspicions, too! The fact that I was better educated—that meant for her that I belonged to another class—convinced her that I wanted nothing to do with the others. I was not her enemy because I was an American, but because she thought I belonged to a different caste. Lola had uttered the very same suspicion concerning Margot many times, although Margot's education was more limited than my own. I had bent over backwards to convince her that education was a useful tool, but not necessarily a creator of class barriers. It was ironical that a society that attempted to destroy class barriers was the breeder of more vicious ones. By constantly making people aware of a class struggle, one originated where it might not have occurred naturally. It was just this class consciousness that built walls between men, dividing them from each other. It was more deeply rooted in educational differences than in material ones.

"She thinks she's better than the rest of us," Lola repeated many times, referring to Margot. "Just because she's been to school a few more years."

"I think you have a complex about education," I had answered her. "Why? Is she really any different from you? Margot is a name-dropper and throws around the things she knows, because she is an unhappy and insecure person. She's obstinate, because she is unsure of herself."

The two women were burdened with complexes that were just the opposit in nature. Margot felt little at home in her simple human nature—her academic German background alienated her from it. Thus she had to meet people with her learning, and not with the spontaneity of her feeling. Lola, however, who lacked the learning, was suspicious of it and secretly felt inferior because of the lack of it, but she was very much at home in her nature.

"Education is only a tool," I continued reassuring the matron, "to invest in the work of humanity. One person makes his contribution with his body and another makes his with his mind. One is no better than the other. They have only chosen different ways of doing the same thing!"

"Well," she started, reassured by my words, "there are some prisoners

who feel that way about education. You know who I am talking about!"
She meant Margot, and I was sure that Lola had planted that mistrust in her
mind against Margot. However, I wanted to let sleeping dogs lie, and I responded with a simple, evasive statement.

"Yes, some people feel that way."

Margot's difficulty was old-maidish pedantry and not the idea that she
was better educated, although in the beginning she had confided in me her
disdain of the others, calling them silly, stupid females, not to be taken
seriously. No, I did not feel that way, I had assured her. Every human being was to be taken seriously, no matter what his station in life. Perhaps
that had started the class struggle between the women—on the one side,
the complexes about not having enough education, on the other, a certain
arrogance and intolerance of the stuffy well-bred. Curses on the class struggle!

"Well, if you think you might want to go back to the others, you had
better talk to the liaison officer, since he was the one who decided your
solitary confinement."

"I'll report to him Monday," I answered with a sense of relief. Not finding any other topics to deal with, she departed and left me alone in the
shadow of her words.

I had been surprised by our encounter. The matron had uncovered a
very sensitive warmth and understanding that I had held her incapable of.
She had struck me as a burly, buxom, blunt policewoman, with little comprehension for anything other than enforcing the law—like those people
who hide behind the law, substituting it for their own conscience. Our talk
had revealed another person. The soft mass of the tortoise had left its
shell. Love had won a victory for both of us! Now I understood her better,
and the origin of her prejudices, which were deeply rooted in the doctrine
of her state.

Although I rejected the evil doctrine, I could respect her for her dedication. She had a mission, and it lay outside of herself.

Something was living within her state that our sick world longs for. A
brotherhood, a sense of solidarity between men, a community spirit. They
were working together in their state. Of course, many were forced to, many
resisted, but many took up the challenge and got involved in the struggle.

They *believed in* something and sought to propagate their message with all the missionary zeal that the early Christians experienced in their fight against the Roman Empire. It was not to be stamped out with force, nor exterminated with weapons. Whoever tried to do so would just be adding martyrs to the world. They were willing to die for it!

The real issue between America and the Soviet Union had been avoided: the romantic revolution versus pluralistic individualism; the missionary zeal of a people inflamed by ideology versus the passive indifference of representatives of a consumer society. And we were so ignorant as to try to fight it off with weapons! Did no one recognize that we are engaged in spiritual warfare? And we, in our detachment, were helpless without weapons, for we had nothing to offer against their religious fervor—unless, unless it really was freedom! But how many really believed in that freedom? Or had it just become another word in our political vocabulary?

How could America charge out as the white knight of freedom on a crippled horse? Had America's children grown indifferent to that freedom? Or did they stifle, choke, and suffocate voices that rang out in criticism, craving rather to be lulled into the security of self-complacency? Or considering every sound that had a different tone from its own, a tune of the enemy? That was the cheapest of all—there was a dangerous tendency in certain circles to brand everyone who criticized society, the Establishment, or the American Way of Life with the label of Communism. These people made themselves heard among the ignorant, the naïve, the prejudiced. For they knew not. . . . But real democracy could only thrive on freedom, or destroy the very factor that assured its existence. Not to criticize society constructively meant crippling the very motor that kept it running and maintained its growth. It was the spirit of the new frontier, forward, progress!

Was freedom alone enough? It was the other side of the coin that really frightened me, though. The whither of the young people. They were a lost generation, the American youth. And while their young voices were crying out in the wilderness that surrounded them, they were not heard. They had to turn to protests, rioting, orgies, drug addiction, crime. Of course, they rejected the selfish excesses of their fathers, the passive indifference, the national apathy. Their voice of protest was a legitimate one. But they only carried a burden of despair for the past. They knew not where to turn to the future. They knew they were free. They were free. They were blessed with an abundance of freedom. But freedom for what? Free to do what? What did they *believe in?* I wanted to pound my pillow and scream out. What did they believe in? Where were they going? Did they really know?

Yes, there are those who would *die* for a lie, but where were those who would *live* for truth?

And what was worse, people were killing other people. Not politicians killing other politicians. People, simple people, who really wanted understanding and brotherhood—not power! Peasants and farmers from villages were being killed just because they *believed in* something. Cowboys and hillbillies were dying because they had to. They were taught; yes, they had to be taught to be enemies. One had to teach hate to get men to fight wars. Oh, my God, my God, why have You forsaken us? One voice crying out in the wilderness. . . . A generation of lost sheep without a shepherd. . . . How could a Christian take up arms, in our times, knowing that he might kill a brother or a sister in a foreign land? Had he been taught that the brother is his enemy—could he believe that? If there is not brotherhood in Christ, where then is it? Are Communists killing *each other?*

I was filled with a *Weltschmerz,* a weariness of life. It hurt me even more to see that so much of the evil nations involved themselves in was the result of misunderstanding. Time and time again. An *einandervorbeireden.* They talk *at* each other and not *with* each other. They conduct their dialogues with themselves *about* their partner, not *with* their partner. Nowhere was that more evident than in East Germany. How could other nations conduct a dialogue with her when they did not even recognize her? What about Red China?

There were two spirits alive in the world that appealed to youthful adventure, the sense of dynamic progress, creative growth, and the healthy destruction of the past. One was good, and the other was evil. One was constructive, and the other was destructive. One was truth; the other was a lie. One was love. The other was lawless rebellion.

Monday passed, and the liaison officer did not send for me. Tuesday arrived, and in the morning hours, hardly eight o'clock, a guard told me to put my jacket on—I was going to the director's. The director? I had asked

to report to the liaison officer. I had never spoken to the director personally, and I had only seen him once outside.

I arrived at his office and waited until I was told to enter. I crossed the
threshold of a large room with a long, narrow table. The warden was seated
behind his desk, a small man, probably in his early fifties. The furrows of
his brow spoke of a soft wisdom, and behind the half-framed glasses, a
pair of lively, intelligent eyes assuaged my fears. His gaze was directed
downward at a paper he held in front of him, and I could see my prison file
lying on the desk before him. He was slow and deliberate, reflecting upon
each word he chose.

"I have a letter here that you have written. . . ." He did not look up.
The tears silently rolled over my cheeks, and I sat quietly awaiting the
words of reproach that would follow. ". . . in which you . . . uh . . .
speak of thoughts of . . . self-destruction." He waited, unsure of the next
words. I remained silent. He continued staring at the letter, and then lifted
his clear eyes to meet mine squarely. "I want to *help* you!" he said. "That's
why I have called you here today!"

I looked into his eyes. They were glowing with a clarity and sincerity
that revealed he was telling the truth. "I'm unaware of what the trouble is,
but I want to find out and see if we can do anything about it for you." How
different he was from his representative, the man who had spoken to me on
entering the penitentiary. It was genuine. His face glowed in warmth, and
he continued:

"We once had a prisoner, a young man, who felt that he couldn't go on
living any more, either. We entered his cell and found him hanging from
the bars on the window, strung up with a necktie. We cut him down, just in
the nick of time, though. You know something? When he returned to consciousness, that was the happiest man alive! He was so grateful that he had
not succeeded in what he had attempted. Now, he's out of prison, and he
has returned to his studies; he completed his doctor's degree not too long
ago. No one loves life any more than he does.

"Besides, I see from your letters home that you believe in Christianity.
Then you can't lose hope! You must keep up your courage. Christianity is,
after all, a *way of the cross*. It involves suffering, struggle. It's no easy
way." He paused again, giving me opportunity to answer.

"I know you're right," I said, ashamed to be hearing the words from a Marxist, for I was convinced that he was one. "I do believe that. But your own poet Goethe has said, 'I have *two* souls in my breast!' That is the difficulty. I was not sure which was stronger. I recognized what my responsibility was, but my weaker side made me unable to be what I would like to be." [How much that sounded like the Apostle Paul's words when he said, "For I do not do what I want, but I do the very thing I hate."]

He glanced down again. "I see from your record that you have been in solitary confinement for more than three months now, at your own request. It is our experience that prisoners in solitary confinement usually go through some sort of crisis or difficulty. Maybe we can work out some adjustment, where you won't have to stay alone all the time."

"Oh, I didn't really *want* to go into isolation at all. There is one prisoner who denounced me and distorted things I had said, prejudicing Frau Meister against me. She had been informing on the other prisoners and continually putting them in bad light with the matron. I tried to defend the others and warned her to stop. Then, when I was away in Berlin, she did the same thing to me. Later, I moved into her cell and found a note, reporting on Prisoner Winter. She made the whole atmosphere unbearable for us all. I wanted to have a good relationship to the personnel, but Frau Meister, especially, was prejudiced against me."

"And you *should* have a good relationship, too. Sometimes prisoners tell us things, but you certainly don't think that we make reprisals for things that prisoners tell us! We more or less know how each prisoner thinks. After so many months of contact, reading the letters home, observing the work, we can make a good evaluation of the character of a prisoner. Prisoners who report on others feel that it is the only way they can prove themselves, but we see through it. Sometimes the guards, on the basis of what a prisoner says, undertake some corrective measure, but certainly that is just a part of prison life—that is part of the suffering involved. You are right. The Meisterin was somewhat prejudiced against you in the beginning, but that will be different from now on. It is hard to establish the proper relationship to prisoners, not knowing them, but now we have come to know you better."

"It all made the atmosphere unbearable!"

"You can rest assured that it will be changed. Why didn't you come to me earlier? Why didn't you come and talk to me about it before going into solitary confinement?" he queried.

"I was afraid. I tried talking to the liaison officer, and he was not objective either. He was influenced by the matron's words before I had a chance to talk to him. The other women suffered from it, too, but they were afraid to do anything about it. They were afraid of the matron and the prisoner who did the informing."

"Well, the next time you have any difficulty, you know you must come to me with it. I am the one to discuss it with. . . . Now, I see in your letter that you say another Christmas in prison would prove unbearable for you. Christmas for us Marxists, as it is for you Christians, is a time of joy, goodwill, peace on earth. We try to make it as nice as possible for our prisoners. There will be a Christmas tree, and I am certain that you can share joy with the others under the present circumstances. It is the time of hope! Don't lose your hope now. . . . Yes, I agree with your statement that your life does not belong to you. It belongs to others, to society, and more than anything else, you cannot take your life, because it would be a tragic loss to others. Everything in you strives toward progress, and you can pass it on to others. . . . You state in your letter that you are not getting younger and you still have a lot of education to complete. Now what would you say if I told you that I am still going to school?"

"I think it's wonderful," I answered, "but I don't want to *take in* all my life; I want to *give out* to other people from what I have already taken in. You are also in a position to practice your profession; you are giving to others at the same time you are taking in."

"But you can give to others, too. You can give to your fellow prisoners! I want you to go back to them and to give them *hope* and encouragement." His declaration took me by surprise. Incredibly, this Marxist was giving me, an American, a mission to the others!

"You're right," I said. "One can always give, in any situation. I recognize this, but I was impatient. I retreated too soon."

"Now," he continued, hesitating, "from your letter I see that you had set your hopes on a release by September. That was somewhat presumptuous, since even your attorneys can't say when you'll be released. For *your sake*, I do hope that you will be released earlier, but that depends on the decision of the officials. Let us hope, but you *do* know that you were sentenced to four years. . . ."

I was unable to answer, for he did not know when I would be released. He was repeating the prescribed formula. "You mentioned the Powers case, and the fact that it took two years to negotiate. Your case is different; you cannot compare it to that one!" he continued.

I didn't know what he meant. Negotiations were negotiations. I had simply wanted to say that it took two years to put them through governments and bureaucrats. If people were working on negotiations for me, it could take just as long. The thought of two years was a few days short of eternity for me. I was unable to bear it.

The warden glanced at his watch. It was late, for our talk had lasted more than an hour. "I'm afraid I am going to have to close now, but you have decided to return to the other women. I'll talk to the Meisterin, and if you have any requests that we can fulfill, don't hesitate to express them. We want to make your life here as bearable as possible under the conditions."

I reported and dismissed myself. He led me to the glass partition, where a guard was waiting to take me upstairs. The tears that had stained my cheeks during the conversation had been transformed from bitterness to sweetness.

I returned to my cell to meditate on the deep joy of our meeting. His parting words had been uttered with deep heartfelt sincerity. "You know," he said, "it is so seldom in one's lifetime that he has the opportunity to talk as we have to each other." There was warmth in his eyes as he spoke, and I knew that he had received even a greater blessing from our dialogue than I. And I thanked God for the crisis that had brought it about.

A genuine dialogue with a Marxist! We both had tried our best to understand each other, and we had succeeded beautifully. At no moment did I feel that he was unable to find his way with compassion into my thinking. And I had experienced empathy with him. There was so much we had not talked about, but that had been silently said with our attitudes and approaches. We had much in common, perhaps more than we had in disagreement.

A genuine Marxist, though, rare as they were to find, was no shrewd, power-hungry politician. He was an idealist. This man probably criticized many of his own government's policies, as any idealist would criticize the discrepancy between his ideal and practice, between the reality of human frailty and the ideal of infallibility. But then, the idealists were the architects of society; the realists were the builders. The success of the building depended on their successfully coordinated work.

"I believe all the genuine humanists of the world can engage in dialogue together," I thought. Of course, they do not have to *agree* with each other. But what about China? Fanaticism was idealism on the rampage. When idealism lost its reasoning power and blindly strove for its goal, subordinating man and principles of humanity to attain its aim, it became fanaticism— a seasoning that turned sour.

A Marxist had been the human answer to a prayer in a time of crisis. I could rejoice in knowing that the ears of love were never closed to any human being of God's creation.

The power of love had broken through another wall.

19

THE RED WITCH

"AFTER BEING LOCKED UP so many months in this stinking outhouse, I think I could even sleep with *Piepse!*" Lola tilted her head back in satanic laughter. "Even the balding doc would be a good partner at this point!"

"Ugh! That slob?" Lise questioned.

Lola's eyes twinkled, titillated by her own vulgarity. She was obsessed by sex, and in freedom she ran indiscriminately after every promise of gratification. She suffered most of all under prison's imposed abstinence, and hardly a day passed without her describing some man in a lascivious manner. Moreover, she loved making attacks in abusive language. Her choice of words would have startled any seaman, and she took immense pleasure in shocking us with violent affronts in vulgar language. She derived keen satisfaction in telling filthy stories and watching us blush.

Lola was the mother of four illegitimate children—all by different men. She was officially married for the second time to the father of her last child. Lola boasted with apparent pride that she had been raped twice in her life, once when she was sixteen and once when she was pregnant with her second child. The first story was a "Lolita" affair, where the man was much older. The second had been a distinguished old gentleman who had mysteriously offered her a ride on a snowy night and had taken the long way getting her home. He had swept her off to a secluded villa in West Berlin before the Wall. To our inquiry why she had not reported it to the police, she asserted that she could not remember where he had taken her.

Lola was a shrew in every respect, and I was very much afraid of her. In secret we called her a monster, a beast, a shrew, the red devil, for she was all of those. My favorite title for her was "the red witch." Although my reason questioned the possibility of such an occurrence, I began to suspect that the mysterious powers of evil had planted the devil in our midst to tempt and try us.

When Lola threw her head back and laughed diabolically, revealing two sharply pointed eyeteeth, I cringed with a shudder of horror at the creature. She launched into attacks on certain guards, and without our noticing it, we all found ourselves burning in fury at her injustices. Someone would end up scolding the guard in her absence, and Lola had material for her reports. She knew how to manipulate us subtly into the palm of her hand.

I resented Lola's cunning in getting out of work details. She always found some special job that had to be taken care of as trusty, when the rest of us were on our hands and knees scrubbing. She usually had to get the dirty laundry ready to send off, or arrange the clean linen on the shelves. Her favorite method of getting around an unpleasant task was going to fetch linen from the attic storeroom. The more naïve of the guards, which included most of them, let her get away with it, because they were unable to see through her. It also provided Lola with the opportunity to get off by herself with a guard, who always accompanied her to the attic, and pump her full of information about the other prisoners.

The thing that irritated us most about Lola was her dishonesty and irresponsibility with respect to production. Every day she "miscounted" the quantity she produced, and finally the production guards were down our throats for writing up higher quantities than we had produced. It reflected on all of us, but we suspected who was responsible for it. Nevertheless, we were helpless about doing anything against it, or even proving it.

When we received a portion of real butter, which was twice a week, she cut off a bigger chunk for herself, and one of us ended up with a hair-thin slice, until we discovered what she was doing. Then we posted either Lise or myself to watch her dish out the food in the evening. We were unable to do anything about the soup, though. She took our servings off the top and scraped up the meat, if there were any, from the bottom for herself. Since the guards were always standing around, if we had even made the claim she was doling it out unfairly, she would have made us out to be the liars. Lola was able to do that, too.

The green-eyed monster of envy pushed his horny head into our group, too. Competition invited him. Lise and I had the highest output, and that meant we earned a couple of marks more each month for our purchases. Lola was extremely envious and continually tried to play down the importance of output in general. It was not a matter of pushing myself, as it was with Lise, in order to earn a couple of extra pennies. It was my long, slender fingers that had been exercised on a piano and a typewriter. After a certain period of breaking them in at the production of relay contacts, I was inclined to a natural manual dexterity. Lise, however, literally worked herself up into a sweat every day to accomplish more and more.

Margot had the least ambition in every respect. Wallowing in self-pity, she had sort of withered away. The guards were continually grumbling at Margot, who brooded for long hours over their complaints. She soon developed the conviction that they were picking on her, and they were.

Margot did not offer a challenge to Lola until she changed over from the contacts to the screws, which she mounted on a metal board. After a couple of weeks of training, and a few helpful hints from Helga before she left, Margot was achieving a record performance with the screws. Lola then demanded that Margot make something else, in which she exhibited less skill. If Margot resisted, Lola screamed "insubordination" and threatened to confer with the matron about Margot's behavior. This frightened Margot into sullen cooperation, since she knew that Lola and the matron stood on the best of terms with each other.

Again hell took on a new meaning in the days following my return to the circle of companions.

This time it was the paltry pettiness of the other women, Lola's hysterical ranting and raving when anyone crossed her, Margot's chronic lying to cover her fallibility, Lise's rigid obsession with her output and performance, Ingrid's inability to do anything right, the constant complaining about illnesses, and the incessant bickering between Margot and Lola. It was enough to drive any soul to destruction.

Moreover, we all suffered under the tyranny of Lola's power, and it was the constant theme of conversation among us, excluding Ingrid. We were afraid to trust Ingrid, whom we knew to be suffering, too, because she shared a cell with Lola. I had to fight to keep from becoming embittered, especially in the evening when I entered my cell aching from the heavy carrying that was often pushed off on me or Lise. Margot always managed to disappear when loads were to be carried, or get out with the explanation that she had abdominal pains, which no one could prove or disprove. Yet, there was nowhere to go with those complaints. Lola had the matron twisted around her finger, and we all had to suffer silently.

It was impossible to retain the soul-penetrating intensity of the love I had encountered. I had to continually return to the source of its power and be regenerated. Nevertheless, having tasted the sweetness of its victory, I again attempted to meet its challenge. Yes, to love is to suffer. To suffer is to love. I recalled the director's words, "Christianity is the way of the cross!"

In my thoughts I recalled a book by a Polish author I had read in Berlin. He had quoted Bishop Sheen's remarkable insight, "America accepted Christianity without the cross; the Soviet Union accepted the cross without Christianity!"

What infinite wisdom in those words! What did I, an American, really know about the cross? And yet, it was central, the key, in the very middle of Christianity. It was the universal and eternal symbol of Christianity. Its crosspiece was a yoke of open arms, extending into life horizontally, reaching outward and joining man to man in the uniting expression of brotherhood. Its vertical beam symbolized the oneness with nature, with the womb of life, reaching upward to the eternal, to the spiritual, to God! The temporal and spiritual intersected, and all on a frame of suffering.

Yes, ". . . let him . . . take up his cross daily and follow me!" But didn't one go out of his way to avoid suffering, to get around it, to climb over it, to ignore it, to flee from it? To make life as easy as possible—that had become the goal of living. Men would go to any length, just to achieve the line of least resistance; would yell, complain, rebel, withdraw, all to avoid suffering.

What did we Americans know about suffering? Had our country been ravaged by war? Or had peace allowed us to be lulled to self-complacent sleep? Had we ever suffered the pangs of hunger that the starving know? Or were we all forced to count calories because of the round pot bellies of an abundant economy? When had we been politically persecuted? Or had too much freedom that was taken for granted made us drift into detached indifference, national apathy? Had it become a push-button world of zooming automatons, where men just did not suffer any more because they did not really *feel?* Where they would even take a marriage to the divorce courts rather than endure one ounce of suffering in order to save it?

Yes, as I had entered prison, I had passed through the portals of a whole new world of suffering—not just my own suffering, but that of others—a world heretofore unknown to me. I had heard the cries of the newly arrested prisoners, protesting the injustice that had brought them there. I had met them. What were their crimes? Had they stolen or robbed? Had they attacked or beaten? Had they murdered? No. They had simply sought their birthright. They had tried to attain their freedom. Freedom to go to brothers, sisters, mothers, fathers, fiancés. That was a crime! Its price was suffering.

But then, what did it mean—The Soviet Union had accepted the cross without Christianity? It was something I had begun to understand in my time at Bautzen. Perhaps it really became clear for the first time when I chatted with the matron that night in my cell. "We sacrificed for our state. We built it up from the ruins of soot and ashes," she had said. "Soot and ashes" and "sweat and blood." There was the strong sense of suffering in her words. Sacrifice and discipline were in them. The people had done without, had relinquished personal gain to the advantage of the community, for the welfare of the state. They had taken on the yoke of the cross! And, yet, they denied Christianity. They rejected the saving power of Christ.

That was a heavy burden—the cross without Christianity! How could one carry it without love, forgiveness, faith? No wonder they became embittered, aggressive, filled with hatred, even psychotic, by projecting all their own evil desires onto their enemies. They wanted to rid the world of evil, social injustice, exploitation, all without forgiveness, without love. It was an impossible task. But, what was Christianity without a cross? It was merely a noisy gong or a clanging cymbal! It was a brittle shell, a vain tradition that was observed with form, but empty of content, meaning, of ultimate concern. Christianity without a cross, or a cross without Christianity were both doomed to bow down to God's greater designs for man.

I, too, had cried out, protesting man's inhumanity to man that had locked me in the confinement of prison walls, but there was one who did not cry out "I am not a criminal" as they arrested Him.

Even as they sentenced Him to death, death on a cross, He cried out, "Father, forgive them; for they know not what they do."

That was a paradox. The greatest love had taken on the greatest burden of suffering voluntarily. And the symbol of suffering became the symbol of love. The sweetness of this realization, in spite of all the anguish and doubt of life in captivity, enabled me to say, "My presence here has a purpose. Lord, help me fulfill it!"

One evening after my work in the factory was finished, I was given the job of cleaning the steps down to the basement. I took my scrub bucket, tattered rag, long-handled scouring brush, and headed for my job. Renate was on duty, and she let us go about our housework with little supervision. Some of the guards stood behind us when we were taking care of cleaning jobs, annoying us with their critical stares or complaints. When Renate had nothing else to do, she was the world's worst, and she invariably knew a better method of doing things. On this particular day, however, she was busy with filing a report, and that gave me the free run of the stairway.

When I had reached the bottom, just inside the heavy glass door, I began wiping the dusty floor with my wet cleaning rag. At the bottom of the door was a space of about six inches, which was free of partition, and I could peek under and observe the activity in the main hallway of the prison. Next to the lock in the door was a hole where the glass had been broken, allowing just enough room for an eye to peer through. I could hear a group of men swishing away on the other side, and I banged about with my pail, clanging and clattering, to inform them of my presence. I was afraid to peep through the hole, because I feared supervision on the other side.

Suddenly an eye was staring at me. *"Guten Tag,"* came a deep voice from behind the door. Was it a trick? This was an opportunity of a lifetime to be able to talk to the men through the door, but if I got caught I knew I could be severely punished. This fear raced through me, but my feminine curiosity and daring were stronger than the fear of punishment. I answered.

"Guten Tag."

"Hey, keep an eye out for old Rog! I've got a gal here on the other side," the voice shouted across to another prisoner. *"Wie heisst Du?"* He asked me my name, addressing me with the familiar *"Du."* Prisoners always spoke with the familiar form.

"Hellen," I replied, wondering whether I should give my real name. "And what is your name?" I inquired.

"Gert. How long you got?"

"Four years. What about you?"

"I got ten. Espionage."

"Oh," I sympathized, "mine's escape help."

"Is your husband in prison, too?" he inquired.

"I'm not married."

"Wait a minute," he advised. He left the door, and I thought a guard must have entered. I busied myself with my scrubbing, glancing up the stairwell to see if I could detect some sign of Renate. If she had wanted to do so, she could have observed me from the fourth floor by bending over the railing and glancing down the long shaft. Or if she were standing at the top of the steps she could have heard the conversation. She was the last guard to tie up with, too. Renate would absolutely explode if she caught me talking to the men. I was taking a big risk that could maybe even endanger my early release, but "Never venture, never gain" continued to be my motto.

Gert returned. He had only gone to get his friend Alfred, who was also single. He introduced us, and Alfred struck me as a very polite, clean-cut young man in his twenties. He was of medium stature, and his muscular build, his round baby face, which was framed with closely cropped blond hair, gave him the appearance that we had come to classify as the "cuddly" type. Alfred had a life sentence for espionage.

"How do you feel about the approaching Christmas in prison?" he asked, not knowing what else to inquire.

"The atmosphere is pretty depressing with the women. What about with you? I do think that it's even worse for me, though, being an American so far away from home with foreigners."

"You say you are an Ami. I'm sure it's bad, but it is hard for us, too. Which of the relay contacts do you assemble?"

"I make the double ones. Does your group get our work?"

"Yes. We're responsible for assembling them into motors," he explained. He glanced around quickly, and someone motioned him back to his job.

In a few seconds Gert returned and took a seat in Max's office, which he was supposed to be cleaning, directly across from the glass door. He signaled me to write a note and send it down with the material, but I shook my head a violent No. I was afraid of really getting caught, and maybe the men had a Lola in their group, too. If I had not tied up with her type once already, I would have done it. Then he rushed to the door, and told me to put some strands of hair in the relay contacts when I assembled them. I agreed I would, and I heard an outside door open and a guard enter. Gert disappeared quickly, and I rushed up the stairs.

Everything was in order. Renate was still in the guard's station, taking care of a report. I returned to the bath with my pail and cleaned it as if nothing had happened, but I was burning with victory. I could confide it in Lise and Margot, but I dared not reveal the meeting to Lola and Ingrid. Lola was sure to spoil my little party, and I wanted to try it again. I would try to get stair duty every time, but it would probably never coincide with the same group of men again.

Some days later I was working on the stairs again, and Margot was a couple of flights below me. She was working on the basement steps, and we both could hear men on the other side of the door. I winked at her, since I had already included her in my little escapade. An eye appeared at the hole in the door. I went up to the door only after a voice said, *"Guten Tag."* It was Alfred, and my heart jumped that we had met again.

"Thanks for the hair," he said, as if it had all been for him. It had been. Every day I had included one relay contact in my case with a long strand of hair. He had found it. Through the tiny aperture our fingers could have touched, or we could have exchanged messages if we had known the meeting would come about. Neither of us dared. There was something so clean-cut about Alfred, so warm and gentle in his manner. He was anything but one of the brawny bullies we had observed a couple of times, who were probably responsible for the vulgar sexual signs we often found written in the sand outside. His eyes sparkled through the opening, pure and friendly, with a healthy reservation. I wanted to tell him so many personal things and break down the barrier between us, but I was too shy, and the softly snatched phrases we dared whisper through the opening were often repeated, because the sounds in the big building swallowed them up.

Margot had gone upstairs, because we had been cleaning the steps a suspiciously long time. Inge was on duty, and she was supersensitive about our not seeing the men. I decided that it was high time for me to return or it would strike her attention what I was up to. I had gone up two flights when I heard the glass door fly open and sounds of footsteps rushing up the stairs. I sprang to the railing and cast a quick glance down to the door. The men were coming up to pick up our work! How had that mistake come about? I was still standing on the steps! Usually, the guards carefully locked us in a cell before the men were allowed to mount the stairs. I was excited and terrified at the same time, because I knew the repercussions would be tremendous. But it was Inge's mistake, not mine.

I waited a few seconds until the men came into sight. Immediately wolf whistles and catcalls sounded. The group of men, five or six in number, were only three or four steps away. At once I was frightened when I stared into the blazing eyes of one of the men I had never seen. They were burning with animal lust. My heart raced, and I felt that I was facing a pack of hungry wolves. What had I gotten myself into? They appeared ready to spring upon and devour their helpless prey. I was the victim.

I had no time to think. I spun around on my heels and darted up the steps with all the swiftness my feet could muster. It was as if I could hear their panting behind me.

Inge was waiting for me at the top with an ugly scowl, untypical of her usual friendly peasant round face. A cell door was standing open waiting to receive me, and she hurriedly locked me in with the others, who sat gazing enviously at me, as if I had just been informed of my release.

"I've just seen the men!" I panted, trying to catch my breath, which I had lost more from fear than from running up the stairs.

Lola looked at me with eyes glaring a deep green and reflecting "If anybody gets to see them, I'm the one!" Then she asked, "How did you do that?"

"I was on my way up the steps . . ." I stopped to catch my breath. My heart still pounded from the unexpected encounter. ". . . and I turned around and they were charging up the steps." I whispered the account, because I imagined Inge standing outside the door, listening to discover how she had overlooked me. Her frowning face had been suspicious, but it had been her fault. The men always called before coming up.

"What do they look like? Any good-looking ones in the lot?" Lola probed further. She was envious.

In the following days I could not get Alfred out of my mind. He was so nice, and it hurt me to think that he had a life sentence. He seemed optimistic in spite of it, radiating youth, health, and comradeship, and I knew he could not be an informer. But there could be one in his group, and as much as I wanted to maintain contact with him, word always traveled too easily through prisons, and sooner or later it was sure to be discovered, especially since I was an American. If it were one of the other women, it would be more difficult to determine which one, but if the word got around that he had contact with an American woman, there was only one. Nevertheless, I wrote out a note and stuck it in my bra, in case another meeting came about.

On the following day Inge traipsed along behind me while I was cleaning the steps. She stood and watched me wipe every step, and when we reached the landing at the bottom, she stood in front of the hole in the door. The men were noisy on the other side, and she informed me that she had come along to "protect" me from them. She had put an end to my meetings through the glass door.

I simply had to devise another method of seeing Alfred. In the evening I could hear men shouting to each other out the window. Although it was forbidden, that failed to disturb their conversation. Alfred had told me that he lived on the upper floor of the wing that joined ours perpendicularly, and I could probably see his window from mine. I was sure that Alfred was not one of the men shouting across the court, because I was unable to recognize his voice.

I climbed up on the headboard of my bed, and by stretching my neck, I could just peer over the window that was open at a forty-five-degree angle. I could see all the rows of barred windows, some with food standing on the ledges. But no face was to be seen. Finally, I noticed a face peering out a window on the second floor, but it was not Alfred. After several attempts I gave up that possibility. It was too dangerous, anyway, because the guards sometimes slipped up to the door and peeped through the opening without my awareness. If I shouted out the window, I was sure to be discovered, too. I would have to rest content without any communication with him.

I sat nibbling on a piece of black bread, for I did not eat the sausage that evening. I never ate the blood sausage we received once a week. I looked up and noticed that the lid to my spy hole in the door was cocked a bit, allowing a view of the corridor outside. I rushed to the aperture and peeked out the crack. With some strain, twisting my head around to the right, I could see the bar gate at the stairhead, and just outside the bars stood the cases of work we had completed for the day.

I wondered why the peephole cover failed to fall closed, but I calculated that paint had dried in the minute crevice that separated it from the hole. If the guard did not make her rounds before the men came to pick up the material, I could watch them on the landing. Usually, the guards did not come around before supper, so I waited hopefully, anticipating a glimpse of Alfred. Sure enough, he came up the steps with the others and I caught a quick view as he stooped down to hoist the heavy load up to his broad shoulders. I resolved to make that my daily routine, but I had to make certain that the lid was slightly to one side of the glass eye.

When I left the cell in the evening to get water and supper, I made a quick survey of the corridor to determine whether anyone was paying attention. I shoved the lid to one side, just enough not to be evident. It worked. Alfred did not always show up with the others, but most of the time he accompanied them. I was thrilled to see him, and I got a chance to see many others I had never seen. I longed to communicate with them, but that possibility was no longer open. I could only continue to send down long strands of my hair, but I had to stay on my guard against being detected by Lola.

The contact with Alfred and the other men prisoners reminded me that a year had passed since I had seen Sammy.

20

. . . NOR IRON BARS A CAGE

LOLA WAS A SHE-DEVIL, but I decided on a new way to deal with her. "Resist the devil and he will flee from you." If I had encountered the devil in the first few days with fear and trembling, it was only when I decided not to let him get the best of me that I could outwit him—by not getting upset at all his escapades and intrigues. I began to sense victory. I ceased to fear him, because now I knew I had access to superior powers, and if I called these into action, I could cripple and paralyze him into the helplessness of a babe. The devil was only a shrew that needed taming.

Thus, I began a new relationship to Lola, a relationship of love. It was then that I learned that her soul was not ebony, but scarlet—just like my own. No, it was not a relationship of simpering sentimentality, but one of firmness, cleverness, and wisdom, calculating what her superior needs were and not giving in to her weakness. Above all, I criticized her openly, or better, told her my real opinion, but tactfully, and she began to respect me for doing what everyone else was afraid to do. She even began to develop a slavish attachment to me, taking my word for gospel truth.

The petty bickerings, silly squabbles, and senseless prattle became meaningful discourse, and every day Lola came to work begging for spiritual food to eat. She would in the most unexpected moments and in a very innocent, childlike manner pop up with a question like "If there's a God, why do babies die?" Then she would rant and rave for minutes, cursing fate and denying any divinity, claiming that she had abandoned her faith when her first child, which had been born out of wedlock, entered life physically handicapped. She had been ashamed of its harelip, and had rejected her child because of its ugliness. The baby, a daughter, was a hemophiliac and already, at fourteen years of age, had nothing to look forward to but death. Yet Lola had never done anything for the child to make up for its handicap; she had not even accepted it as her own, and had left it in her mother's care. After she had married its father later, however, only to discover that the marriage was a mistake, Lola had fought for the child in the divorce court. It had been a nasty fight. Her husband tried to prove her to be a Lesbian, but without success. Finally, she won custody of the child, but only with a sense of victory that her rightful possession had not been taken from her, not with a mother's joy at not being separated from her child.

"Yes," Lola said bitterly, "when the priest told me that the child was a punishment for my sins, it made me sick! I gave up anything that resembled faith!" She informed us that her mother was a nominal Catholic and her father a nominal agnostic. She had been a nominal Catholic until the priest had called her a sinner. Now, she loathed the church, called it one of the worst exploiters of human beings, and refused to enter its portals. She had the wholehearted support of Lise on the topic, too.

Lise had been brought up in the Protestant Church, but she claimed that all pastors were hypocrites, after she made the discovery that her pastor stole. Then she committed the unpardonable sin in the village; she withdrew her membership from the church. "Everybody in the village is a member of the church and a member of the party, too," Lise stated as a matter of course. One would be ostracized if he were not. I was amazed at this discovery, though. The people understood neither the ideology of the party nor the theology of the church, but they held on to the church because they were afraid to let it go. It was a deep-seated tradition, ingrained in the folkways. The superstitions of the womenfolk demanded that their babies be christened, and everyone had to have a church wedding and burial. Then, if one faithfully paid his church tax, which he could not get around if he remained in the church, he had a safe and secure insurance policy for the hereafter. That was the way it went. The party, on the other hand, offered many economic advantages to members. One could get better housing, a more lucrative position, and the approval of the local authorities. A sheer pragmatic approach had tied many peasants to the party.

Ingrid, however, was completely unprejudiced in her approach to religion. She had never known it. For her it had never existed one way or another. Her mother had been a staunch and devout party member, and Ingrid had grown up in the aura of the party line. Whether she had undergone the naming rites a party member's newly born child is usually exposed to, I was uncertain. It had replaced the church's christening sacrament and was a formal ceremony, naming the child after birth and dedicating its life to the state. The service was conducted by party officials. Ingrid had undergone the "youth initiation" rites, which was the state's version of the church's confirmation. Lola described it as being a "highly political" ceremony, in which the youth confirms his loyalty and dedication to the state.

The next step in Ingrid's political growth was the FDJ—the young people's political organization—which prepared them for membership in the party. Later she joined the Communist Party.

When I talked with the women I was astounded to realize that Communism was nothing more than the perverted Christian church at work! The evidence for me was that its appeal spoke to something basic in man, something deeply rooted in his nature and needs.

"What do you need churches for anyway?" Lise grumbled. "They only exploit people!"

"Because I think that community is a necessity for men. The church is really no different from the Communist Party—a group of people, who accept a common belief, and commit themselves to a common goal," I answered.

"Hmmmm, I never thought of it that way," Lola interjected.

"Yes, apparently man is endowed with a community spirit, the deep need for participation with others, because where a community does not exist, men tend to create one," I responded.

All the rites and rituals of the church—symbols and tangible evidences so that people could visualize their faith—were present in the party: the glaring signs advertising socialism, the youth initiations, the parades. The regular church services had become the party meetings, accompanied by the feeling of obligation to attend. The party named a newborn child; it performed wedding ceremonies. And it was held to be infallible! They claimed that it was impossible for a group of people with a common goal in history to err. Man had a need for assurance, to know that the object of his concern was unconditional, infallible; a pope had only been superseded by a party.

"You know, you Communists are obliged to be missionaries for your conviction, too—yes, for your faith. In fact, a believer, or a 'convinced' Communist, maintains the inevitability of Communism, just as a Christian accepts faith in God. The difference is that Communists displace the Christian God with matter, and it dwells omnipotently in the state."

This time Ingrid reacted, although I was certain she had not caught the full significance of my last statement. "That's true," she replied, "a true Marxist is like a Christian should be. He is supposed to love his neighbor."

"As long as his neighbor does not belong to the bourgeoisie!" I observed.

All eyebrows flew up. By now the women sensed that my remarks were made in goodwill.

"No," I continued, "I am really impressed with the international solidarity or brotherhood of the Communists, where proletarians of all nations unite in an effort to promote justice."

Margot frowned. She always kept her mouth tightly buttoned in these discussions. If she responded, it was with sarcastic grins.

"Yes," I thought to myself, "the people are really searching for salvation. Indeed, the Communists themselves. Their horizon is history, and salvation is found in the historical transformation—where peasant and farmer will be filled, where the last will be first! Where there is no night, no class, no tears! All will be one, united in brotherhood, sharing and loving. . . . That's what the people are promised. . . .'"

Perhaps it was significant that the Protestant Reformation, with its industrial ethic, never made it to Eastern Europe, and a miscarriage of history had come about, impoverishing the people in the Eastern countries and depriving them of their rightful economic growth. Even today, the countries that have failed to clasp Protestantism are the potential converts to Communism, which replaces the church with little effort. All the articles of faith have been carefully displaced, removed from the "afterlife" and restaged on the earth in the present time.

Margot refrained from taking part in our religious discussions, and committed herself neither one way nor another. If it had been one way, it would have been of one who accepted the truth of the matter, but remained indifferent to its significance, representative of most of the Christian world; of those who could say, "Oh yes, I believe in Christianity" but felt no commitment to it. Such people are uninvolved in Christianity as *a way of life* rather than an ideology or dogma that one has to accept intellectually. These same people who "believe" in Christianity also believe in Einstein's theory of relativity, the existence of Red China, or the necessity of world peace, but the decisive question is, Have their lives been changed in any way by believing in those things? Or are they untouched by the reality that things of ultimate significance can take on meaning for their daily lives? In our age it is too simple to become a head without a body—a kind of automaton, running around feeding on theories that never get around to becoming truth, reality, a way of life. That is how one head can be full of conflicting theories, and still go on living as if none—or all—of them are realities. . . .

We had become involved in a discussion of this very problem, when

Lola asked me to explain what I meant by a claim I had made that most Christians don't *really* believe.

"Let's take Puerto Rico, for example," I began carefully. "It is a beautiful island in the Caribbean. I can describe it to you in detail—its whispering palms, the coral reefs, jagged shoals protecting the shore; the glowing bay of phosphorescent waters, that sprinkle a thousand stars when you let a handful slide through your fingers; the pounding surf with its ceaseless comings-in and goings-out, surging with power; the sun-baked, lively natives, who parade the avenues in the afternoon, with congenial smiles and calm courtesy; and all the typical scenes of life on a tiny tropical isle. . . . You form an image of this island, a pleasant one, in this case, and you say 'Yes, I've heard about Puerto Rico. I believe it's a beautiful island.'

"Then I proceed to tell you about the tumble-down old shanties that house families of twelve or thirteen; the barefoot beggars, brown-skinned children in tatters; or even the shark-infested waters of the sea, that forbid you to swim or splash in their surf. You don't like this side of the picture. Nevertheless, your picture of the island becomes varied, you may keep most of the bad, or even the good, depending on your own needs, forming your own image of the land. And when someone asks you about it or mentions it, you respond, 'Oh, yes, I know about Puerto Rico.' And you begin to describe it as you have understood my picture and adapted it to your own needs.

"Thus, the picture is passed on to others, and perhaps becomes more and more distorted as it reaches more ears. It's a secondhand account that is passed on. What's the matter? Why you haven't *experienced* it, have never really known it for yourself! It has never become significant in your life, and consequently, you believe only that *there is such an island* as Puerto Rico. You even know something about it, pleasant and unpleasant, whichever you choose to retain, and you convey your impressions, based on what you've heard or the picture you've painted for yourself. But you don't know it! It hasn't become a living reality for your life!

"Can you understand, then, how it is with many Christians? They believe that Christianity is a religion, that it exists, and many even go to the churches, but their lives remain untouched by its reality. Christianity is not a list of 'truths' that you either believe or disbelieve, thus accepting faith or rejecting it. It's *a way of life!* Anyone who claims to be a believer may be tested by his works, for 'by their fruits ye shall know them.' "

"But who can accept a book of fairy tales in the twentieth century?" Lola demanded bitterly. "Science has cleared up those myths and old wives' tales!"

"Yes, fortunately. I can't accept myths either any more, but only living realities. . . . You know, when you were a child, you were taught about God with pictures you could understand, images that meant something to you. But when you get older, you must mature, and put away childish things. How many people do that in the twentieth century? When they get older they decide they must reject their childish notions of Christianity, and they throw the whole thing out the window—the child with its bath water! Of course, we cannot continue to accept immature concepts of Christianity, but we can grow in our understanding! But I still think that those images you find in the Bible are very important today, and we cannot do away with them, since they speak for realities. For after all, Christianity is a religion of the people—people understand these pictures and images better than they do dogmatic statements about them. Christianity must not become an intellectualized religion. Although thinking people can believe, they can translate the images into their understanding."

"But how can any intelligent person today accept Christianity?" Lola argued. "You are the first person with any education I know who takes it seriously. . . ."

"You know what's wrong?" I inquired. "Many so-called educated people reject on hearsay something they have never explored on a mature level. Let's take an English professor, for example. Perhaps he knows little about nuclear physics, but he does not reject the whole science of physics, just because he is ignorant of its laws or because he doesn't like the sound of some of them. The physical laws continue to operate in the universe, whether he accepts them or not! The same is true with the spiritual laws, with Christianity."

"But, what of this God you tell me about . . . One isn't able to see him," Lola probed.

"My dear child," I began, "can you see electricity? or air? or even gas? No! Nevertheless, electricity is at work in our universe. It is there whether you can see it or not! We know about its workings. . . . Would you deny that love exists?"

"No."

"So even though you cannot see it, you do not deny its existence. You say that love itself cannot be seen, but the evidences of it can be seen. Just as electricity cannot be seen until it flows into some appliance. We must first turn on the switch!"

Ingrid had almost stopped her work. She was deeply engrossed in the conversation. It seemed to bother Lise, though, for she scowled and nervously continued pushing herself to maximum performance. Large moist beads collected on her brow.

"The average individual sees only the burning light bulb; he doesn't recognize the laws at work behind it, that is, until his interest is aroused or someone tells him about them. Then he looks into the principles and forces at work behind it. He investigates them. Thus it is with man— when he sees the beauty and harmony of love at work in a human life, he wants to know the source of it, especially when he recognizes his lack of it, his need of it, and the power it can produce in his own life. Especially when he understands that this is power and energy for his *own* life, meaning, and direction, the ultimate solution to his existence. And without it, only death! Then he wants to discover the source of it, know it, and go to it. But how? He learns of the significance of it in other lives—however limited that may be; and he discovers that much can be learned about it in a book that describes it—the Bible. However, the reality of it is to be found in a person. The person of Jesus Christ, the first man, completely born of the will of God!"

Lise interrupted when she poured out a huge carton of finished contacts. She began to count them slowly, causing us to postpone our discussion until she had completed. She rejected such topics, and she seemed deliberately to cause more noise than usual when we got off onto Christianity, which was happening every other day. Lola had not exhausted the topic yet. For it was Lola who always dictated what topic was up for discussion. All eyes darted in Lise's direction, impatiently demanding that she discontinue her crashing with the gadgets. It always irritated me that she counted five or six times, and usually when we were in the most intense heat of a conversation, but I restrained myself until she had finished.

"Yes," I continued, "it sounds fanatical to 'worldly' wisdom—as the apostle expressed it, 'a folly to the wise and a stumbling block to the Jews' of his day, who considered themselves to be good, righteous, pious people already. These two groups of people still exist—they are not limited to nationality or race: those who by their own reason and knowledge find the gospel of Jesus Christ to be silly and unbelievable, and those who believe themselves to be Christians because of their pious morality, which they have usually grown up with anyway. Neither has found Christ, nor His love. Everywhere this love is found, there is a healing—a renewal, a regeneration of human beings, a new being, born of the will of God—which is rooted in this love."

"Well, I must say . . . you present it differently. How many Christians believe that?" Lola inquired skeptically. Her tone had lost some of its harsh aggressiveness.

I glanced up at the peephole. Someone had just looked. I wondered whether our discussion had been overheard. I knew the matron resented my talking to the others about Christianity. Also Max was against it. One of my letters from home had contained the good advice: "In your day-to-day associations with your fellow prisoners, you are getting more education than can be found in most books. And, just as important, you are teaching others, if not by words, by your actions, what you and your country stand for." That had been marked out. That was an indirect admonition not to teach the others what I or my country stood for! Nevertheless, that would not stop me—not now—now that I was convinced that it was my real purpose in being there. Besides, the director had said, "You go back to the others and give them encouragement, *hope*. Teach them to give!"

There was nothing detrimental to their state in my message. To the contrary, I wanted to help them learn to contribute to the community of mankind. I was sure the warden understood this. If I was called in again for "influencing" the other prisoners, I could explain myself to him, and I knew I would go away with his blessing!

"You know," I said, directing my statement this time to Ingrid, "Christianity and Marxism have much more in common than most people give them credit for. It's the politicians and governments that don't get along with each other. Already in many countries discussions have begun in which Christians and Marxists come together. Christians have neglected their social responsibility around the world, but they are slowly waking up to this fact. They are engaging in the new challenge that Christian love affords—they will not stand by and let social injustice or exploitation cause privation or the denial of human rights. In fact, Christians can join hands with the Marxists in this struggle—so long as it does not entail weapons!

"I also have had a chance to work with the student congregation here in East Germany, and they find that they have an opportunity to serve as citizens of a socialistic society."

I dared not discuss the unchristian aspects of the regime, such as the removal of freedom, nor the evil hatred that was taught, but, there again, was it the more idealistic Marxists who were responsible for that or the shrewd politicians, who were exploiting their own beliefs? The Marxists were not running the government, as far as I could see. They were the ones who had withdrawn in disappointment when the fanatic regime took over. I had even heard remarks of bitter disappointment from Marxists of other countries when they had seen what man had made of Marxism. Christians could cry to the same tune—a look at the history of the Christian church would reveal man's fallibility.

"Another thing," I continued, "most people misunderstand what it is to love. For centuries the Christian commandment to love your neighbor has been falsely apprehended by those who have approached it seriously, attempting to cast themselves away in self-denial. They end up with a neurotic, weak, milk-toast type of personality. I know so many of those who discredit any claim to a genuine healthy self-love. And they are all sick! The commandment is to love your neighbor as *yourself*. Of course, you have a right, an obligation to love yourself. Self-denial is only secondary self-love, not self-abandonment. That means that number one and number two just become equals, and your interests are just as important as mine!"

I had emphasized an explanation of love for Lola's benefit. I was aware that something in her rebelled against the sickly, too soft variety of sympathy and self-denial. Love was too weak in her, causing her to become encrusted with a hard shell that resisted its pain. And this gave rise to her exploitation of the same weakness in others. I wanted to show her that Christians should be strong and powerful in their love, not the exploited, the browbeaten, the brooding and self-pitying who had been trampled down by the hard strokes dealt by life.

She did listen to my message. Something in her was moved, but Lise's resistance remained. There was a sore spot, a wound, that had been caused by her loss of faith in her pastor, and she referred to it in every discussion on the subject. Finally, I decided to pull her into the discussion, overcoming her resistance, or at least, destroying her irrational argument.

"It seems to me," I said, "that your whole faith in Christianity was tied up in your minister! He disappointed you, and you gave it all up. How absurd! Why do you demand perfection from him? A pastor is no different from any other man! It's you Germans yourselves with your absolute attachment to authority who have put him up on a pedestal, accepting him as a god! Bring him back down to the common people, where he belongs, serving them! He is not any different from you or me. He only has a different mission to perform. Don't expect more from him than you would expect from yourself!"

No wonder many in Germany felt as Lise did. The pulpits of the old churches still protruded on pedestals high above the congregations, just as the pastor stood academically high above his flock—perhaps much too high. He had to descend to his congregation, to their problems, to their lives here and now, come down out of the clouds of his romantic imagination, and his aesthetic appetite, and speak to *real people*. Real people caught up in the cogs of an industrial machine. At least, that was a central problem I had observed in the churches. The pastor had not descended into his own human nature to discover his commonness and oneness with the people—that basically he had the same problems as they. An academic heritage in the study of theology had separated it from life, and alienated theologians from themselves, exalting theology only in relation to scholarship and not in relation to life! Such theologians were responsible for the empty pews, the retreat of the workers from the congregations, the middle-class, "tradition-minded" residue who still clung to a dying past. I recalled a poem that must have originated with the folk:

A village priest of antiquity
Climbed up in a high church steeple
To be nearer God, that he might hand
His word down to the people.

So day by day in his high church tower
He wrote what he thought was given
And dropped it down on the peoples' heads
Two times one day in seven.

One day God said, "Come down and die."
And he cried out from the steeple,
"Where art Thou, Lord?" And the Lord replied,
"Down here among my people."

Lola soon looked upon philosophical discussions as her favorite sport, and she had found a comrade in me. She, with her interrupted education, never completing even junior high school, had more instinctive, spontaneous, natural talent for human beings, even when it was used to exploit their weaknesses, than most university professors had attained with their years of comprehensive education. I held a fearful admiration of her ability to sense out others, but I hesitated to reveal just how much of a nose for people she had, for I was frightened to show her the significance of her power. She was coming to respect me, to look up to me with an attachment and admiration I had never known.

Lola was bothered about the origin of the universe. "Where did it all come from anyway? That would answer a lot of questions about God. . . ."

"Don't begin with the universe!" I advised her. "If you want to find faith, begin with the human condition. The search for God did not begin with philosophical speculation about the universe, with hypotheses respecting its origin, or disputations on the Genesis account in the Bible. It began simply with the human condition and God's answer to it. Christians and Marxists could begin there at the same point, for there it is that they agree. They both want to rid the world of evil, and they both agree that man is a captive of selfish human nature that binds him within himself. However, the two diverge when it comes to a solution. Marxists think that the solution lies in changing man's environment, in setting up heaven on earth. How can they do that without changing man himself?" I addressed the inquiry to Ingrid.

"What do you mean?" Ingrid inquired seriously.

"Well, we've seen how many years of socialism? And has man gotten any better? No, there is still evil and crime in the world. Your country has done away with starvation and distributed its wealth to a certain extent. Yet, still the problem of evil exists. There will always be someone who acts in his own interest, for his own advantage, even when it harms others. A classless society where everyone has had his fill has still not solved the basic problem of evil."

"Socialism is not perfected yet!" Ingrid defended her belief. "When that perfect society exists, then there should be no more evil."

"Do you *really* believe that? Do you really believe that human beings will stop being selfish and change their nature, just because the social structure has changed?"

Ingrid looked puzzled. Lola jumped to respond. "No, I don't think that will change them!"

"But there will be no need for crime when the pure socialistic society exists," Ingrid contended.

"Now who's talking myths?" I asked. "Besides do you believe that man's only need is economic? What about murder from jealousy? What about sexual crimes? What about the thirst for power?"

"Well, . . ." Ingrid hesitated, searching for an answer. She considered it her responsibility to defend the party.

I continued, aware that she had no answer to man's sins that had no economic origin. "I find that faith in God is the only answer to the human condition, the only way to get out of ourselves."

"I don't think that you have to accept Christianity to believe in God," Lola stated. "You can just accept a powerful force in the universe. Why do we have to give it a name?"

"Yes, but then you make religion anything you want it to be. You have your own private picture of God, and make Him out to be just what your needs are. If there is a God, why wouldn't He try to reveal His nature and wishes to man? If there is some almighty power that is responsible for creating humans, why shouldn't it communicate with them in some way? Anything else is certainly what the psychologists call 'wishful thinking.' That is making one's own private religion.

"You know it has been claimed that man made God, because he needed Him—he projected his need for a father into the universe, affirming a personal-father type of God. I would just invert those very charges, claiming that those who destroy faith in this God, or who find it necessary to tear down that revelation of Him, do so because they have a need to justify their own evil and selfish desires. God makes them uncomfortable because He calls man to responsibility for his actions—faith is the thorn in the flesh of modern, comfortable, complacent life. And I mean *real* faith. No wonder man finds it necessary to tear down religious faith, for he will go to any extent to get around his responsibility—to keep from bearing a cross! It is man that rationalizes away the existence of God, not who rationalizes Him into being!"

There was a stillness in the work cell. Were they following me? They seemed to be eager and open. "What about heaven?" Lola asked.

"There is certainly something to the idea of heaven on earth. It was the Marxists who shook the Christians out of their false 'hereafter' approach to life and brought them back to confront the 'here and now.' I mean, no Christian can claim he has faith, if he does not accept the responsibility for his life on earth. God has revealed to man that He's not found just beyond sunsets and at the end of rainbows, but here on earth—also in the midst of slums and ghettos!

"I guess I have best observed it in my work in psychotherapy. People just have to keep on growing, or they become sick and die spiritually. Yes, there is some force that propels man forward, that promotes growth, and resisting it, stopping its progression, means that one becomes ill. Burdened by guilt or anxiety, one stops growing spiritually. Everyone needs to cleanse his mind and his heart. Daily our minds take in certain nutritive ideas, just as the body takes in food, processing it, extracting the essentials for growth, and expending the waste. Our minds have to rid themselves of waste, too, and sort out what is needed from the useless and harmful material that passes through.

"Living in faith allows us to be continually purged by forgiveness, and to take in the constructive food for our growth. Of course, it has to be faith that involves our whole person, and not just our intellect. It has to be faith that reaches down into the depths of us and penetrates our unconscious mind, transforming our way of life to an ever better one, ever re-creating, renewing. When one accepts that kind of faith, one is reconciled to himself, to his fellow man, and to God. When man really experiences that kind of faith, he can live with himself with a deep sense of joy, he is free to give to and love others, and his relationship to God is renewed. God has offered man his reconciliation on a cross, there again, through Jesus Christ. . . ."

"Just who was Jesus Christ?" Ingrid inquired. She had heard only that he was a wandering prophet, and Lola called him a politician, since I had pictured him as one who wanted to go about changing men, creating a new way, the way of love, reconciling men to each other, to themselves, to God.

"Jesus Christ was the revelation of the Word of God. It was His person —the Word of God made flesh—that unveiled the Creator to creation. You see, God showed man that He no longer resided in temples made with hands, but in the human heart. That our bodies were His temples. Men could become new beings by believing in Him, born of the will of God, new creatures who had overcome evil. The church lives within each believer. But it was Christ Himself who condemned the hypocrisy of the so-called pious of His day, the hard-hearted moralists, and went through the world spreading compassion, healing broken spirits and bodies, teaching love and forgiveness."

Finally we reached a deadlock in our discussion. "All right," I said, "let me ask *you* three questions. First: Where are you when prosperity arrives? Will you be happy, or apathetic, indifferent, or complacent?"

"There is really still too much work to be done to take the time to consider an answer to that question." Ingrid was immediately on the defensive.

"Second question: What about all your anxieties and guilt? Where do you go with them? Even the god Matter has a conscience and demands one of his followers. In this game of life, you are sure to disobey the rules and hurt someone, and where are you when you are burdened by the weight of your guilt? That's a huge cross to bear, one that would break even healthy backs."

This time there was no answer. They all reflected silently. That was my cue to ask the last question.

"What about the ugly archenemy death? What are you going to do when he arrives at your threshold? You may shut him out of your consciousness in your youth, but when age overcomes you, will you have overcome him? He is another burden to carry through life, and the impersonal god Matter offers no assurance of 'well done, good and faithful servant.' "

I had lost them, but even though we had gotten philosophical, that question was an existential one for Ingrid. She was obsessed by death. I wondered—with the inevitability of death, how then could Communists be reconciled to life? Did they have to seek life selfishly for themselves? Or could they lose it and thereby find it?

The awareness that *they* were trying to say many of the same things Christians were, that they were really longing for salvation, was an insight that filled me with hope. The object of their faith had become displaced; the peasant had become weary of his heavy burden, and had risen up to demand his own. Communism had appeared with a promise. But oh, what a wolf in lamb's clothing.

It proclaimed peace, and incited to revolution. It cried freedom and built walls. It demanded democracy and set up dictators. It spoke of love and engendered hatred. And yet, people believed. But we did have something in common. We who had the lighter burden could reach hands across the sea and alleviate the peasant's load with all the love we knew. He could give us his cross, and we could give him our Christianity!

If our daily topic left religion, it revolved around release. This subject was painful for all of us, but no one could resist engaging in the self-torment of considering release from all aspects and angles. We even played guessing games, cast clairvoyant views into the future (at least Lola did) and drew lots to see who would be released first, second, third, fourth, and last. Three times the women dropped names in a box, and three successive times the same order repeated itself: Margot, Lise, Lola, Ingrid, and myself! Although I was not superstitious, I was disturbed by the results. I had not drawn from the box, but allowed the others to do it for me. I suggested another go-round just to challenge the results of the three drawings, but this time I suggested the procedure and drew from the box myself. I recommended a number system, which should be more accurate than the names. We were to take five slips of paper and write the numbers from one to five on them. Lola performed this, carefully following my directions, and dropped the folded pellets into a carton, shook them rapidly and passed them around. Everyone opened his paper slowly. I had drawn number one! That was enough of a trial for me!

21

MENDING WALL

IT WAS APPROACHING the Christmas season. The air was filled with an electric vitality and excitement, but a heavy weight hung around the neck of each prisoner. How could one bring the spirit of the season into all the suffering that surrounded him?

Outside we had long been wrapped up in the heavy, deep-blue, double-breasted overcoats that robbed us of the last trace of feminine vanity. Our heads were bound in faded blue scarves, and our hands encased in old gray woolen gloves. We never refrained from laughing or making some comment about our appearance as we waddled down the staircase, bundled up as poor "matchgirls" or Salvation Army refugees, and we were happy that the corner window outside remained closed. The humiliation would have been greater if the men had seen us.

Winter had arrived early, greeting us with splotchy white flakes on the first day of November, and when it repeated its performance on my birthday, the twenty-first, I could not help recalling that same day just one year before.

Seated on the assembly line we talked about the coming holidays. It was supposed to be *the* holiday in the *Knast*. The guards and the officials went all out to give prison a cosy seasonal atmosphere. They tried to make up for all the rigors of prison life on one day of the year. We were to get a Christmas tree, too. There would be icicles, lights, and good meals. We had already put in our cake orders in advance. German fruit cake. It was not so rich as American fruit cake, but somewhat drier. Raisins, nuts, and —if we were lucky—chips of candied lemon peel. There would be good television programs, too. We could watch TV all day.

"I read in the paper that *Carmen* is going to be shown on Christmas Eve. With Mario del Monaco!" Ingrid announced with wide eyes, clapping her pudgy fingers in childlike delight.

"I'm not going. I'm just gonna stay in the cell by myself." Lise's mood contradicted Ingrid's delight.

"I'm going to stay in my cell, too!" Margot chorused with Lise, with a deliberate stubbornness that informed us she would not change her mind.

"*Carmen!* I can hardly wait!" I supported Ingrid's enthusiasm. "It's one of my favorites."

"Ugh!" Lola dampened our spirits. "It will be a dreadful atmosphere here at Christmas. Christmas in the *Knast*. How can we all get excited about that? It turns my stomach just to think about it."

"We can make the best of it, though," Ingrid insisted.

It was probably the tenth time we had engaged in the same argument. The forces were clearly divided. Lise and Lola were resigned to spending an ugly, suffering, lonely Christmas in the *Knast*. Ingrid and I were determined we would make the best of it. We were even looking forward to all the advantages of Christmastime: more television, good food, a chance to sit around with candlelight and celebrate. Margot was sometimes in our camp, but most of the time she was in the other one. She really did not know which one she belonged to. Depending on her mood, when she was stubborn, she wanted to suffer. Ingrid and I always ended up telling the others to wait and see before they made any sweeping decisions about their behavior at Christmas. It might not be so bad after all.

"Why can't we just enjoy celebrating Christmas with each other?" I asked, obviously the wrong question for Lise and Lola.

"You don't have any children at home waiting for you!" Lola responded heatedly.

She was right. I didn't. She and Lise did have the worst time of it. Lola with four children, and Lise with two. Ingrid had her tiny son, but he was still a stranger to her. She had received pictures of him, and he had grown up to be a little man. Her mother had brought the plump little doll along on the last visit, which had been just a short time before.

"My little Andre," Ingrid had remarked with a puzzled expression of doubt. "It's a horrifying feeling," she said, "to take your son in your arms, and feel that the child belongs to someone else. I don't feel any inner relationship to the baby. He's a stranger."

We encouraged her to believe that her reaction was normal under the circumstances. After all, the baby had been taken away from her when it was only a couple of weeks old. Now it was over a year old. The child had been removed in the most critical time when a mother develops a deep relationship of love and kinship to her child. She had tried to nurse it, but since she was unable, mother and baby were separated.

"Is Andre really *my* baby?" she asked on numerous occasions. But the pains of childbirth were still a reality to her, and she cringed when she described them to us. As in all the Communist countries, she had undergone natural childbirth without anesthetics. The tiny creature that had been taken from her womb was now a stranger to her. A little being, alien to its mother and who would probably never see its father. He had to begin life in the state nursery, sharing his affection with scores of other babies. But he was a happy little fellow. Ingrid said that he greeted her all smiles, bouncy and active. She had bought him a teddy bear and a chocolate bar for the visit. That had been all the Christmas he would receive from his mother. He knew his grandmother better, but she was really a stranger, too, who did not have time for him. Grandmother worked, and baby had to live in a home for children like him.

Ingrid was obsessed by guilt because she did not have the feeling of love for her child. "How could you?" we asked her. For the child was just an abstraction for her. There was no living, growing relationship between mother and baby. Only a picture of baby, and baby grew in leaps and bounds. Poor baby. He had entered the world fatherless, as a prisoner, and then he was taken away from his mother. What kind of life awaited him outside—in the larger "concentration camp," as some of the East Germans called their state? Ingrid expected her love for her child to be something instinctive, something inborn because she had borne the child in her body. It was hers. Didn't that assure automatically that love grew along with it?

I tried to differentiate between a selfish, possessive mother "love" and the dynamic growing relationship of genuine love between any two people. Many mothers loved and cared for their children as a middle-class bureaucrat loves and cares for his first automobile. It is his possession, and he would do anything in his power to protect it from all bumps, bruises, and scratches that the outside world might inflict on it. He would even fight with some careless motorist who had bumped his fender by backing into his car. But that was not love. Most mothers had a certain amount of that kind of concern for their little possessions, which too often became obsessions.

"No, Ingrid, any love is a growing, interdependent relationship of giving and taking. It is living, dynamic, giving of itself, not self-seeking."

From children we wandered back to the theme of Christmas. It was really a children's holiday, and for children to experience it without their mothers was tragic. We always concluded our violent arguments on the subject by deciding that if anyone took part in the celebration, he was not permitted to cry. Crying would be done in the cells alone. It was more or less an unwritten prison rule for Christmas.

Ingrid had received some candles and Christmas paper from her mother, and she shared them with us. The others refused to decorate their cells. The guards had also set up miniature trees, wide wreaths, and tiny

Santa Clauses in the culture room. The spirit slowly arrived on the scene, even if some of the women resisted it.

The air was full of hope and expectation. Therefore, it seemed natural for me to expect some sort of surprise at Christmas. Surely, the East Germans would not be so cruel as to keep me another Christmas! Christmas was *the* holiday for the Germans. Maybe, just maybe, they might reward me with a release. Could that be possible? Margot thought so. She even feared it, because she felt that when I left the others would all turn against her again. Lola was also afraid that I would be released. For the first time in her life she had come to a deep understanding with someone, and she confided in me and sought my advice. She was afraid that I would suddenly be snatched away. As much as I hoped, a twitch of doubt told me that "the time is not ripe."

When Christmas Eve finally did arrive, I was lying flat on my back in my cell. Already, I had been excused from work for several days. One day I had gotten up with what at first appeared to be a crick in the neck. I worked that day and asked to see the medical orderly. He gave me some rheumatism liniment to rub on it, and the next day it had extended down through my shoulder and back. It was a pinching sensation that did not disappear, and the doctor was finally called in.

They informed me that I had probably been caught in a draught of wind which had inflamed the nerve. Rest was the only way to chase it away. Thus, I was confined to bed rest and prescribed tablets that were for rheumatism. I began to worry.

What if I did have rheumatism at my age? I was really done for. The guards had been complaining about my physical condition. They claimed that I ate too little. I did. Lise was the only one who ate very much, and she shoveled it in with a farmer's appetite for three. I never touched the blood sausage, the pork fat which we sometimes had every three days. That was all. Pork fat and black bread. Or the bitter sauerkraut, or the boiled potatoes we were served in scores. The Germans piled their plates high with them and could not understand why I disliked them. Just what did Americans eat? They wanted to know.

Ten pounds had already disappeared, and I had to request a new uniform. I worried about becoming a shriveled-up old woman by the time I got out. That same fear hovered over every one of the women prisoners. Every woman was haunted by the ghost of age and decay. We were a slovenly and pitiful lot, and our favorite expression became, "You should see me outside." It was always followed by a descriptive list of luscious clothes, latest hair styles, all the "little" things women go in for. "Oh, to be a woman again!" We discussed it in all its phases. Admired, appreciated, in the presence of some man, preferably the husband.

Now I was lying on my back. The pain did not go away. I was sure that it was nothing serious, but I was afraid that they would not allow me to get up for the Christmas celebration. Everything would be ruined if they did not. But everyone was being especially nice to me. Renate even told me to remain in bed when she entered the cell. Some of the guards babied me, brought me food, and even advised me to take it easy. There had been such a change. Even Tosca appeared to be concerned. Inge had been especially worried, and she inquired about my health each morning when I went out to fill my two water buckets.

As I lay on my back, I had time to think. My mind traveled. . . .

Five women. What stroke of fate or plan of Providence had overlapped these lives with each other? I marveled at the diversity of the women. Lise, a simple peasant; Ingrid, an anxious unwed mother; Lola, a comical misfit; Margot, an educated pedant.

I was drawn to these women. I wanted to give to them what their state had denied them. A taste of freedom. To share with them all the worlds they had never explored, worlds they were shut off from. Not just the worlds of countries, but worlds of ideas. I felt compassion for them. They were not just prisoners of the penitentiary, but they were enclosed in a huge penal colony, shut off from the world by a wall. . . .

I was eager to meet the challenge afforded me, to share with them the inner realities of faith, hope, and the greatest of these, love—translated into action, expressed in clarity and simplicity. But there were so many walls to clear away. Heaps of rubble, devastations of war, that had desolated the soul—opinions, prejudices, attitudes that had estranged them from themselves and from each other. Besides, was I overestimating my own energies and ability to give? Any encounter meant a two-way exchange, and I must always be tuned to the partner of the dialogue. They were hungry for the travelogues, but more avid for the exploration of the world of ideas. They even flooded me with questions concerning my faith. I trembled at the recognition of my responsibility—that of a missionary in a Communist prison. There was the danger of punishment if I taught against the state, but my gospel was one of love, a constructive one. I felt the same strong flow of love that had been revealed to me before. It was the most elemental spark of life.

Our little factory table had become a sounding board for all the currents of life—love, marriage, childbirth, religion, philosophy, politics. The petty and significant were aired, argued, debated, and discussed. The walls of our work cell overheard a cross section of life with all the thoughts, desires, emotions, motivations, and impulses that woman had ever known. Nothing through which the ceaseless flow of life had streamed was left untouched. All the impenetrable mysteries from the cradle to the tomb took their course in our tiny world away from the world. Unable to experience the real world outside in a tangible way, we lived it in our consciousness that was made alive with the exchange of all the individual lives that our circle represented. Each of us became a part of the whole, and the whole became a part of us. We could give to each other and receive in return.

I took the others on trips to countries they had never seen, for them exotic lands far away, awakening a longing to be free. I painted pictures of the pigeons in the San Marcos Square in Venice. We breathed the exhilarating free air of the Parisian Latin Quarter, or we shouted out a chorus of exuberant "olés" at the Madrid bull ring or stomped out a flamenco. I carried them along with me on my wanderings through the romantic hills of Ireland's Killarney, with a rucksack on my back, or we sat out on one of Stockholm's tiny islands grilling shish kebabs over a crackling fire. We threaded through a maze of dark alleys in the Kasbah of Tangier, or went mountain climbing in the Bavarian Alps, or watched the monkeys in the sunset on Gibraltar. We stood gaping as tourists before the Empire State Building or drove through the rolling hills of San Francisco. In the evening we rested in a hammock in the Pacific twilight of Acapulco.

I could experience all the horrible pangs of childbirth and the deep joy that followed with Ingrid's account of her tiny son's entrance into the world in a prison hospital. I lost myself in the vivid descriptions of the stinging pain, which felt like "the whole bottom was falling out." Lola's accounts of her love affairs were real scenes in which we all became aware of our own loneliness and womanhood, as woman suffered away from man. We lived together the provincial life of Lise's lazy village and were distressed with her to experience her husband's stepping out on her, or the children's terror when their parents were dragged away from them by the police; and the tyrannical tirades of Margot's father, his denouncing her to the Security Police, his exploiting her financially while she was locked up in a prison cell, brought tears of pity to all our eyes.

Or we could probe into the secrets of faith, awakening an awareness of ourselves—for to know oneself was to find God.

There was just one life for us all now. It was *our* life, and even if there was friction, we were all forced to climb out of our protective shells and meet each other nakedly with the raw stuff of life. In the tiny prison community there was nothing that could be hidden—character weakness, foibles, pretenses, roles that each had assumed in life, masks that had been worn for protection, even the past—all was stripped off and revealed in the bare present. Thus, all reservations were removed and nothing that life was bold enough to engender was taboo to our begetting minds. Each member confessed that she had never lived with such intensity, openness, and sincerity as she had experienced in our little prison factory. Life had become more alive there than it had been on the outside!

We could mend all the broken family relations from our long work table, which was covered with a thin corrugated plastic cloth and usually piled high with material for production. Lise's relationship to her husband, in which her puritanical fear of expressing her feelings as a wife had clouded their happiness, could be made new. She had learned through our many discussions that her own failure as a wife had driven him to adultery. She could no longer blame him, but sought the source in herself. She would leave prison with a new relationship to her husband. Another wall came tumbling down.

Ingrid was obsessed by a deep-seated fear that she was unloved, unwanted, that she was inadequate, and she confided in me a fear that she had never told anyone about. She had invented illnesses for members of her family and had spread tragic stories to others to arouse their sympathy. She desperately needed to be loved and accepted, and she had decided that she must have gone "crazy" in order to have done such a thing. I helped her discover that her needs were absolutely normal—that her craving for love and affection had prompted her to gain what had been denied her, through invented stories and fables that had become realities for her.

Another of Ingrid's obsessions was a fear of death, and all her nightmares were filled with ugly, black pictures of death. The day she revealed her carefully guarded secret to me, she felt a surge of relief. A heavy stone had been removed from her breast. Another wall had fallen.

I tried to familiarize Ingrid with her inner world, to engender faith in herself, which was so far away and foreign to her. She always listened to the "outer voices" to determine her behavior, but I encouraged her to call on the "inner voices." Yes, that was it. She knew I was right. She knew that, all her life, deep and far-reaching self-confidence had been lacking, and she had always tried to adjust to first one person and then another, never taking her own real inclinations into consideration. As I encouraged her to think and act for herself, she began to rise up against Lola's tyranny over her.

Lola more than any other became deeply engrossed in our discussions of the "psychology of living." She was longing to discover herself and had a passionate need to do so. Daily she posed thousands of questions, and more and more I broke through the actress, the clown, and the hussy, to something soft, sincere, and genuine, which really yearned to give of itself, but was too weak and underdeveloped to do so. I encouraged it, daily complimenting her instinctive *Menschenkenntnis*—her natural understanding of human nature—of which she was still unconscious. She was delighted. She had never considered herself anything but a sort of failure in life, she confessed, and had to become a roaring performer to overcome it and win people. She confided that everyone considered her to be a gay, optimistic extrovert, but in reality she was a potential suicide candidate. I encouraged her to let her quiet, still self grow, to dare to look inside herself, instead of always tuning in to the outside world. . . .

I heard a heavy swishing sound outside the door. The women were dragging something up the steps, something heavy. It swept past my door. Then they returned. The same swishing passed the other way. What was happening? The Christmas tree! But why were they brushing back and forth with it? I picked up a copy of the *Berliner Zeitung,* and began to read. I was interrupted when the door flew open. It was Aneas.

"Get your clothes on and come and see the tree." She was grinning from ear to ear with her usual roguish smile, half concealing her joy behind the authority of her policeman's uniform.

I grabbed my clothes and in a few short seconds she returned. Frau Meister was standing outside the door and told me to bring along my dishpan. I knew what that meant. There was a package for me. My Christmas package had arrived!

"Well, you'll have enough for your birthday and Christmas, too," she said, cutting the cord on the heavy brown paper. Two boxes stood boldly on the table before her. I was embarrassed to receive so much, because the size of packages was usually limited. I had been given special permission to receive a larger one, since my birthday and Christmas were only a month apart. Besides, it was part of the concessions that were being made since I had my heart-to-heart talk with the director. I had also received my wristwatch only a couple of days before.

Another generosity had been shown me some weeks before. I had written on the weekly purchase list "milk," and "when not available, *Babysan.*" If there was anything I craved in prison, it was milk. I knew prisoners could not buy milk, but I thought I would still give it a try. "Never venture, never gain." Babysan was the DDR's brand of powdered milk, and it was a special preparation for babies.

When my list landed with the policemen in the office downstairs, they got a big bang out of it. They called upstairs and wanted to know who had ordered it. I confessed, not knowing whether I would be punished for trying to be smart, or complimented for my sense of humor. Nothing happened, and a couple of hours later Aneas was taking orders for milk. We could now order milk each week, and the quota had been gradually raised to a maximum of three half-liters.

The matron tore the brown paper off the package. Santa Claus had arrived after all. I had been afraid that he would be denied entry into the DDR because he was a capitalist, but apparently they were being generous. Although not with the West Berliners. No *Passierschiene,* I had read in the papers. That meant that the West Berliners would not be able to visit their relatives at Christmas. The price had been too high. The East Germans were demanding political recognition as the price.

The box was filled with toilet paper. Ah, what luxury! My mother and father had certainly guessed what situation I was in, even though they had probably used it for the packing. Almonds, Hersheys, canned meats, peanut butter, a fruit cake, crackers, my favorite "chocolate turtles." This would be the greatest Christmas ever. I piled all the things together and carried them into my cell.

It was hard to find room for all the new things in my cabinet, for I had already stocked up with purchases from the money I had earned as an extra bonus for working overtime. We had also picked up some extra cash from darning socks for the men prisoners. All of the others had received packages, too. Christmas would be a grand celebration, after all. I had enough food to last for a couple of months, and plenty to share. No one would go hungry.

Aneas took me back to the culture room. Lola and Ingrid were fussing around the tree. Since it was Saturday, Lise and Margot were busy in the work cell. Lola refused to help decorate the tree. No, she couldn't, she protested. She knew she would break down and start bawling. I watched in blissful admiration while Ingrid did the decorating. There was even a long string of electric candles, and that was the first time I had seen electric candles in Germany. Usually the Germans decorated their trees with wax candles, which they lit on Christmas Eve. They all disliked the electric lights and called them *kitsch.* That was in West Germany, though. In the DDR people were more open-minded about technical progress, and they were not so tradition-bound as the West Germans. Science and progress. The Communists encouraged and promoted both of them. The West Germans were still too romantic about their traditions to think about introducing technical devices into them.

In the afternoon at about two o'clock, we all traipsed into the culture room, our arms piled high with candles, cake, coffee, and candy. We took the old white sheet-tablecloth, shoved the two square tables together, covered them, set three tall, red candles in the middle, and scattered bright Christmas napkins on each place. I broke off a couple of green sprigs from the Christmas tree when no one was looking, and arranged them in a tiny bough around the candles. Bits of greenery popped out here and there, followed by splashes of bright color, and we turned off the lights. Ingrid lit the candles and connected the tree lights. The room filled with a warm glow.

We sat around the table a few seconds in an unspoken agreement to observe silence. Everyone inhaled the fresh biting aroma of evergreen, the melting candle wax, spicy Christmas cake, and freshly ground coffee. A deep sense of joy surged in my blood. I knew it did in the others, too, despite the sadness of separation.

As soon as Ingrid had arranged the table, everyone was sipping a cup of coffee and nibbling on cake, while Margot sat in silent withdrawal. I waited until the opportune moment when everyone was still and settled and pulled out a surprise for each of the women. I had wrapped an individual gift in pink and yellow Kleenex tissue and tied it with thread from my sewing kit. Announcing that Santa had come, after all, I placed a Christmas package at each place.

At first Margot refused with reluctance, but I assured her she would spoil my own fun if she did not accept, and she finally agreed. Then I passed out a piece of "chocolate turtle" to each of the women—my favorite candy of caramel-and-chocolate-coated pecans. The women did not know pecans, because they were foreign to Europe. All of the faces glowed in grateful delight, and they all issued "thank you's" at one time, lining up to hug me.

I had given Ingrid and Lola each a ballpoint pen, since I had several on surplus. Lise received a bar of chocolate and later a pen, too. Margot was the most surprised. Some weeks before she had almost begged me to swap some of my Crest toothpaste with her for something else. I had held out. Now she was thrilled with a tiny tube of it.

Margot was the least generous of the women, and she seldom shared from her packages, although she had permission to receive more than any of us. It was Margot who brought old Scrooge into our cosy celebration. But for that very reason, I was happier to show her the significance of giving. It appeared that Scrooge's heart softened after a while.

Lola boasted she would never use her pen—it was a real American one! She would keep it as a souvenir, a keepsake of prison. An American pen in the Knast! Who would ever dream of receiving American articles in an East German prison?

Supper came, and we enjoyed the traditional Christmas Eve supper in East German prisons—Bockwurst and potato salad. Afterwards, Lise got up from her chair and asked the guard for permission to return to her cell. Big drops trickled down her plump peasant cheeks. Lise wanted to be alone "with her children" on this Eve. She would light a small candle for them.

When we all returned to our cells, we were elated by the presentation that had taken our minds away from their grievous broodings. Now, in the still quietness of her cell each could retreat to her own meditations on the Silent Night.

I climbed up on the headboard of the bed and gazed out the window. The court was silent and deserted. There was no sound from the noisy machines that usually buzzed and hummed away until the early hours of the morning. A thin, gauzy blanket lay on the asphalt surface of the inner court. Even the tearful harmonica had stopped singing. Now and then a gust of wind picked up white flakes from the roof and shook them, like a veil, over the open court. A man's bass laughter enlivened the still night; then it faded and died. The soft sobbing of a woman seeped over the window ledge.

Lise. It was her third Christmas in prison. How long, oh God, can one stand? Her spirit is broken, and she is a nervous wreck. Hasn't she been punished enough? Dear Lise. She tries so hard, too. . . . I dropped down onto the bed and stretched out.

"Silent night, Holy night! . . ." Once upon a Christmas ago, I sat with a Weasel . . . "All is calm, all is bright. . . ." With candlelight and Communists . . . "Round yon Virgin Mother and Child, . . ." Oh, dear, dear Lise. "Holy infant so tender and mild, . . ." Ingrid, your baby is crying for you. "Sleep in heavenly peace. Sleep in heavenly peace." Drowsiness engulfed me.

At once I stood on the threshold of a new heaven and a new earth. All the prison gates of the world flew open. All men were free! They had won another chance. There was no more crime, for each was a brother to the other. The hungry were filled and thirst was quenched. Men dwelt with one another in peace, for they needed no war. The Wolf and the Lamb lay down together in peace. . . .

The flashing light aroused me from my state of drowsiness. Had I been awake or asleep? Had I been thinking or dreaming? Awake or asleep? It was no matter. Men *could* be brothers! *We* had grown to understand each other. Even the guards were having their joy from our Christmas celebration. Yes, I had grown concerned about the other women, their little worlds had become mine, their problems were my problems. Not just because we shared the same lot, but because we had become a part of one another. "I am a part of all that I have met." I loved each of the women, and I suffered with them and grew with them.

I sensed a profound truth that went beyond East and West Germany, beyond the United States and the Soviet Union, beyond Communism and anti-Communism. It transcended prisons, walls, barbed wire, laws, and institutions—it was a *new way*. It was the way of forgiveness, reconciliation, peace. Yes, a new revolution! It was the way of "love your enemy," for thereby you conquered him and swallowed up enmity. Loving him opens your ears to his voice, your eyes to his needs, and your heart to him. You are able to understand him. To give to him. To learn from him.

In the approaches between countries lies a truth that transcends governments, principalities, powers—it's people, *the* people. They are really no different in Leipzig from in Memphis; in Dresden from in Liverpool; in Weimar from in Buenos Aires. My encounter was no different from meeting Mr. Brown, Herr Schmidt, Señor Gonzalez, or Monsieur Blanc, who have their respective attitudes and prejudices. Why must they become different when they take their offices in Washington, Bonn, Paris, Moscow, or Berlin? They are still people. The same principles hold true for them. Why could they not engage in a dialogue, too? Governments consist of men—dialogues take place between men. . . .

Yes, I had planted a seed in the East. I knew I had. I had showed them that many of their ideas about Americans were misconceptions. I showed them a new way. Maybe I had been one tiny candle in the dark world that knew no freedom, but still that candle gave light and warmth. . . . But I had learned from them, too. I understand many of their needs now, their doubts, suspicions, fears.

Yes, I'll be released one day. . . . Then I must tell them: You *can* love your enemy and thereby conquer him . . . dialogue is possible . . . time . . . patience. . . .

I was swallowed up in sleep, where a dream took on reality. . . .

Then I saw a new heaven and a new earth; for the first heaven and the first earth had passed away, and the sea was no more. And I saw the holy city, new Jerusalem, coming down out of heaven from God, prepared as a bride adorned for her husband; and I heard a great voice from the throne saying, "Behold, the dwelling of God is with men. He will dwell with them, and they shall be his people, and God himself will be with them; he will wipe away every tear from their eyes, and death shall be no more, . . . for the former things have passed away" (Revelations 21:1-4).

22

CHRISTMAS, 1966

LOLA STOOD BEFORE ME with tears in her eyes. "You know . . . just wanted to tell you . . . I'm glad I came to prison because I have met you!"

I could only respond with a deep sense of humility. "Your giving me that honor has reconfirmed my purpose for being here!" I extended my arms and we hugged each other. Tears of joy swam in my eyes. Love had won another victory! We had grown to understand each other. Another wall came tumbling down! I discarded the idea that coincidence or a strange play of circumstance had brought us together. "Thank you, Lola, for the greatest Christmas present I've ever received!"

Christmas Day was another festive gala like the afternoon of Christmas Eve, only this time Lise remained with us. Our Christmas table was piled with cake, cookies, candy, coffee cups, and candles. The prison direction had bestowed several pieces of pastry on us, and for our holiday dinner we had schnitzel, green beans, potatoes, and gravy. We had also whipped up a pudding with mix Lise had received from home.

The soft illumination of the room was from miniature electric candles shining through a huge deep-green fir tree that stretched up to the ceiling, and warm-red Christmas candles that flickered and danced with their flames. No one seemed to notice the heavy bars that cast their long, black, ugly shadows through the tall windows. Everyone was intoxicated with the spirit of the season, and perhaps with an even greater awareness than its celebration outside would have brought. An exhilarating breathlessness seized each of us, and when we refrained from exchanging conversation, we sat silent, drinking deeply of the evergreen smells; savoring the smoke play of the candles, the flickering fire, the aroma of fresh coffee, cheese and fruit cake, oranges and apples, and the very air filled with the spirit of love. Joy. Peace. Goodwill.

Occasionally one of the women would gaze off into the distance, with a nostalgic veil over her eyes, where tears welled up in the corners. Then she would be recalled to the moment, to the present, and the drops would roll away into a soft smile.

No one dared talk about her family. That was taboo. The family was present this year; we were the family, our tiny circle of women. I thought of *Little Women*. Yes, that was what we were, even though the other women did not realize the full impact of the discovery. I knew it was there—the tacit bond of brotherhood. For I sensed it, felt its presence, experienced its power. For them it was still an unconscious, unverbalized feeling, something vague and distant. It was mingled with melancholy, unexpressed longing, a tinge of sadness that tinted the moment. For me brotherhood was not just the sadness of the situation, but the sympathy aroused by suffering with the others, and the sensing that one day I would leave them. One day, who knows . . . maybe they would leave me first. . . .

I did not know whether it was the hope of the season or a premonition, but I had a strong sense of anticipating a release. I even dreamed about it for the first time in prison. I sniffed it in the expectant air. There was no concrete sign of it; no one made me aware of it—no letter, no indication from the guards, no tangible signs of this hope. But Margot constantly re-peated that she knew somehow that it would come soon. Lola expressed her fear daily. "I know something is going to happen. Something big." It usually did when Lola had that feeling. But, of course, that certain some-thing did not have to pertain to me.

In the afternoon, we stationed ourselves around the television and viewed the West German film, *Uncle Tom's Cabin*. Of all the films I could have seen on Christmas Day, that was probably the last one I should have seen. I was forced to leave after the film and I returned to my cell where I wept bitterly.

It seemed that from prison the only contact with my country was the heated accounts of the war and the racial problems. Only its shadow side, its imperfections, its injustices. No wonder I not only asked myself "Whither Germany?" but "Whither America?"

America, I weep for you! The indifference and apathy of the masses; the naïve "black-white" foreign policies; the citizens' being denied their rights because of race, fanaticism, intolerance, prejudice, crime, cor-ruption. The empty shells losing themselves in the pursuit of pleasures. The masses of students that desperately sought something to believe in, something to cling to, something to hold on to, in an age of indifference and ignorance, of doubt and cynicism, of emptiness and nothingness. They became cynical and rebellious, and indulged in demonstrative protests. Had it become "they" who ran the government, not "we"? Yes, give the government back to the people, that's where it belongs in a democracy. It is our government! It is our voice!

But that was only one facet. It was too easy to forget the growth that one had undergone, when one lost herself in self-examination and self-criticism. This freedom was still alive in America, but the raging fire our forefathers brought us had dwindled to a tiny flame. But it was not yet extinguished. It must be kindled, kept alive, until it became a roaring bonfire once more. America was still blessed with it. Our system was still superior. We could still demonstrate, protest, voice an opinion, even though it might be ignored. But that was only as long as people participated.

To become indifferent invited the death of the system. It simply turned *our* government over to *them,* to politicians who ended up representing *their* interests and not *ours.*

Yes, our youth were ready and willing to engage in an understanding of the enemy—to dare a real dialogue, a genuine exchange—to embark on a new revolution. They were hungry for justice, equality, brotherhood, reform, but they found themselves powerless because their voice was not heard. Many who became involved were cast off, ignored, or stereotyped as beatniks, hippies, hoods, because of beards, blue jeans, or Beatle haircuts. Their protests were sincere, and that was only the outward expression of involvement.

The tragedy was that too often in their willingness to engage in a dialogue with the enemy, many forgot to engage in a dialogue with their own government. They forgot that they had been arguing with ideology and not with people. They often lost themselves in rebelling, protesting, condemning without stopping to try to understand their own government, without sitting down at a discussion table, without having written their congressmen! They were impetuous, impulsive, and impatient—but they were citizens. Their vital interest in their society made them aware of the mistakes that had been made, of the errors and failures of their fathers. Someone must listen to them!

But someone must remind them that we are growing, that progress can still thrive in our system. No matter what our failures are, our people do not have to be walled into the country, guarded and supervised; they do not receive high prison sentences when they speak out against the government, nor do Russian tanks come to silence them when they strike or demonstrate, as they did to the Berliners on the 17th of June, 1953.

No, they cannot abandon the ship now in lawless rebellion, because she is outworn, broken, or sinking. It is their responsibility to revive her. To patch up her leaks. Someone must listen to them!

They have a right to criticize, not just a right but a responsibility, for they live in a democracy. In a genuine democracy, the system can only thrive and grow on constructive criticism, and that criticism is participation, concern, involvement. But their hair is too long, their voices too loud, or their faces unshaven. Has someone stopped to ask why? Ignore a child and he gets aggressive. He seeks attention. He will go to any length to get it. Someone must listen to them! Oh, wake up, America! I plead for you!

These thoughts rushed through my head as I lay on my bed. After some minutes I returned to the others.

"Why are you so sad?" Lola asked.

"Oh, I get so involved. That movie set off many things inside. The injustice to our Negroes hurts me every time I experience it, even though I do feel that the race relations are improving in my country," I explained to her and the others.

"You are too sensitive," Lola replied, unable to understand my tears.

"I don't think people should ever become insensitive to human suffering, individual rights, injustice, fanaticism, prejudice. I've seen so much of it in my life, man's inhumanity to man. I'll never be indifferent. I guess it's that same sensitivity that brought me *here*. . . ."

"You ought to become a Marxist," Ingrid interjected.

"My interrogator advised me the same thing. No, I don't think they have the answer. Not to the human condition. How are they going to change men's hearts? No, I think Christianity has the only answer. I mean *real* Christianity with its message of love. I think that this love is the *only* answer to the human condition. Only by believing in it, daring to live it with one's whole person, giving, serving, working for the community of mankind and not just a select group, can life have purpose and meaning, goal and direction, and can peace with all men be attained. The Marxist talks about love, too, but how are men going to be able to love if they believe in a struggle between classes? When they are taught hatred of their enemy? How can men love if they cannot forgive?"

Our evening conversation closed when the television was again switched on. On Monday I would return to the workroom. The nerve in my back still twitched, but the pain had gone away. The tree would remain standing a week, stretching out its firry arms in a coat of tinsel, reminding us that we had enjoyed a special holiday; but otherwise, the routine and humdrum of the assembly line would return. Life would go on, picking up where it had suspended its monotonous repetition, losing the sense of time in the revolutions of a wheel, so that one would ask herself whether it was yesterday or tomorrow. Nevertheless, it was today, and somehow today was different, because there had been yesterday and there would be tomorrow.

When the following days brought no evidence of the nearness of a release, and the Christmas season had faded in spirit, my hopes wilted and withered, even though Lola kept repeating, "Something terrible is about to happen. I just know it is."

In the monotony of the machinelike work in our little factory, we had spent much time speculating on when a new prisoner would arrive, when the first one would be released, whether this or that guard would be replaced. . . . Any change was welcome, even if it were a change for the worse.

One afternoon Ingrid, our avid and devout newspaper reader, informed me that she had read in the paper that Jack Ruby had died. I had already expressed my concern about the Kennedy assassination earlier, telling the women I had met Mark Lane in Vienna and had tried to arrange for him to speak in West Berlin about his investigation. After hearing about his findings, I was curious to learn more. When Ingrid announced that, I immediately took interest and requested the article. I had glanced at the paper, but somehow I had overlooked that article.

When she brought it the following day, it opened up a lively discussion. There I read, in an East German newspaper, that Ruby, the "last witness" to the assassination, had died of "cancer." They had put cancer in quotation marks. Then the article charged that the American secret services were in some way involved. At first I supposed that it was preposterous propaganda. But then I started considering the facts as I had become aware of them before my arrest and drew the conclusion that it was not impossible. I shared my concern with the other women, and they were amazed that I openly spoke out on some of the problems of my government. They did not dare to do it against their own.

"Oh, you've got to get rid of the notion that governments have to be infallible before you can support them!" I addressed myself to Ingrid and Lola, who tended to cover up any mistakes the regime made. It was that need for self-justification that had pounced out again.

"I'm right and you're wrong. Well, maybe we are both wrong. Or, maybe we are both right." There were other possibilities besides "I'm black and you're white." We are both gray! If there was any political truth I tried to impress on the women, it was that.

"Our President is just a man, and not even a superman. He makes mistakes, too. But that doesn't mean that we have to give up our system," I went on to explain. Totalitarian governments, especially, felt the necessity to declare their infallibility to the people. Otherwise, the people might start to doubt, and instead of just "trusting" in the government, they would rise up and participate themselves. That was the reason that criticism was suppressed and stifled. The people just had to trust. Never ask questions. It was a "just leave the government to us" attitude—you are only the people.

I had often wondered what had become of the investigation of the Kennedy assassination. I knew that Mark Lane was writing a book, and I had mentioned this fact to the women, who were eager to learn the details. Even the East Germans had admired President Kennedy, and somewhere I had read an account of the tearful reaction in Moscow and East Berlin when they had learned of his assassination. In spite of political differences, they had respected his judgment and his dedication to a peaceful coexistence.

We were in the middle of just such a discussion when the door flew open. It was the matron. *"Strafgefangene,"* she motioned to me. She seldom said my last name, because she felt insecure pronouncing a foreign word. *"Kommen Sie Mit."*

What did she want with me? I became worried, because I was expecting no mail and knew of no other reason to be called out in such an earnest voice. She led me into the culture room.

"I just wanted to tell you, *Strafgefangene,* to make yourself pretty for tomorrow. You'll have a surprise." Her eyes glowed in warmth.

I hesitated a minute. My heart had never raced so quickly. "How big a surprise?" I asked. Was it a release or just a visit? Maybe neither.

"Oh, just a surprise. I can't say any more. You have permission to roll up your hair tonight."

"Thank you, Frau Meister, for telling me. Prisoner Battle dismissed." I reported and returned to the others.

I was too excited to work. The little gadgets slipped through my fingers, and the tiny coils were flying through the room. Should I tell the others? Whatever it was, I had to share it.

"The matron just told me to make myself pretty for tomorrow. A surprise awaits me!" I blurted out.

"What?" They all exchanged glances, and their eyes dilated in anticipation of the Great Day.

"Yes, but I don't think it could be a release," I clarified.

"No, I don't think so, either," Margot agreed. "The other women said that they don't give you any advance warning if it's a release. They just come and tell you, 'Get your things together.' You leave the workroom, and that's that."

"What could it be then?" Lola asked excitedly.

"Oh, maybe a visit in Berlin with my interrogator. Maybe with my attorney from Washington. In fact, that's probably what it is," I answered.

"Maybe it's your father again," Ingrid speculated.

"No, it couldn't be. We don't have that kind of money," I contradicted. "Besides, if it is, that will mean I am really here to stay for four years!"

"But a release . . ." Lise questioned. "Maybe it really is."

"We can see. Tomorrow if I have to take my things with me, you'll know that I'm going to be released."

"Yeh, that's right," Lola confirmed. "If you're gonna be released, you'll probably leave early in the morning, too."

"Who knows?" I asked. "I imagine I'll have to stay in Berlin a day or so anyway."

"Why don't you leave something in the workroom and come back and get it when you find out where you're going?" Lola asked.

"I don't think that would work," I assured her. "I'm sure that the matron would come and get it for me."

The rest of the afternoon was spent in speculation about what my surprise could be. The prison authorities were unaccustomed to telling prisoners before a release, so I counted on some visitor. We all thought up ways to make me look attractive. Since my lipstick had been taken away when I arrived at Bautzen, we came upon another possibility. Margot, who had some colored pencils, offered me a red one. I marched up to the mirror, touching the pencil to my tongue a couple of times, and started rubbing the point across my lips. All eyes were fixed on me. Work was disrupted for the afternoon. I returned to my seat with glowing lips.

"It's great," Lola remarked. "You look better with a little color."

"Shall I leave it on?" I asked.

"Oh yes," they all chorused.

"But what about the matron?" I inquired. "Maybe she won't like it."

"She doesn't care," Lola reassured me. "She knows I put shoe cream on my eyebrows and my eyelashes. She asked me where I got my mascara. When I told her, she just laughed."

"All right," I agreed. "She's in a good humor, anyway."

That evening after we had finished our housework and had eaten supper, we met again for needlework in the culture room. I entered with my hair rolled up, and Renate assured me that I could only get away with wearing my "radar," as she called my hair rollers, this one time. I had also smoothed hair remover on my legs and went with bare legs. I was scolded for having no stockings. "But Frau Wachtmeister, just this one time?" I pleaded. "I have to let it dry." She glared severely, grimaced, and decided that she would let me get away with it just this once. But no more, mind you. Renate enjoyed bestowing grace on the prisoners. She exercised it little, and when a prisoner was nice and pleading with her, she succumbed.

I brought some vanilla wafers along, and we brewed a pot of coffee. Needlework was still not one of my hobbies, but I always went along for the relaxed social hour. In the workroom it was usually too hectic to concentrate on both production and conversation. We sat in a circle around the table, and each of the women took out her bag of needlework.

Margot was crocheting a piece of lace to trim a hanky. She hated the work, but had taken it up in self-defense. Lise was busy knitting a stocking

cap to go with a shawl and mitten set for her little boy. Ingrid was working away on the second sweater for her tiny son, although Lola ended up
doing all the work for her. Ingrid, who had learned knitting only in prison,
had caught on after some weeks of struggle and a scrawny looking first attempt at a sweater. Lola, who was very creative, made up her pattern as
she went along. When she wasn't occupied with Ingrid's piece, she was
knitting a dress for herself.

Lise laid her cap aside, and pulled a finished hanky out of her bag. She
went over to the table in the corner, took an old blanket and sheet, and set
up for ironing. She carefully pressed the crocheted lace on a handkerchief
she had made for her daughter. Then when the lace was just right, and she
had pressed the folds together neatly, she came over to me and said, "Here,
I want you to take this. I don't know whether we'll ever see each other
again. It was for my daughter, but I can make her another one. I wanted
you to have one anyway."

"Thank you, Lise," I said as I hugged her, "thank you very much."
Moist drops formed in our eyes. I did not try to refuse her daughter's handkerchief, because it was a love token from Lise's own hand.

"You need a crying rag when you arrive in freedom. It oughta be a nice-
looking one, too," Lola added.

I laughed. "You all don't know whether I'll be released. I don't think
it's a release. I won't get excited about it until I know."

"I wanted to make you a hanky, too," Margot added. She had already
had me pick out the color. Now maybe it was too late. It was supposed to
be my wedding handkerchief, she said, and it had a wide, sweeping, intricate, white lace border.

"You can send it later," I laughed. "First I have to find a husband."

"I was going to make Hellen a hanky, too," Lola joined in. She had
spoken about giving me a keepsake to remember her by. She had promised to knit me a sweater if I bought the wool for it, and we both had been
considering it seriously.

"Wait a minute, you all," I interrupted all of their affectionate well-
meant attentions, "I'll probably be back. You don't have to worry about
making the gifts yet."

"We'll send 'em to you, if you don't come back," Lola answered.

They all wanted to lavish presents upon me, tokens of remembrance. A pang of sorrow went through all of us, and I sensed a faint tinge of envy that something new had entered my life. But they tried to overcome it.

"You know, I guess we are all envious when something happens to another one of us, but this time I couldn't have wished it for a better person," Lola told me. I knew she meant it. Whatever awaited me, she shared my joy now, and anticipation. The others did, too.

Our session was interrupted when Renate came for us to return to our cells. Each of the women came up to me, put her arms around me, and hugged me tightly. We were all choked up. Lola noted that it was irregular to have a needlework session on Monday. It must have been planned by the matron as one last hearty session for us together. If that was really the case, then we had all traveled a very long way down the avenue of understanding. I liked to think that it was.

The night was one long breath of anticipation, with little sleep. In the morning long before darkness merged into the illumination of dawn's first rays, I lay with open eyes. When the light flashed on, I sprang from my bed and busied myself with my hair.

I slipped on the same old slovenly uniform, the sagging skirt, the faded blouse, the heavy stockings. I rubbed my lips with Margot's colored pencil, only briefly considering the danger of poisoning which for the sake of vanity on such a special occasion was worth the risk.

The routine of the morning was just as usual. I joined the other women in the workroom.

The matron noticed my lips as I left the cell. "Where did you get the lipstick?" she inquired.

"It's a colored pencil," I answered sheepishly, awaiting the reaction.

The matron grinned. She showed no sign of anger. In fact, she was in an exceptionally good mood, but I still had trouble making conversation with her.

When by eleven o'clock nothing had happened, I began to wonder whether anything was going to happen. We still buzzed away in wild speculation about what the sudden trip could be. We had all concluded that it was definitely not a release, for it would have been carried out differently.

The time slowed down to a creeping pace, and the morning passed in twice the time it usually took. Finally, the door swung open. Inge motioned me to come along, and her usual pleasant face was clouded.

"Macht's gut!" one of the women called out.

"Have a good time!" came another voice.

"Take it easy!" Margot said. Despite the excited confusion, I knew it could only be Margot. That was always my advice to her, along with "keep smiling." Margot was oriented in all the Americanisms long before I had met her.

I almost waltzed down the corridor to my cell, which Inge opened awkwardly, still with a serious expression.

"Well, get yourself ready!" the matron who stood in the doorway ordered. "Take along just enough for a day or so," she advised.

"Do you know how long it'll be?" I asked with an effort to hide my deep disappointment.

"Probably a couple of days," she replied, indicating she had no idea herself.

"Do you know who's coming for a visit?" I went on to probe.

"No, you'll find out soon enough," she replied with her usual policewoman's closed distance. Nevertheless, the matron was in a friendly mood. I felt more secure with her when she radiated some warmth. I had never been so surprised as I was to learn that she was a mere thirty-four years old. Her heavy stature, her stern manner, and her sober expression left the impression that she was at least in her late forties. She commanded the respect of an elderly matron, and she had been employed in a prison with criminal prisoners before taking on her position with the "politicals." Although the state did not recognize this distinction in the types of crime, the prisoners did.

I dropped a few cosmetic articles into my shopping net with great haste. This time I was not going to forget my hair rollers. The last time I had gone to Berlin for a visit, the matron had stubbornly refused permission for me to take them along.

In an instant I was reminded of my written accusation—all the pages of fiery charges I had copied down. I had folded them up into a tiny ball, covered it with a plastic bag, tied it with a rubber band and immersed it in an empty deodorant bottle. Then I had removed the plastic roll-on top, that appeared to be made onto the bottle, and had poured pink hand lotion into the slender bottle. In addition, I had a list of addresses of all the people I had met while in prison hidden in my large can of body powder. I had pried the lid of the metal tin loose, and had pushed the tiny slip of paper down through the powder. Should I take these things with me this time? Against my better judgment, I decided to leave them at Bautzen.

Weeks had elapsed since I had finished taking the potent vitamins I had kept stashed away. That meant a hundred days had passed since I had received them, and I had rationed them out to one a day. I was confident that they were responsible for the good health I had enjoyed up to that time. When my supply had become exhausted, I noticed the difference in my disposition and endurance. I fought exhaustion and depression and had much less energy than before.

The matron stalked down the steps. We repeated the same procedure we had gone through on the previous trip to Berlin. I picked out the clothes I wanted from the personal effects, and then changed into them. Nylon stockings, red checked wool costume, green ruffled blouse. I doffed the ugly garments that robbed me of my identity and donned the apparel that belonged to me.

Again I felt proud and feminine, as I admired myself in the mirror. If one did not look closely at my skin color and the dark circles under my eyes, it was not evident from a hasty examination that I had spent more than a year in prison. My hair had darkened and lost its sheen. No sunlight, little fresh air, a dusty workroom. I was surprised that a crop of gray hairs had not sprung up as with Margot. She was ten years older, though.

The matron cleared the corridor of prisoners and then gave me a go-ahead sign. A large group of guards stood leisurely at the end of the large hall, scrutinizing me with curious stares as I made my exit. I saw the eyebrows rise and the tongues begin wagging. As I walked past, I pranced out with the proudest stature that my tired, resigned body could hold. I was no longer a number, a *Strafgefangene,* I was a *person.* Just like them. "Clothes make the man." Of course, I knew they did not, but they lifted my drooping morale. Once more I had stepped into ladyhood and left behind the prisoner, the scrub woman, the unskilled factory hand. And now I was treated like a lady, too.

I was locked in the visiting room for lunch, and then introduced to my group of police escorts who were to take me to Berlin. This time it was high protocol reception, and I speculated on its significance.

When Gummi Ball greeted me in Hohenschoenhausen I only nodded this time. He led me to a new cell a few doors away from the medical station. The cell, which had housed no guest of the state for some time, was coated with a blanket of dust.

After some minutes Bowlegs came and handed me bed linen through the slot. "You can lie down," she said, "but don't get undressed, because they might want you for something."

I imagined that remark to be routine, too, and I really expected no visitor at such a late hour in the afternoon. The trip was still shrouded in a cloak of mystery for me.

I made my bed, found a stiff old rag to dust off the furniture, and stretched out across the bed.

Again I was overcome with a feeling of tormenting uncertainty. Everything struck me as anticlimactic now. A visit would be a welcome change, but I longed only for a release. All the long weeks of hope had been crushed when I learned I would have to return to Bautzen again. The weight of resignation prevented me from even looking forward to the purpose of my coming to Berlin. I was afraid to hope.

23

GUEST OF THE STATE

As I LAY ACROSS THE BED, staring up at the ceiling, I heard the spy hole on the door click open, remain open a few minutes, then fall shut. Suddenly, the metal key clanked in the lock.

I hopped up from the bed. In Berlin I could skip the ridiculous reporting, but I did have to stand erect. When the door was flung open, there stood the same old suspicious runner who had become just another of the fixtures of the place. He smiled at me, but a mute smile. He was serious and reticent. The faint smile said, "So you're still with us."

I followed him along the familiar path through the prison. I wondered whether I would be welcomed by the Weasel. We passed his door, and stopped short of the last door on the left. This was where I had celebrated my first Christmas. The other interrogator. . . .

I entered, and the double door was closed behind me. *"Guten Tag,"* he welcomed me, extending his hand. A faint recognition glowed on his face.

"Guten Tag," I answered.

"Wie geht's?" he inquired.

"Oh, I'm getting along all right under the circumstances," I answered, using the prison formula.

"Take a seat." He motioned to the soft chair in the corner. He proceeded to take a pipe from his desk and filled it with tobacco. He lit it and then took a seat across from me.

"Well, I'm still around," I said with a smile, starting the conversation.

"Yes, I see," he replied with strains of reminiscence. "I didn't know you were still with us, until I got a call that you were coming up from Bautzen."

"I didn't know you all would keep me so long. . . ."

"If anyone had been interested in getting you out, they could have let us know. But that isn't the case," he interrupted.

"That's not true," I replied. "My parents have already written me that their petition for clemency was refused."

"What?" he asked. He poked around in his pipe bowl. "It would have to pass through my hands. The Security Police would have to give a report on you. I know nothing of such a petition."

"That's what they wrote. Maybe there is some misunderstanding." I was baffled, because I was certain he was telling the truth.

"No, I don't know of any petition, and I am sure I would have heard. But if your countrymen were interested in helping you, they could send some official over here to inquire about you or request your release," he continued, with a note of irony.

"You're aware of the difficulty in that," I answered, "when they don't even recognize this state."

"We're not begging for recognition," he said firmly, "but Americans claim that they are interested in the welfare of their citizens. In your case no one has shown any interest."

"I'm afraid I can't do anything about that, though."

"Well," he continued, puffing lightly on his pipe and gazing into the distance from time to time, "the reason for your coming here today . . . first, let me say I am assigned to you as your host, so to speak . . . is that you are to receive a special visitor." He hesitated some seconds and observed me closely. After so many months of passive obedience I had become callous to taking orders; I had learned to take what came. I had no reaction to his words.

"We did not know what kind of . . . what . . . uh . . . connections you have. Someone has written, claiming he knows you, and requesting a visit. Let me ask you, do you know a Mark Lane?" His penetrating scrutiny probed suspiciously to determine whether it was not all part of some move, perhaps, for someone to get in to see me. Reporters had tried and had been refused. Students in West Berlin had tried unsuccessfully, too.

"Oh, yes, I know him! I am very much interested in his investigation of the assassination of President Kennedy. I tried to arrange for him to speak in West Berlin before I was arrested. Is *he* coming for a visit?"

"Yes, . . . uh . . . no . . . actually, I don't know who is coming. Someone from England."

"England?" I was amazed.

"Yes, Mark Lane wrote a letter, informing our officials that he knew you and that he had contacted Bertrand Russell on your behalf. Lord Russell has written Walter Ulbricht, requesting an emissary to come in to visit you. We just got the letter, and everything is still tentative. We don't know when the visit is to be. One of the assistant general attorneys called me about it today."

I was overwhelmed, and after long months of buried hopes, a new expectancy surged forth. Not even realizing the significance of the visit with respect to procuring a release, I was especially excited to learn about the latest developments of Mark Lane's investigation. "Then I'll be able to find out about the investigation," I stated. "Do you know whether his book has been published?"

"I . . . uh . . . am not informed," he responded, somewhat embarrassed by his lack of information. "See this letter, here—it is from Bertrand Russell. It is addressed to the President of our State. A man as renowned as Lord Russell can address a letter properly. Why can't your government officials do that?"

"It's not my fault," I answered. "I wish they would. I am only a victim of governmental policies." And certainly I was. If there had been some official recognition, I might have been out of prison months earlier. At least someone would have instructed my parents to submit a petition for clemency, but, as I had feared, apparently no one had told them to do so. The lawyers had probably been too busy with the prospect of negotiations to inform my parents of the possibility of such a maneuver.

The door eased open, and a striking man with dark wavy hair entered. My interrogator introduced us and we shook hands. The stranger wanted to have a word with him in private. The interrogator locked his safe and left me sitting in the room alone. It was highly irregular and a golden opportunity stared at me. He trusted me, though, and nothing in the world would have made me violate his trust.

I sat quietly gazing around the room. The bookcase. Good books. The thin carpet. Potted green plants. The joy. The hope. It was the first concrete sign that offered promise. No, I wasn't forgotten. Somewhere people were still working for me. Now I was to receive a visitor—from Bertrand Russell. A flood of gratitude. I felt unworthy.

I was still unsure whether the visitor might be Mark Lane himself.

My interrogator returned. He had been talking to the man who was assistant general attorney. He had shaken hands with me! Me, a prisoner! There had been no condescending look, no expression of scorn. He had almost been friendly.

"I think I am a bit better informed now. The visit will be either Friday or Saturday, and it is not from Mr. Lane, but from a Mr. Colloms. Do you know him?"

"No . . ." I thought a moment, wondering whether it made any difference. I would have said "yes" if the visit were about to be canceled because I did not know him. "No, I don't know him."

"I hope you realize that this is quite irregular. Normally, only the relatives of a prisoner are allowed to visit. You have Walter Ulbricht to thank."

Two small pots of coffee were delivered, along with two fat slices of fresh pound cake. He poured coffee into my cup, a polite gesture he always performed for me. "You had better hope that something can be arranged about your release," he said. I had long since become passive regarding doing anything about securing my own release. What could I do? That was the irony of it all in prison. The prisoner himself was the last one to help himself get out. He was totally dependent on others.

"I just asked regarding a petition of clemency. The General Attorney's office knows nothing about it," he explained, wiping his glasses. He left them off a few seconds and stared directly into my eyes.

"That's strange . . ." I wondered. "It must have been a misunderstanding." But what a misunderstanding! It had almost cost me my life! I had been desperate when I had read the letter from home. That kind of foolishness was over, though.

The stocky interrogator got up, ambled over to his desk and took out a pack of cigarettes. He lit one, poured another cup of coffee, then changed the subject.

"One of my colleagues told me that he was surprised at how nice you are. You know the man who talked to you at Bautzen."

I thought back a moment. Yes, I recalled a well-built, handsome interrogator who had come to Bautzen just to question me about another American who was imprisoned in Berlin. I had known the American, having met him on a charter flight from America to Germany. "Yes, I remember him," I answered.

"He was surprised at your behavior, because you . . . uh . . . sort of have a reputation of being a 'wildcat' around here. After that big scene in your interrogator's office."

I smiled. "Is it that bad?" I asked proudly.

"Well, let's say everyone in the whole building heard you screaming. They all thought that you were pretty wild after that."

"I've heard lots of people screaming," I said, somewhat surprised that they could even find my behavior strange under the circumstances.

"Yes, but a woman of your background. . . ."

"I'm no different from anyone else," I immediately broke in.

"In any case, I assured him that you had just become hysterical. It's not always the prisoner's fault, you know. It depends on how the interrogator handles him. I really don't think I would have had that difficulty with you. . . . But, understand what I mean here. I mean that I think I understand you better than your other interrogator." He smiled warmly.

"Yes, I'm sure you're right," I agreed with him. "You know I cannot even imagine you as an interrogator. You're much too kind and much too sensitive."

"Oh," he laughed, "I have a reputation for being one of the worst ones around."

"You?" I asked in unbelief. "That's not possible. You're much too kind-hearted."

"I'm afraid it's true."

"I guess it's because we've always had a different relationship. You have never interrogated me. You've always been my 'host.' But one thing is bothering me. How can you reconcile your occupation with your conscience? I mean torturing confessions out of people?"

He glanced away a second with an embarrassed pause, and then a look of dubious confidence fell over his face. "With *our* people I am doing a *duty* by getting them to confess. It is their responsibility to the community of this society, and we can only help them when they are willing to cooperate with their state. Besides, for themselves, for their consciences, it is better to accept the responsibility for their actions."

I thought of Catholic confession as he spoke. Here again I was met with the religious nature of the ideology. An interrogator was a sort of priest, an official of high standing, who exacted the truth from the sinner, the criminal who had acted against the greater community.

"It is my ethical responsibility to the whole society to get criminals to confess. It is our belief that it is always better for the person himself and for the society he has acted against. For example, I once had a woman who was very bitter and who refused to cooperate. She did not know it was a matter of life or death for her child, who had been given a sleeping medicine on an escape attempt. Several of my colleagues tried to get her to confess, but her reaction left the impression that she was a cold, hard woman. She laughed indifferently when we questioned her about her child. Actually the woman was trying to conceal her real feelings, her fear and anxiety concerning her child. I finally got her to confess, then she assumed a completely different nature."

He snuffed out his cigarette stub and poured coffee into my cup. He seemed to be satisfied with himself. It was his ethical responsibility to get people to confess. He did not explain how it was with foreigners, though, with those who did not live in his state, and those who did not believe in his ideology.

Yes, his ideology. He was an idealist—he believed. I glanced at the complete works of Lenin on his shelf. I posed some question about Communism. Now we were at the heart of the matter. When I spoke of the "goal of world domination of Communism," he corrected me.

"It isn't the goal. Marxism-Leninism has no goal. It is the *inevitability* of a certain historical development. History *must* take a certain course."

"Why do you try to propagate your belief, then?" I asked. "Why do you try to convince people of it if you are sure that history must follow that course?"

"To encourage people to *go along* with history, instead of resisting it. To speed up justice. To accelerate the process of progress. Therefore, it is our attempt to make society more democratic where the party has not yet come to power. That's why our newspapers devote so much space to criticizing the West German Government, to answer your question. When the structure of society is democratic, the prerequisite for Communism is established, and the process will hasten its course. It is difficult in West Germany, for example, because the Social Democrats have very clever economic policies. It makes it hard for the Communist Party to gain a foothold."

"What about America?" I probed cautiously. I was keenly interested in his answer. "I heard the other day that Gus Hall, the First Secretary of the party in America, was here for a visit."

"As far as I am concerned, he is just a front—to bring the party out into the open and get the names of all the members on a list. I don't know about the party in America, though. It is not my specialty. I am more familiar with the party problems in West Germany. Nevertheless, there is a *subjective* and an *objective* preparation for the attainment of Communism. The objective exists in America, that is, the wealth is concentrated in the hands of a few. But the subjective is not ripe yet. That is, the minds and hearts of the people are not inclined to accept Communism."

"And maybe they never will be, as long as *real* freedom exists," I thought to myself. He got up, sauntered over to the desk, and looked through a couple of drawers, apparently looking for his pipe tobacco. What he had said had stirred up my appetite to learn more about his way of thinking—how the believers in the system really thought. This urge prompted me to ask him the next question.

"Do you have any books telling about your state? I would like to read them. Or your side of the story about the Wall, about Berlin? I've only listened to the other side till now."

He went over to his bookcase, slid a panel to the side, reached in and unlocked the glass panel. He rummaged around a couple of seconds, producing a paperback documentary. "This is the only thing I have around," he stated, handing me the book. "It's published by the press agencies of all the socialistic countries."

I looked at the cover. *Tatsachen*—"Facts." I had seen a similar book with a paper cover in West Berlin. Only this was about the East. I leafed through it quickly, and pictures caught my eye.

"It deals with cases against French, British, American, and West German intelligence agents and their activity. Mostly with Americans, though." He took it from my hand, glanced at a couple of pictures and then handed it to me.

"Here, look at this. It is a communications tunnel that the Americans built under the Wall into our territory." I examined the picture of an elaborately equipped tunnel, outfitted for wiretapping. They had tapped Russian military phones by means of the tunnel. I knew how he felt about it, so I said nothing. It had been discovered by accident, when one of the walls began to cave in.

Then he turned over to another picture. It was a photocopy of statements made by a Bulgarian citizen. He had claimed that the CIA had tried to blackmail him into working for them when he had gone to West Berlin on a visit. There were statements from several citizens of other socialistic countries who made the same claim.

The interrogator looked down at his watch. "I am going to have to leave now. You can take this book along to your cell if you'd like. Is that sufficient?" he asked.

"I think it'll do for a while," I responded.

"I'm sorry I can't talk any longer, but I have an appointment. I'll see that I have another chance to talk to you again Saturday after your visit." He picked up the phone receiver and requested the runner to come and pick me up. When I left he squeezed my hand tightly.

When I returned to the cell, supper was waiting for me. I had no trace of appetite. I was still too much up in the air about all the developments of the last few hours. So much to digest. What did the visit mean? What could be done? Then, there was so much to comprehend about our conversation. Confession. Communism. No, now the visit was more important.

On the day of the visit, I did my best to make myself attractive. I had received permission to shower and wash my hair the previous night. The guard had even offered me hair rollers, but I assured her I had my own. The officials were going all out to accommodate me on this visit to Berlin, and the guard who had allowed me to shower without supervision had brought me a mirror and a razor after bathing. She let me take my time about it, too.

The visit was scheduled for nine o'clock. Shortly before that my interrogator sent for me, and we enjoyed a cup of coffee together.

"You had better hope that something develops from this," he had told me again.

Of course I hoped, but what could I *do?*

"Bertrand Russell is a man who is highly admired and respected," he had also told me.

Of course, I knew that. What was he trying to say? That he was someone they could not refuse?

My escorts and I piled into the Wartburg, and I noticed once again that

I was entrusted with a door with a handle. Previously, that had not been the case, but it was all part of Cinderella's being transformed into a lady. . . . With a certain nostalgia that struck me on every visit to Berlin, I enjoyed the scenes that passed my window, as I watched for familiar signs that marked the way to Magdalenenstrasse.

Saturday morning was shopping day in East Berlin. Life filled the streets, notably contrasting with the weekdays' desertedness—especially now that every other Saturday was a holiday.

The panorama from the car window. Just one pane of glass that separated me from my freedom, that tortured me with a preview of what one day would be mine and a reminiscence of what had been taken from me. A fine drizzle fell, and it was one of those typical ugly, scowling, continental days. No one outside seemed to mind the rain. They were accustomed to it. I wouldn't mind it either. Just to be outside. Suddenly I was surprised by a recognition. Not of one of the many unfamiliar faces that indifferently passed by—unaware that an American prisoner was being transported in their presence or they would have stopped and gaped. We were not driving to Magdalenenstrasse!

We were crossing through the city, and I began to recognize familiar signs of the center of the city, or rather the area not too far from the Wall, territory known to me as a tourist. The bombed out ruins of the old cathedral rose up on the horizon, the parade grounds where the May Day celebrations took place, the classic opera house. From my window I viewed tourists with their cameras dangling from their necks—within speaking distance when we stopped for a light, an intersection, or a sign. Were they Americans, too? A U.S. Army car drove through the streets—so near and yet so far.

We stopped before a huge complex of buildings, apparently governmental offices, with stories, rows, and sections of stern architecture. The driver pulled the car into a private entrance in the courtyard of the compound, and I examined the sign on the door. *General Staatsanwaltschaft*. I was being taken to the General Attorney's office! It had to be a high echelon visit, for not even Mr. New nor my father had been paid such a reception.

We all climbed out of the vehicle, and the driver took the car around back to park in the lot for employees. The other two escorts led the way into the building. As we approached the entrance, I saw a familiar face in the doorway. It was the first prosecutor who had been assigned to me. He nodded a friendly *"Guten Morgen,"* and I replied the same. I was afraid to offer him my hand, for he had treated me with a condescending manner on our first visit.

We went immediately to an office. I looked for a name on the door, but I found none. A secretary briefly looked up from pounding her typewriter, mumbled a *"Guten Morgen"* and went about her work. My prosecutor told us to be seated for a while at the round table in the corner, and entered an adjoining office, from which several voices could be heard.

I started to remove my own coat, since the man guard was busy helping the woman escort. Prisoners usually did everything for themselves, and I expected no gentlemanlike gesture from the guards. To my amazement, the guard rushed to help me with my coat, and took it and hung it on the wall with the others. I was so accustomed to being treated as a second-class citizen, that the brief intervals of interrupted prison treatment were good for my sense of selfhood. I was another person again, not a number that had to obey, but a person, a special person, even, since I was receiving an important visitor from England.

I wondered whether the secretary knew I was a prisoner. She seemed not to. Did I look like one? No. Dressed up, nylon stockings, elegant costume. No one could see I'd served more than a year.

The door to the adjoining office, a thickly padded door, opened slightly, and my prosecuting attorney nodded, "Miss Battle."

The guard seemed to smile, "I'll keep my fingers crossed for you"— with a tinge of hope, which I probably read into her anxious expression. I walked across the room and entered the office. The door swung closed behind me.

My eyes quickly scanned the room. Seated at a head desk at the end of the room was the assistant attorney I had met two days before. On his immediate left was an attractive interpreter, a young redheaded woman who smiled sweetly when our eyes met. On the right of the assistant sat Mr. Colloms, the attorney sent by Bertrand Russell, a man who reminded me of my father in every way. He had dark wavy hair with touches of gray and warm smiling eyes that spoke through a pair of spectacles; he appeared to be in his fifties. To his right was my original prosecutor, another assistant General Attorney. I shook hands with everyone. This time I dared.

At the assistant's request I was seated next to the interpreter. The sole condition of the interview had been that an assistant General Attorney be present with an interpreter, so that no material that "might threaten the security of the state" could be exchanged.

Mr. Colloms proceeded to question me, first concerning my health and treatment. Then I was to describe my crime to him. How did I feel about it?

I explained to him that I recognized the necessity to respect the laws of another country, but I also felt that they must be questioned in regard to their interest for humanity. No, to advocate violating laws would be advocating anarchy! I was no advocate of lawlessness. Nevertheless, when personal rights were being denied because of laws, one had to suffer or break the laws.

I interpreted the questions he addressed to the assistant General Attorney, who spoke some English himself and usually understood our comments in English. What were the legal possibilities of an earlier release?

Dr. Wendlisch, for the assistant's name was repeated by Mr. Colloms, informed us that according to Section 346 of their law, there were two conditions under which I could be released earlier. The first entailed a decision by Walter Ulbricht, President of the Republic, granting remission only after a formal representation had been made to him. I was informed that neither private individuals nor government representatives had done so in my case. "If your government were interested in you, they could do something about it!" I was again informed, and this time in no uncertain terms.

"What can I do about it?" I asked, unable to withhold the tears. "It's not my fault. Why do you have to take it out on me?" They implied that if either an American official or some member of my family or even any citizen had requested clemency from the president, perhaps I would already have been released. That had not been done. No one. Not even my family. That was a bitter recognition that made me feel completely abandoned, if what they were saying was true.

"I know my family would submit such a petition requesting my pardon, if they knew it were possible," I assured him. "They must be getting poor advice from my lawyer or the State Department."

That was it. My family did not even know, and my fear of months had been confirmed in one statement. Why had no one told my parents to submit a petition, a request for clemency? Of course, my family wanted to get me out, and they could perhaps have spared me months of suffering. The lawyers were more interested in negotiations, because they were in their own interests.

Suddenly I had the horrible feeling that it had been my lawyers who had kept me in prison. Just one early word to my parents to write a letter requesting my release could have gotten me out. Was I naïve in believing that? Were they just saying that? No, it was in their interest, too, to grant such a pardon, for it would show the world that they were capable of showing mercy. Were they really? If that were not true, then I had only been kept so long as a prime object of barter. . . .

"We understand that you are not responsible for the policies of your government concerning our state," Dr. Wendlisch answered. "We are not vindictive, either. We will be happy to see the day when prisons no longer exist. But a sentence has more than one purpose. It is also to frighten others who may be inclined to commit the same crime," he explained.

"I hope what you say is true. But I have certainly learned my lesson. It did not take fourteen months to convince me of the authority of your state," I replied. "I had learned that after one week of interrogations."

But the last part of his statement struck me as an injustice. I was an example to all others. I was being used to show the rest of the world what would happen if their idealism and involvement in freedom led them to taking the step I had decided to take. No, that was a gross injustice.

The other possibility for an earlier release was a remission on recommendation of the Attorney General, showing that the criminal "had been on good behavior, had shown remorse for commission of the crime, had shown that he recognized the error of his ways, had been rehabilitated and could find his proper position in the society." They informed me that this latter portion of the law was usually limited to citizens of their state. In certain "exceptions" it could even be applied to foreigners, for they did not want to discriminate against foreigners. Dr. Wendlisch agreed that the section could apply in my case, especially since my crime had not been committed out of a desire for material gain or out of political enmity against the state. They concluded that I had acted without having given the matter thorough consideration.

They were right. I had been torn between two desires. One was greater, nobler—that of seeing a divided Germany reconciled—of encouraging understanding between people where enmity divided them. Any open act of resistance to the German Democratic Republic meant I was acting against this desire, but not as an enemy of the state. On the other hand, my sense of personal freedom, my desire to help an individual, assumed automatically that I would help Sammy attain his freedom if it lay in my power.

There were legal ways of getting people out, as I learned from Mr. Vogel. They were long and wearisome but they existed in a few cases. However, for Sammy there would have been no legal possibility of reaching the West, Mr. Vogel informed me. There remained only flight.

Were laws holy? Or were human beings more holy? Which was nobler, to act for society, a vague, undefined mass of individuals or to act for an individual? There had been no promise of a productive future for Sammy in his state—neither for society nor for the individual. There remained only flight.

We concluded our talk after a couple of hours. I informed Dr. Wendlisch that as a result of my imprisonment I had learned considerable about his state. I realized that I had held many prejudices concerning it, and I felt that my decision to act against his state had not been consistent with my own approach to reconciliation. However, as long as the citizens were denied their freedom the problem would exist.

I asked Mr. Colloms to request Bertrand Russell to submit a petition for clemency for me, since I felt that it was the only possibility for my release.

The return to Hohenshoenhausen was filled with hope. I saw no streets, no cars, no people. They all melted away in one blurry mass of blending hopes, anticipations, and expectations. The first concrete sign had appeared. There was no return now. Something had to develop.

When the door to my cell slammed shut behind me, I fell down on my knees, and poured out my heart in gratitude before God.

24

ICH BIN EIN BERLINER

SATURDAY, January 21, 1967. Sunday passed, Monday passed. Tuesday, Wednesday, Thursday, Friday. The days ticked by in long wearisome waiting. Seconds, minutes, hours. I tried to concentrate on my reading. I paced back and forth. I played games with my fantasy. Saturday, Sunday, Monday. One thing was certain. I had remained in Berlin. Something had to happen. Tuesday. Wednesday. The door opened. To my interrogator's.

"Sit down," he said, taking a seat opposite me. The coffee stood waiting. "I'm sorry I couldn't take time out and talk to you sooner, but I've been busy. I did promise you we would talk again before you returned to Bautzen. How are you getting along?"

"I've run out of reading material," I replied. "And I'm starving. This time the food is not so good. Since I have been consigned to hard labor, my treatment has gone down several notches. I would like to request some of my things to be sent up from Bautzen."

"Well . . . I . . . uh . . . don't think you'll be needing them. You won't be here with us much longer. . . ."

"What?" I asked, awaiting the verdict. The decisive words were about to be spoken.

"No, you won't be with us much longer. I have word that the Big Day will be coming soon. I don't know exactly when, but soon." His quiet seriousness gave way to a broad smile.

"I can't believe it! I won't believe it! Not until it really happens!"

"It will happen."

"How soon?" I begged.

"I don't know. Say, this weekend, for example."

All words left me. Stunned to silence, searching for some word, some thought to break the stillness, I gazed at my interrogator. I wanted to hug him, share the joy of the moment with someone. Anyone.

"Your things are being brought up from Bautzen tomorrow. I have already sent for them," he explained; it was the final word of confirmation for me.

How the conversation went from this point, I could never recall, for the news that had been announced put me in a state of shock, near oblivion to all that happened afterwards. I do remember that as I left his office, he took my hand, grasping it firmly, gazed into my eyes with deep sincerity and wished me *"Alles Gute"*—the best of everything. "I won't say *Auf Wiedersehen*," he stated with an amused grin, for those words meant that we would see each other again. . . .

I saw that perhaps I stood on the threshold of freedom. The first thing I wanted to cry out was "I am a Berliner!" as John F. Kennedy had proclaimed to thousands on a hot June day in 1963. For to be a citizen of the free world is to be a citizen of Berlin. Kennedy had said:

> *You live in a defended island of freedom, but your life is a part of the main. So let me ask you . . . to lift your eyes beyond the dangers of today; to the hopes of tomorrow, beyond freedom merely of this city of Berlin, or your country of Germany, to the advance of freedom everywhere, beyond the wall to the day of peace with justice, beyond yourselves and ourselves to all mankind. Freedom is indivisible, and when one man is enslaved, all are not free. . . . All free men, wherever they may live, are citizens of Berlin, and, therefore, as a free man, I take pride in the words* Ich bin ein Berliner.

When I participated with the thousands of Berliners who commemorated Kennedy in a torchlight ceremony after his assassination, and stood, almost squeezed to suffocation in the crowd that had turned out for the renaming of the West Berliner square where Kennedy had spoken, I began to sense that I had become a part of Berlin and Berlin had become a part of me. Then, after having stood in an East German courtroom, I knew that I had earned the right to be called a Berliner. I could nevermore remain indifferent to all those who were being denied their freedom.

Yes, John F. Kennedy had been a Berliner. I knew that now I, too, was a Berliner. I had paid the price for believing in that freedom, had become a victim for daring to become involved. Although John F. Kennedy had died for what he believed in, his spirit lived on in many young hearts. One voice of courage in an uncommitted, detached world of men—a voice of courage to dare freedom in a world of bigoted, intolerant fanaticism—a voice crying in a wilderness. To engage in a struggle—to swim against the mainstream—to take up a cross—to become involved—to sacrifice. Those who were afraid to dare to be free, those who dared nothing, were nothing and became nothing. But, they killed him. Did that flame of freedom die out with him? No, it still burns on his tomb, with the unextinguishable flame of the spirit he proclaimed, kept alive in the hearts of those who believed in his message.

No, I could not and cannot remain indifferent to freedom. In the dark world of prison bondage, I had encountered many of those East Germans who had sacrificed everything for freedom. I had been moved by their cries and shouts against injustice, protesting the tyranny of a regime that denied them their innate right. I had become a part of their suffering, too. It was those I would leave behind, still contained within stone walls, behind iron bars, who would obligate me to keep the flame of freedom burning in the hearts of men. In the middle of the twentieth century, a century that boasts the greatest progress of mankind, freedom and human rights were still living issues to which no citizen of a democracy could remain indifferent.

Yet, there was another burden I shared. It was the lot of the peasant, the worker, the farmer, the rejects of society, the "little ones" of the world. I knew that these, least in the world, were being misled and seduced by the spirit of evil that promised them their salvation. And they had become weary with their burden; their backs had bent and broken under the weight of their own crosses. I wanted to cry out to them:

"Arise all you farmers, workers, peasants, neglected, rejected little ones, for the last in the world will be first in the kingdom. Turn away from the false god of Materialism and accept the living God, in whom we move and breathe and have our being Only His *love* has the power to restore, to make sick men whole, to cleanse, to make every man a new creation. For there was one who suffered and yet He could say: 'Come unto me, all ye that labor and are heavy laden, and I will give you rest. Take my yoke upon you, and learn of me; for I am meek and lowly in heart: and ye shall find rest unto your souls. . . .' Indeed, to love is to suffer. To love is to forgive."

Yes, that discovery was born in prison—from the cold, dismal darkness of a prison cell! It was a paradox, but I experienced it. It was Love, a magnificent obsession, the shaking of the foundations, the deep and penetrating revelation in the soul. It held the power of peace, to stop wars, to dare a dialogue, to give of itself, to unite man in brotherhood, to create justice, to say in spite of its suffering, "I can love." And as the waves that draw from the source of the depth and fullness of the sea must empty themselves, so must the soul that ever drinks from God's impenetrable depths pour out its love, spilling over on all creatures. There is no enmity among men—only imperfections and misunderstandings that can all be cleared up with one sweep of the arm of love. In spite of, no, *because of* the stone walls, the iron bars, I could experience love. It was not vague and mystic, but powerful and real. It made me encounter the present, the other human beings that surrounded me, with understanding and acceptance. The wall between East and West, friend and foe, you and me, had been broken down, and we were able to engage in an understanding dialogue between equals. Just as men could meet and understand each other with this spirit, so could nations. It was not utopian, but a real, living, dynamic force in the universe!

The following day my things arrived from Bautzen. I immediately dug through the huge heap that Gummi Ball had stacked up on my bed, searching for the deodorant bottle with the hidden charges. It was not there! I also discovered that a jar of expensive face cream was missing. A knot twisted in my stomach. So, so. They had discovered my little hiding place. I no longer needed it, anyway.

When I found the large can of body powder, still with the addresses, I decided that they probably had not found the charges, after all, but had decided to help themselves to my best looking cosmetics. This conclusion was more likely. What disturbed me most of all, however, was that all the written pages of my diary had been ripped out of my notebook. Not a single written word of all those weeks of trial remained. If I had only brought all the things with me to Berlin, it never would have happened. Such suspicion and fanaticism in Bautzen. . . .

When I complained to Gummi Ball, he grimaced apologetically, but there was nothing *he* could do about it. I could have my lawyer write the penitentiary protesting, but that was out of his jurisdiction. That was the *Vopos,* he made clear to me with a lift of the eyebrows and a shrug of the shoulders. That was the second time a secret police officer had made that distinction. Apparently, the *Vopos* even had a bad reputation with the secret police.

That evening the runner appeared in my doorway wearing his usual sober mask. This time I followed him in a new direction, to the administrative offices of the prison. I entered a bare office—the same room where I had undergone that horrid physical examination on my first night in Hohenschoenhausen. A new face received me, staring across a desk. I sat down.

With a grave air the voice that went with the face spoke, "I have been given the task of informing you that you are to be released on Friday, February 3, 1967." He lifted his eyes from the paper, eagerly awaiting my reaction.

No response.

"What do you have to say to that?" he inquired, awkwardly trying to get me to register some reaction.

I had calculated Saturday as being the earliest possible day of release, and I was unsure just how I would be able to live until that day arrived. Then, it dawned on me. "Friday? Why that's tomorrow!"

I had responded with such vigor and surprise that he had to laugh. He wanted to share the joy with me. "Yes."

"Oh, I have a request! Can I request a sleeping tablet for tonight? I haven't slept a wink the past few nights, and I know I'll never live through this one!"

"Yes, of course." He grinned again. "Do you have any other wishes?"

I thought half consciously a moment. "No." I could think of none. Just my freedom . . . that was all.

The following morning at seven o'clock, Gummi Ball and I trudged out to a sputtering vehicle with our arms loaded with bags and suitcases. A couple I had never seen before were sitting in the front seat. Gummi Ball nodded a last melancholic "Good-bye." I replied.

I climbed into the car. Why, indeed, it was the same car that had carried me away to captivity on a snowy night in November of 1965! At least, it resembled the impatient Wartburg. My curious gaze immediately examined the door. No, this time there was a handle.

As the car leapt forward, I did not look back—only forward, into the new day. It was bleak, gloomy, rainy, but it was a new day. As we drove away, the massive complex of Hohenschoenhausen loomed up before me for the last time, through the misty morning. We went through its heavily protected portals, past the sentries with their slung machine guns, and onto the open streets of the city of Berlin. "Adieu," I whispered to myself.

The couple rattled away in dialect. I hardly understood a word. "It's gonna be a great day in West Berlin today!" the driver exclaimed, glancing back and nodding his head with a friendly gesture. "Lots o' celebratin'!"

I smiled. Something was sure to go wrong. Can't afford to get excited too soon.

"*Ja!* You'll be meetin' the others for a party, eh?"

"What others?" I inquired, puzzled.

"You know, your buddies." He glanced in the rear-view mirror.

What was he talking about? "Oh, you mean the other Americans!"

"Yes."

"Are they being released, too?"

"Four o' ye."

"Oh! I didn't know they were going to be released, too!" He apparently thought that we were all part of a little clique. "They have nothing to do with my case," I explained.

"Mr. Vogel might not be able to pick ye up till this afternoon," he explained with an impish grin.

"Are you kidding?" I asked.

"No, I'm serious."

"Really?" Maybe it was his dialect, or his wide-eyed expression, but I was sure he was pulling my leg. He finally convinced me that he was telling the truth, and I choked down my disappointment.

When we arrived at Magdalenenstrasse, I waited until he inquired inside about the latest word from my lawyer before unpacking the car. He returned soberly. "He can't come till six o'clock."

"Oh, no. He's always late, and today of all days!" My face fell, and with it my eager anticipation. Tears trickled down my cheeks in big drops.

"Do you want to wait here, or do you want to return to your cell in Hohenschoenhausen?"

I reflected a moment. I hated the filthy, ugly, stinking cells of the Magdalenenstrasse prison, but go back—never, never, never! "I'll wait here."

While we unloaded my things, an officer conferred at length with the driver. Finally, the driver informed me that I was entrusted to the special care and kind consideration of this gracious and charming officer. They had whipped up a special cell for me, too—one for VIP's, only with a bucket—but for the eleven-hour wait, it would certainly suffice. If I needed anything, the dashing officer was at my beck and call. I requested water for coffee—I remembered I had some instant with me—and a knife, for I still had some leftover fruitcake tucked away.

If the day was not the longest in my life, it was the second longest, second only to the day of my arrest. I lay down, got up, paced back and forth, read a few sentences in Jung's *Psychological Reflections,* looked at my watch, lay down again, got up again, paced the floor again, read a few more sentences, looked at my watch. Ten minutes had passed. The next problem was whether Mr. Vogel would come on time.

He didn't. At six o'clock, the handsome face of the officer appeared in my doorway. "Get your things together. You can wait downstairs."

I waited in a dumpy corner room, where a scratched, dirty, ash-stained table top provided a rest for my weary head. The two guards who were to turn me over to my lawyer were impatient, too. They were already off from work. They were anxious to get home to their wives or go out with their girl friends, but they had to wait, too.

In another room only two doors away, I could hear the loud voices of the men. Three other Americans. Seven o'clock. Still no Vogel. At 7:15 I went to the guards, who were standing outside smoking. "Please let me go to the men," I begged. "I can't stand this waiting by myself." The last lap was the hardest.

"I'm afraid we can't do that," one of the two men answered. One had escorted me on the trip to Neustrelitz when I had had the lively conversation. The other had been the desperate driver after my trial.

"We'll keep you company," the more lively of the two answered. We spent the next forty-five minutes chatting about the inevitability of Mr. Vogel's arriving late and even made bets. We also discussed East-West politics at great length. I could not repeat a word of the conversation, for only my mouth participated. The rest of me was preparing itself to accept the inconceivable freedom that was awaiting just over the Wall. Beyond the Wall. . . . After fourteen months without it, I could not imagine what I would do with it. I wanted to rush out and embrace the whole world in one huge hug of gratitude for it. That much I knew, but it was not quite there. Just beyond that Wall. . . .

Mr. Vogel finally appeared after 8:00 P.M. I climbed into his Mercedes, and suddenly three men's heads popped up behind me. I reached into the back seat and shook each hand with a congratulation for what was about to come. Lovett. Herrin. Matthews. All three Americans entered my life in person. We already knew *about* each other, and now they were realities for me.

"We want to thank you," Herrin said and Matthews seemed to echo his words. "We're sure you're the one who got us out. Mr. New said that you had agreed to being part of a 'package deal' for all of us. We really want to thank you! You probably could have been out sooner if it hadn't been for us." The two Negro men poured forth their deepest gratitude.

"I'm truly glad it was possible," I answered, "for us all to leave here together." I had no idea at this point how it all had come about, but if I were really responsible for their being released too, I was grateful for the couple of months of extra time I had served.

We tried to exchange as many tidbits as possible about penitentiary life. They were surprised to learn that I had been in Bautzen, too. They laughed when they realized it was my hair they had received in the relays. The plush Mercedes was bubbling with stories that now seemed to be from a distant past, vague memories of a nightmare that sticks in the mind after awakening.

We arrived at Mr. Vogel's office, which was buzzing with activity. Then I entered an inner office, where a distinguished-looking gentleman, with rich black hair, sat at a coffee table. He welcomed me with a great smile. Mr. Vogel sat down, and I took a seat between the two men.

"This is Maxwell Rabb," he announced in German, "who is responsible for your release!"

Suddenly my head was spinning. Mr. Vogel continued to address me in German, and I began, in German, to address Mr. Rabb—who replied only with a blank expression and nervous nods. It was all so unclear, so unexpected, under the circumstances, and the anticipation of crossing the border was so strong, that I was unable to comprehend what was occurring. Besides, the hour was growing later. It was approaching eleven. I acted as an interpreter for the two men, but I still had not grasped that this gentleman seated at my side had negotiated my release, along with the release of the three other Americans.

We finally piled into the car again and headed for the crossing. Arriving at the Invalidenstrasse, a new crossing for me, Mr. Vogel sped around the concrete barricades, weaving through the obstacle courses where a guard just glanced into the car and greeted him with a friendly *"Guten Abend."* No passport control, no car inspection, we just zoomed right through. I looked around at the others; they were holding their breath, too. Then we rolled by the last gate. We were free! Thank God! We were free!

"Freiheit!" I shouted. "Sweet, blessed, longed for, beautiful, beloved freedom!" The men shouted too, and I reached into the back seat and shook hands of congratulations with them. *"Vive la liberté!* Freedom! *Libertad!"*

Our reception was a cloak-and-dagger one. As soon as we had arrived, the headlights of a black official car, parked in a side street, flashed on. Mr. Vogel answered with his headlights. Another black limousine pulled in front of us with a U.S. State Department license, and we followed it into a side street. There we all piled out in a kissing, embracing, hand-shaking ceremony. I was immediately met by Mr. Livingston from the Eastern Affairs Department, and Mr. Stange, my West Berlin attorney, who shuffled me off to another State Department car. Four official black limousines awaited our glorious reception. Each of us was escorted away separately.

A drizzling rain fell as the lights of the city flashed by. As we drove to drop Mr. Stange off, a whirr of new signs, people, life, activity, West Berlin, freedom, rolled by the window. It was all too much, inhaling the exhilarating air of the fresh, new, reborn freedom. My head was swimming with a thousand new sensations. West Berlin. I love it. I am a part of it. My bond with the Berliners was stronger than ever. . . .

We were received at a secluded villa in Dahlem, where the meal I had dreamed about for months in prison stood waiting on a beautiful table. A champagne-and-steak reception, suited to the best of royal visitors, with Maxwell Rabb and the State Department officials who had received us.

Afterwards we rushed off to a press conference in the America House. I needed some time before I talked to them, for there was too much to think about, to digest, to consider before meeting the roomful of reporters. I had a lot to say, but the State Department officials indicated I should keep it all as short as possible. What were they afraid of? I wondered. I immediately sensed their strong allergy to reporters. Why did they want us to say little? The press is the agency of a free society, the carrier of ideas. I had experienced its abuse and manipulation in the East. Now I wanted to communicate my message of freedom. No, the time was not right. After giving answers to a few questions—answers that proved to have been grossly misunderstood when they appeared in some of the newspapers—I indicated I was too tired to go on. I was, but I was still burning with a message.

The State Department had arranged for accommodations, apparently secret, so that I would not be "bothered" by the press, and I spent three weeks in West Berlin, in order to arrange for my return to America, to ship back my things, and to enjoy sweet reunions with my friends.

Yes, I had sat in a prison cell for more than a year! I never for one moment felt like a hero—just someone who was involved in helping another human being get access to his birthright, which was his freedom. All of the previous months I had asked myself time and time again whether it had really been worth all the pain, anguish, and suffering. The night of my release I learned something that offered the key to the answer.

Sammy had been released to West Berlin just four months before my own release. "Yes, then it was worth it all," I told the two lawyers as the car rolled over the border into West Berlin. But even before I made the magnificent discovery, I knew that a deep rich meaning and perspective from my encounter in the East had been added to my life. The anticipation of understanding, of a dialogue, of harmony among men, of a new venture in human relations was possible for those who *dared,* no matter how radical their differences might be.

I had journeyed out into the wilderness of lost souls, and I was but one small voice. A wilderness of souls filled with venomous hatred for those they considered their enemies. And I was but a tiny candle set upon a hill, illuminating the darkness. But a voice had spoken to me in the wilderness of my own soul, when apathy, unbelief, or despair had crept in—when I had turned away from the radiant countenance of the only true and living God. "Look to me," it said, "I am the Resurrection, the Way, and the Life. The Hope of all the World, lest any man be led away by false doctrines. *I am Love.*"

And when I turned and heard that voice and accepted it within my own heart, I saw the power and the glory of a new heaven and a new earth. . . .

EPILOGUE

"HELLEN!"

"Sammy!" I rushed into his arms. We stood in a long, clinging embrace, smothering each other with kisses of joy at the reunion.

"Man, you made it to freedom after all! I was sure I would never see you again!"

Laughter, tears, joy, pain raced through me.

"Oh, Hellen. I'm so, so sorry! They lied to me. Those jerks told me that they didn't keep you! I didn't even know that you were in prison until I arrived in West Berlin four months ago. I've been doing everything I could to try to get you out. . . ."

Sammy and I spent hours trading stories and then we arranged for a celebration with Peter and Juergen. We all agreed that I had earned the right to be called a Berliner.

When Sammy and I had the opportunity to review all our months of anguish, I sensed that he was the same old Sammy. Somehow, though, I had become different. The experience had taken us in two opposite courses. Thus, when we had uttered our last "good-byes" to each other, I knew this time that our ways really parted—even though Sammy's life had become a part of mine.

Some days before my departure for America, I received a strange luncheon invitation. It was from a diplomat with the State Department whom I did not know; I did not hesitate to accept. The engagement was arranged through an individual I had learned was working for the CIA, and I assumed the diplomat was, too.

When the diplomat arrived—let's call him Mr. Hunter—I immediately recognized a gentleman who had mysteriously been present at my warm

313

reception in the secluded Dahlem villa following my release. He informed me that his purpose in inviting me to lunch was to exchange German prison experiences. He had been a prisoner-of-war in Germany.

After so many months of confinement I was receptive to the delicious lasagna and the warm, colorful atmosphere of the Italian restaurant. But it was his words that I digested on that day. They remained long after the backdrop of our scene had faded into oblivion.

We spent little time in trading war stories, but discussed Communism and the American way of life. We also discovered that we were on the opposite ends of the personality pole. I loved people and he loved causes. This recognition did not strike me with any significance until Mr. Hunter made a further disclosure.

"You know," he announced with conviction, "I love my country above *everything*. My first loyalty lies with her under *any* circumstance. How do you feel about that?"

I wondered about his purpose in asking. Then I responded. "No, I am afraid that my first loyalty lies elsewhere. My second loyalty belongs to my country. You see, I have brothers and sisters in every nation of the world, living under every race and creed in existence, even in Russia. My first loyalty belongs to God and his people everywhere. . . . But let me ask you a question. Would you be loyal to the American government even if a Hitler came to power?"

He wasted no time in deliberation. "Yes, I'm afraid so. That's my oath of office. No matter who is in power. I cannot forsake my government." He hesitated some moments. "You see, we are sometimes forced to tell lies to the world. . . ."

"Oh, no! I believe that it is unnecessary. Truth is always victorious. It only takes longer. Therein lies the strength of our nation—in our integrity! If our nation deals in falsehood and lowers itself to evil methods, then what really does distinguish us from the Communists? We are then no different from them! It's *only* truth that conquers."

His words stung with a painful recognition. Why, he was no different from a Communist, nor from a Nazi, if his faith was in the state! The American man who sat across from me was a dedicated idealist, and yet I knew he was just as wrong as those East German officials whose Marxist conviction obsessed them with the idea of world domination. He stood for "my country right or wrong!"

When I returned home that afternoon his words were still ringing in my ears. How many Americans had also become inflamed with the faith that America was responsible for the righteousness and salvation of mankind? That their own government was infallible? They had been filled with the wrong kind of national pride and closed their horizons to any other nation or people. America was only a "promised land" as long as she remained with God. And was her government a God-fearing government? Mr. Hunter had implied a confession that it was not!

How many Mr. Hunters were in power? These people knew of no love for their enemy, no love for mankind. Their love was the power of the state. While politicians were speaking slogans about building bridges and daring dialogues, another invisible government exerted its secret influence toward combating evil with evil around the world. No wonder America's youth were disenchanted.

The words stuck with me even as my Pan American jet crossed the Atlantic and the first glowing dots of Manhattan became visible below. Yes, I loved my country, but not as Mr. Hunter did. I loved her for the honest principles that made her what she is. The Statue of Liberty had become a living symbol for me, with her flaming torch lifted high, welcoming any visitor with the promise of freedom. It was a new fire she held in her hand. Again I recalled Kennedy's words in Berlin: "Freedom has many difficulties and democracy is not perfect, but we have never had to put a wall up to keep our people in. . . ."

After a surprise press conference in the New York airport, I boarded the plane for Washington. There I was met by the beaming welcome of Mr. New, Representative John Duncan, and Mrs. Howard H. Baker, Jr., the wife of the Senator. I spent a rushed couple of days shaking hands in gratitude in the State Department, and meeting scores of new faces in the government.

My greatest thrill, however, came when my plane approached the Knoxville, Tennessee, airport. The stewardess came and requested me to leave the plane last. A glorious surprise awaited me. I stepped off the airplane to the tune of a band and met a welcoming committee from my hometown;

my feet trod a red carpet, two dozen red roses rested in my arms, and a kiss was planted on each cheek by my mother and father. Bulbs flashed, reporters shot questions, and I glowed with joy. I was home! God bless America and the Americans!

In the solitude of the evening, long after my weary parents had fallen into bed from exhaustion, I was still in ecstasy over my grandiose reception. The Oak Ridge Twenty-Fifth Anniversary Committee had welcomed me home with open arms, and I felt a bond of brotherhood I had never known with the American people. But there was joy beyond expression when I began to plow through the stacks of letters from the four corners of the country. Almost without exception, each letter said, "Our prayers are with you." Those prayers were Jewish, Catholic, Baptist, Presbyterian, Episcopalian, Christian, Methodist. Another wall had come tumbling down!

In the following days at home, after my blissful mountain-top experience, a heavy cloud of depression began to set in. I spent long and tedious hours at my typewriter, still an alien to the new abundance of freedom. Finally, I reached the floor of a valley where I could not go on—something profoundly necessary in my life was lacking. . . . An invitation that reached me just then to spend a vacation in Ft. Lauderdale held an unexpected answer to this need.

I had been in Ft. Lauderdale less than a week when I learned of a group of dedicated people who knew no denominational barriers and consisted of Jews, Catholics, and Protestants. They were all united in a bond of faith that reminded me of the early church. I was surprised when I received an invitation to speak about my imprisonment at their meeting. I agreed willingly, but with a certain fear.

I had already talked to numerous civic groups and fear to speak before an audience was foreign to me. Who was I, though, to address a group of people who lived in such unconditional faith in God? I had almost taken my own life in despair, and how could I tell them anything?

I approached the meeting with trepidation, and as I spoke, the love in their hearts shone through their faces. Joy was in their midst, and I poured out my message of the paradox of love and suffering to eager ears. Yet, when I expressed the necessity of conquering a Communist with love, which meant engaging in a dialogue with him, opening up our ears to his real needs, some seemed to bristle in indignation. How could anyone venture a dialogue with the hate-filled terrorizers and revolutionaries?

A few were prone to doubt such words from a young woman, and even inclined to chalk them up to naïveté. . . .

When I sat down, another speaker arose—a Negro from Jamaica who introduced himself as having been a member of the Communist party for twelve years. He addressed the group.

"At first I hated the pious, self-righteous Christians I knew because they held only condemnation in their hearts for me when I became a Communist. It was the Communists, though, who assured me they were more interested in the welfare of mankind, and it was the Communists who were out doing things for the poor, the hungry, the rejected, the outcasts—not the Christians."

He spoke with power and conviction. A hush fell over the room. "But there was one thing I could not reconcile with my conviction of Communism. I was taught to hate. And it was only when a Christian came to me in love, with an open heart and acceptance, that he conquered me. I could recognize the superiority of his way. Then I knew that they had the answer, the ones who conquered with this love. . . ."

That evening God had spoken. His message was unconditional love for all men. If I had vaguely sensed in prison what the new revolution was about, I knew of its power and existence there, that evening in a room crowded with love-filled people of all faiths. My eyes traveled across the cross-section of people—an Episcopal priest, a wealthy businessman, a Presbyterian housewife, a Baptist attorney, a Lauderdale socialite, a Methodist mother, a Jewish nurse, a Catholic nun. . . .

I learned that this revolution was sweeping not only America, but the entire world. All of these individuals were united in a common experience of an encounter with the living reality of Christ. Everywhere all walls of class, race, religious denomination, nationality, creed, ideology were tumbling down. They were falling as the result of no man's efforts, but God's!

That night I experienced a rebirth. I enlisted as a soldier in the New Revolution. It was not the hatred, protest, and violence in the grim ghettos that characterized the New Revolution, for without the message of inspired prophets, many had turned toward the messengers of violence and bloodshed to rid the world of evil. It was a revolution that went deeper than any ideological revolution, because the roots were in a change of heart. Therein lay the answer to the human condition. The New Revolution did not begin with society or the social structure, but within oneself. It was a gift of God. It was LOVE.